Foreign Policy of the European Union towards Latin American Southern Cone States (1980–2000)

European University Studies
Europäische Hochschulschriften
Publications Universitaires Européennes

Series XXXI
Political Science

Reihe XXXI Série XXXI
Politikwissenschaft
Sciences politiques

Vol./Bd. 491

PETER LANG
Frankfurt am Main · Berlin · Bern · Bruxelles · New York · Oxford · Wien

Andrea Ribeiro Hoffmann

Foreign Policy of the European Union towards Latin American Southern Cone States (1980–2000)

Has it become more cooperative?

Cases of Foreign Direct Investment and Agricultural Trade

PETER LANG
Europäischer Verlag der Wissenschaften

Bibliographic Information published by Die Deutsche Bibliothek
Die Deutsche Bibliothek lists this publication in the Deutsche Nationalbibliografie; detailed bibliographic data is available in the internet at <http://dnb.ddb.de>.

Zugl.: Tübingen, Univ., Diss., 2003

The author thanks for the permission of reprinting in Chapter 5 of this book contents published previously in:
Joaquín Roy and Andrés Malamud (Eds.)
"European Influence on Latin American Integration: Between Emulation and Cooperation"
European Center, University of Miami (forthcoming)
and in: Luiz Otávio Pimentel (Org.)
"Direito Internacional e da Integração" Florianópolis, Fundação Boiteaux, 2003.

D 21
ISSN 0721-3654
ISBN 3-631-52554-0
US-ISBN 0-8204-7301-4

www.peterlang.de

Contents

Chapter 1 - Introduction

An analysis of recent literature on the relationship between the European Union[1] and the Latin American Southern Cone States[2] suggests that a *rapprochement* between the two regions has been taking place since the mid-to-end 1980's.[3] Several cooperation agreements were signed on a bilateral basis, such as with Argentina in 1990, Uruguay in 1991, and Brazil and Paraguay in 1992, as well as two agreements on a bi-regional basis with Mercosur: the Inter-Institutional Cooperation Agreement, in 1992, and the Inter-Regional Cooperation Agreement, in 1995. In 1999 began a negotiation process for the conclusion of a third agreement with Mercosur, the Inter-Regional Association Agreement. The professed EU intention is to build up a 'special relationship' or 'partnership' with Mercosur, as a means to promote democracy, respect for human rights, the rule of law, regional integration, sustainable development in the Southern Cone, and to increase bi-regional trade and economic relations with particular attention to the importance of social solidarity.[4]

Historically, the First World War interrupted the evolution of relations between today's European Union and the Southern Cone States. Before 1914, the relationship between these regions had a broad character, with Latin American countries taking Europe as their ideological and cultural model, as well as their main economic partner. The United States attempted to eliminate this influence in the course of the 19th century, the Monroe Doctrine of 1823 being the first explicit manifestation of this intention.[5] After the Second World War, the United States

---

[1] For the period before the Treaty of Maastricht which created the European Union, the term EU refers to the three European Communities: the European Economic Community (EEC), renamed European Community (EC) by the Treaty of Maastricht; the European Coal and Steel Community (ECSC) and the European Atomic Energy Community (EURATOM)), and its member-states within the framework of the European Political Cooperation (EPC).

[2]The term Latin American Southern Cone States (hereinafter called Southern Cone States - SCSs) refers to the countries that became members of the Southern Cone Common Market (Mercosur) created in 1991, i.e. Argentina, Brazil, Paraguay and Uruguay. The definition excludes, therefore, Chile and Bolivia, despite the fact that these countries are included in the geographical definition of Latin America's southern cone, and are associate members of Mercosur.

[3] See:Dias, 1999; CEPAL 1999; IRELA 1997,1999a,1999b; de Brito, 2000; Ayuso, 1996; Camerana, 1995; Correia, 1996; Dauster, 1996; Di Biase, 1996; Freres et al, 192; Galli, 1995; Grabendorf, 1999; Gratius, 2002; Guzman, 1981; Marin, 1996; Matutes, 1999; Mix, 1996; Petersen, 1983; Bodemer, 2001; Picerno 1996; Purcell, 1995; Roett, 1994; Ramjas, 1996; Saboia, 1993; Vasconcelos, 1993; Vizentini, 2000.

[4] See:COM (95) 495 final; COM (99) 600 final; Declaration of Rio, 1999; Chris Patten's SPEECH/00/346, 2000.

[5] Independently of what was 'better' for Latin America, i.e., to be under the influence of former colonial states or of other states seeking to increase their own power, the fact is that the Monroe

achieved absolute political and economic hold over all Latin America, considered then a strategic area in Cold War geopolitics.

During this period, the Western-European states initiated an integration process that culminated with the creation of the European Union by means of the Maastricht Treaty in 1992. While the EU is today one of the main economic and political partners of the Southern Cone States, the reverse is not true. The latter have not been a priority in European Union's foreign policy towards less developed countries, unlike Central and Eastern Europe, South Mediterranean states, and the African, Caribbean, and Pacific states that were signatories to the Lome/Cotonou agreements. Relations between the two regions can therefore be defined as highly asymmetrical.

Considering this asymmetry, one would expect that a change in the bi-regional relationship of the last decades would coincide with a change in EU foreign policy. This study, therefore, analyzes recent developments in the bi-regional relationship mentioned above from the vantage point of EU foreign policy. The foreign policy of the European Union is a controversial topic in itself, and it has been criticized for being confusing, incoherent, stagnant, and a failure in terms of creating common policies among member-states. Some conceptual and operational problems with regard to the 'actorness' of the European Union, and the decision-making process in foreign policies will be addressed in this study, but it is assumed that such problems do not threaten the existence of an EU foreign policy neither the possibility of analyzing it.

The present study seeks to answer two questions in particular - whether or not the EU foreign policy behavior towards the Southern Cone States has become more cooperative since the mid-to-end 1980s, and why a change, if any, has occurred. Among the explanatory factors usually pointed out in literature and in the media in general, three are recurrent: the EU intention to balance the US hegemony, the accession of Portugal and Spain to the EU, and the processes of democratization, economic liberalization, and regional integration that took place in Southern Cone States.[6]

Overall, the explanations for this *rapprochement* have not, however, been treated in a methodologically systematic fashion. This study attempts to fill the

---

Doctrine marked the entrance of the US into the dispute of influence over Latin America. See Louard, 1992, p.480-485, and Blum et al, 1988, p.187-188.

[6] For the first case, see Vizentini, 1999, p.155; di Biasi, 1996, p.38; IRELA 1997a, p.3; Hofmeister, 2001, p.9; Nunnenkamp, 2001, p.137; d'Arcy, 2002, p.210; Gratious, 2002, p.11; Santader, 2000, p.48; Stocchiero, 1995, p.31; Bouzas, 1999, p.18; Grabendorf, 1999, p.81 and Giordano, 2003, p.21. For the second case see Pio 1997, p.10; Dauster, 1997, p.113; Alperstein, 1992, p.233; Navarro, 1992, p.60; Medeiros, 1995, p.49 and Vasconcelos, 1993, p.105, and for the third case see Marin, 1996, p.187; Cussac, 1995, p.42; Alloco, 1998, p.21; Vasconcelos, 1993, p.108 and Ayuso, 1996, p.159.

gap, and to develop an in-depth empirical analysis from a conceptual framework based on current IR literature.

The methodology and the approaches used in the analysis and their specific hypotheses are presented in detail in Chapter 4, and a precise definition of the object of study, i.e. the dependent variable, in Chapter 3. Before that, a brief historical background of EU foreign policy in Latin America, and towards Mercosur after its creation in 1991 is presented in Chapter 2. The analysis of two selected case studies, foreign direct investment and agricultural trade, is then carried out in Chapters 5 and 6, respectively. The main findings of the research are summarized in the conclusion.

Chapter 2 – The Southern Cone States in the foreign policy of the European Union: a historical background

In order to analyze whether and why EU foreign policy towards the Southern Cone States has become more cooperative since the mid-to-end 1980s, it is helpful to sketch the general historical background of EU foreign policy towards Latin America (section 2.1), and towards Mercosur (section 2.3) after its creation in 1991. This Chapter also contains a brief description of the main historical and institutional aspects of Mercosur (section 2.2).

2.1) EU foreign policy towards Latin America

The first official contact made by the then European Community with Latin American countries was shortly after the Treaty of Rome, in 1958, when the European Commission sent a Memorandum of Intention to most governments stating its intention of establishing close relations and cooperation with the area, and specifying that the Community's preference for internal trade should not hinder commercial prospects between the two regions.[7] In 1963, following a proposal by the Commission (COM (63)6), the Council of Ministers approved the establishment of a Contact Group between Commission officials and Latin American ambassadors in Brussels. As a development from the Contact Group's meetings, which took place from June 1963 to January 1964, the Latin American ambassadors sent a Memorandum to the Council of Ministers setting forth the need for a comprehensive policy towards the region. The Commission and the European Parliament supported the initiative, with the latter issuing a detailed report known as the Martino Report.[8] As a result, bilateral work groups were formed and held meetings during 1965 and 1966 to discuss specific issues regarding their commercial relations. However, the Latin Americans hope to transform the meetings into a negotiations forum was frustrated.[9] The Council never responded to their demand to upgrade the work groups into a mixed commission, despite the Italian government's interest in promoting better relations with Latin America, as part of its 'triangular policy'.[10]

---

[7] See Yrigoven, 1985, ch.2; Mower, 1982; Duran, 1985, pp.9-17.

[8] For the report see IRELA 1996, p.5.

[9] Cavalcanti, 1996, pp.180-181.

[10] In the 1960s the Italian government adopted the so-called 'triangular hypothesis' in foreign policy, aiming to promote a relationship between the US, Italy, representing Europe, and Latin America, to support the economic development of the latter. The policy was motivated, among other factors, by the concern of the Italian government with the massive immigration to the region, which reached more than 900.000 Italians between 1946 and 58. The lack of US support to the

In 1970, the Latin American countries that were members of the Special Committee for Latin American Coordination (CECLA) issued the Declaration of Buenos Aires calling for an institutionalization of their political dialogue and closer economic cooperation between the two regions.[11] This time the Council responded positively and a regular dialogue was initiated between the group of Latin American ambassadors to the Community (GRULA) and Commission officials.

This dialogue, however, did not advance in any substantial measure, and the Community's official policy was limited to bilateral commercial treaties with the major Latin American countries (so-called First generation agreements), such as Argentina in 1971, Uruguay and Brazil in 1973 and Mexico in 1975.[12] One exception was the policy developed toward Caribbean countries, which were incorporated together with other former European colonies in Africa and the Pacific in the so-called ACP Group and accorded a special regime codified in the Lomé Convention of 1975.[13]

In 1974, an Inter-Parliamentary Dialogue between the European Parliament and the Latin American Parliament (Parlatino) was initiated. Since then, it has been held yearly, and the main concerns usually addressed have been the consolidation of democracy, respect for human rights, and fostering economic development in Latin America.[14] In 1975, the Latin American countries tried to improve their regional cooperation and common representation abroad by founding the Latin American Economic System (SELA). In 1978, SELA produced the Informe de Punta del Este and, in 1979, Decision 44, advancing proposals of qualitative changes in its relations with the Community, which can

---

policy contributed to its failure. For more, see Camerana, 1985. Italian immigration was already strong before this period. Until 1947, there was a total of 1.513.151 Italian immigrants in Brazil, followed by Portuguese (1.462.117), Spaniards (508.802), German (253.846) and Japanese (188.622), see Ribeiro Hoffmann, 2001, p.149

[11] CECLA was an *ad hoc* group formed in 1963 by Latin American countries to coordinate their participation at the first meeting of the United Nations Conference on Trade and Development (UNCTAD). For the Declaration of Buenos Aires, see IRELA, 1996, p.32.

[12] First generation Agreements are characterized by their conventional bilateral and technical structure and their reference to possible reciprocal cooperation. In practical terms, however, these treaties only extended the Most Favored Nation (MFN) status to its signatories. See Lamothe, 1996, p.650; Calderón, 1996, p.682.

[13] The first Lome agreement was renegotiated in the subsequent Lome's II of 1979, III of 1985, IVa of 1989, and IVb (Mid term review) of 1995, and replaced in June 2000 by the Cotonou Agreement. For more, see Chapter 5, EU Development Policy.

[14] Parlatino was created in 1964 by the Lima Declaration as a permanent regional institution comprised by the elected national Parliaments of Latin America, with the purpose of promoting peace, democracy, human rights, economic development, regional integration and international cooperation, among others. It has a permanent seat in Sao Paulo, Brazil, where the annual Assembly and other meetings are held. For details, see homepage http://www.parlatino.org.br.

be seen in the context of the movement of the New International Economic Order (NIEO).[15]

Shortly before assuming its presidential term in 1980, Italy, through the Italo-Latin American Institute (IILA) proposed a ministerial meeting between Latin American countries and EU member-states to foster bi-regional relations, in which Italy would suggest the possibility of concluding a "Lome agreement with Latin America." The meeting never took place, but the Italian government at least emphasized the necessity of intensifying relations with Latin America, and restructuring the forms of dialogue with the region.[16] The Council, still under the Italian presidency, responded positively and established two instruments to renew the dialogue: meetings between GRULA, Coreper, and the Commission, and meetings between GRULA and the Commission. However, the admission of Cuba to GRULA during the same year, and the Falklands war, in 1982, resulted in a suspension of the dialogue.[17]

With the exception of measures related to the Falklands, EU foreign policy towards Latin America remained based mostly on Inter-Parliamentary Dialogue and on bilateral economic treaties. With regard to the latter, a new round was signed (the so-called Second generation Agreements)[18] with individual countries such as with Brazil, in 1980, and with sub regions, such as the Andean Pact, in 1983, and the Central American Common Market, in 1986. [19]

In 1984, the Commission prepared the document 'Orientations for strengthening relations between the Communities and Latin America' (COM (84) 105), setting out proposals to promote closer cooperation in specific areas and the access of Latin American countries to the European Investment Bank (EIB). In the same year, the Dialogue of San Jose was institutionalized between the Commission and the Contadora Group (formed in 1983 by Nicaragua, Colombia, Panama, Venezuela, Costa Rica, El Salvador, Guatemala, and Honduras) to deal with the Central American crisis, triggered by the Nicaraguan Revolution and the US military policy towards it. It is generally held to be one of the best examples of coherence and efficacy in the EU foreign policy, and the first case of an open divergence with US policies in Latin America.[20] Also in 1984, the Institute for

---

[15] See Yrigoyen, 1985, p.17.

[16] See Camerana, 1995; Cavalcanti, 1996, pp.196-197.

[17] About the EU conduct during the Falklands War see Camerana, p.61; Yrigoyen, ch.3; Hill, 1996; Martin, 1999, pp.131-169.

[18] The second-generation agreements reaffirmed the MFN clause and contained declarations about the intention to increase bilateral economic cooperation. See Lamothe, 1996, p.650; Calderón, 1996, p. 682.

[19] The Andean Pact was created in 1969 between Venezuela, Colombia, Equator, Peru and Bolivia, and the Central American Common Market was originally created in 1960 between Guatemala, El Salvador, Honduras, Nicaragua and Costa Rica, and revitalized after the Central American crisis, when Panama became a member as well.

[20] See : Smith, Hazel, 1995; Saraiva, 1996, ch.5; Guttry, 1996.

European-Latin American Relations (IRELA) was created to promote interregional relations with support of the European Commission and the European and Latin American Parliaments.[21]

In 1986, the Commission sent a communication to the Council about the state of affairs in Latin America as well as proposals for the development of a new policy, based on the recognition of the heterogeneity of the region, and in support of the sub-regional integration processes (COM (86) 720). The Council responded supportively and, during the Hague Summit in June, declared its interest in strengthening bi-regional relations, and emphasizing the new dimension of Latin America in the Community as a result of the accession of Portugal and Spain.

After joining the EU, Spain assumed a very active role in promoting Latin America, even if the concept of Spain as a 'bridge' between Latin America and Europe, fostered by then Foreign Minister Fernando Morán, and based on the concept of 'Hispanidad' - stressing common cultural values - had to be replaced by the more modest role of 'catalyst for change and supporter' of Latin American interests. Spain managed to obtain key Latin America-related positions in European institutions, such as the Commissioner for Latin American affairs Abel Matutes, in 1989, and the Commissioner for Development and Cooperation Manuel Marin, in 1993.[22] Portugal has also had a long-term special relationship with Latin America, but its links have been restricted to Brazil. Within the EU, Portugal largely joined the Spanish effort to promote closer relations with Latin America, but with less "enthusiasm." As in the context of the Ibero-American Summit (see below), Portugal showed some reluctance in joining what it saw as primarily a Spanish initiative, which might be seen as a legacy of its historical fear of remaining in the shadow of its larger neighbor.[23]

---

[21] IRELA was closed down in 2002 due to allegations of financial misconduct.

[22] The increased interest of Spain in developing closer relations with Latin America began under the regime of General Franco. The consensus on the priority accorded to Latin America among Spanish political parties is reflected in the Constitution of 1978, in which Art.56.1 of Title II states that "As a Chief of State and the symbol of its unity and permanence, the King shall moderate the regular functioning of its institutions and assume the highest representation of the Spanish State in international relations, *particularly with the nations of its historical community...*" where "historical community " referred both to Europe and Latin America. These priorities are reflected in the structure of the Spanish Foreign Ministry, which created, in 1985, the Secretariat of State for International Cooperation and for Iberoamerica, alongside with its other two divisions, the Secretariat of State for the EC, and the General Secretariat of Foreign Policy. For more about relations between Spain and Latin America see , Schumacher, 1995; Berrocal, 1981; Guzman, 1981; García, 1996, pp.707-711; Baklanoff, 1996, p.110; Atkins, 1995, pp.89-90; Durán 1997; Cavalcanti 1994, 1996.

[23] A major multilateral cooperative initiative promoted by Portugal together with Brazil was the creation of the Community of the Portuguese Speaking Language Countries (CPLP), in 1996, including Angola, Cabo Verde, Guine-Bissau, Mozambique and Sao Tome e Principe as well. The idea came up in 1989 during the First Meeting of the Heads of State and Government of the Portuguese Speaking Countries in Sao Luis, Brazil, when the Portuguese Language International

In 1987, the Rio Group Dialogue was established, as a development of the success of the Dialogue of San Jose, but with the main difference that is was not created to solve a crisis situation, but rather to establish a permanent forum for bi-regional political dialogue. The Rio Group Dialogue was institutionalized in 1990 by the Declaration of Rome, and turned out to be the main forum for meetings at the ministerial level, where security, as well as economic issues, are often discussed.[24] In 1989, the meetings between the Commission and GRULA were resumed. In 1990, the European Commission opened a delegation in Paraguay and Uruguay and, in 1991, in Argentina (in Brazil it had already been opened in 1984).[25]

In 1991, the Iberoamerican Summit, between Portugal, Spain, and most Latin American countries was initiated. Although not an EU initiative, these Summits contributed to consolidate the leading role of Spain, and to a lesser extent, of Portugal, in the promotion of closer relationships with Latin America within the EU. The second meeting, in Madrid, coincided with the 500th anniversary commemoration, the Barcelona Olympic Games and the Universal Exposition of Seville, when Spain succeeded in establishing the concept of "Iberoamerican community," a project pursued by it since the mid-1970s. In subsequent meetings, a number of joint cooperative projects were developed, and international forums positions were coordinated.[26]

Institute, based in Cidade da Praia, Cabo Verde, was also established. The Community, contrary to what the name suggests, does not focus merely on linguistic matters; its objectives include political-diplomatic coordination and economic cooperation. It has a legal personality, an institutional framework and a budget financed by the member-states and private contributions to support the implementation of its objectives. Some of its achievements include cooperation with Timor-Leste, the mediation in the conflict in Guine-Bissau in 1998; the cancellation of Mozambique's external debt with Brazil in 2000, and the development of anti AIDS projects, as well as technology transfer. About the CPLP, see Saraiva, 2001, and for a general historical background of the relations between Brazil and Portugal, see Magalhaes, 1999 and Cervo & Magalhaes, 2000.

[24] The Rio Group was created in 1986 by Brazil, Argentina, Paraguay, Uruguay, Colombia, Mexico, Peru and Venezuela as an intergovernmental group to promote peace, democracy and integration of Latin America. Bolivia, Chile, Equator and Panama joined later. For more, see Saraiva, 1996, ch.6. For the final declaration of the meetings until 1996, see IRELA, 1996, and EU DG External Relations homepage.

[25] The delegation in Paraguay and Uruguay operate in a joint office located in Montevideo. For details see the delegation's homepages (www.delarg.cec.eu.int; www.delbra.cec.eu.int; www.delury.cec.eu.int). About the opening of the delegation in Brazil, which was the first in Latin America, see Cavalcanti, 1996, p.195.

[26] The Iberoamerican Community is qualitatively different from the British Commonwealth and French relationship with former colonies. The longer lag in decolonization time and the relatively more advanced stage of development of the former colonies give a much more symmetric character to the Community, despite Spain's leadership ambitions. For more details, see Seixas Correia, 1994, and for the conclusion of the Iberoamerican annual summits see the homepage of the Spanish Foreign Affairs Ministry: http://www.aeci.es/

In 1993, the European Investment Bank was authorized to finance projects in Latin America and in 1995, the Madrid European Council adopted the document 'European Union and Latin America: the present situation and prospects for a closer partnership 1996-2000' (COM (95) 495), proposed by the Commission, in which the EU advanced a new strategy for its relations with Latin America, based on a differentiated approach, corresponding the necessities of each country or sub-region.

A new round of agreements (so-called of Third generation) was signed with individual countries: with Argentina and Bolivia in 1990, Venezuela and Uruguay in 1991, Chile in 1990, 1996 & 2002, Mexico 1991 & 1997, Paraguay and Brazil in 1992; and with sub regions, such as the Andean Community and Central American Common Market in 1993 and Mercosur in 1995. Negotiations with Mercosur for a new (association) agreement started in 1999. The main new aspects of these agreements were that they were broader in scope and included political conditionality regarding democracy, the environment, and human rights, by means of the so-called democracy clause, and they could be renegotiated with total flexibility, as set out in the so-called 'evolutive clauses'.[27]

Third-generation Agreements must be seen in the context of the creation of a vast network of institutionalized relations in the EU since the beginning of the 1990s. The EU has signed agreements with a large number of countries around the world under the name of cooperation, association, partnership, 'European' agreements, etc. The peculiarities of the agreements with Latin American countries are best understood when contrasted with agreements signed with other countries or regions. In terms of similarities, all third-generation agreements contain democratic and evolutive clauses, being classified under mixed competence, since they cover issues under the competence of the Community and of Member States.[28]

[27] The agreements with Mexico of 1997 (after the incorporation of Decisions 2/2000 and 2/2001), Chile of 2002, and the Association Agreement with Mercosur, under negotiation since 1999, are sometimes referred as fourth generation, since they include FTAs, unlike the other agreements. See Lamothe, 1996, p.651; Calderón, 1996, p.682; García, 1996, pp.725-732 CEPAL, 1999, p.8; COM (95) 216 final; Devlin et al, 2002.

[28] It is interesting to note what while the democratic clause is welcomed by Latin American governments, which see it as a reinforcement of the guarantee against the return of military governments (Mercosur also has such a clause, which was used against the attempts of military coup in Paraguay in 1996 and 2000), most Asian countries see it as an attempt of the EU to export Western values in detriment of Asian values and an issue of national sovereignty. This disagreement, enhanced by the entrance of Burma to ASEAN in 1997 is the main reason why the attempts to conclude a third generation agreement between the EU and ASEAN in 1992 failed. See Lim Paul, 1999, pp.4-11.

Regarding differences among the third-generation agreements, the most important is whether they are "empty" of "full" in terms of legal commitments.[29] While the agreements with the ACP, CEE, and former Soviet and Mediterranean countries contained from inception specific legal commitments concerning topics such as trade, competition, etc., the agreements with Latin American countries were originally empty. Some of these agreements, such as the one with the Andean Community, remained without substantial commitments, but others, such as with Mercosur, Chile and Mexico, were "filled" later, either by the conclusion of a new agreement, such as the one with Chile of 2002 and the Mercosur one, under negotiation since 1999, or directly in the same agreement, such as the case of Mexico, with the incorporation of Decision 2/2000, which promoted the liberalization of trade in goods, and Decision 2/2001, about the liberalization of trade in services and FDI.

The logic behind the execution of empty agreements is their political meaning. One political reason pointed out as a factor for the execution of such agreements is that they were seen as a strategy by the EU to reinforce its presence worldwide and consolidate the international legal personality of the Community as distinct from its Member-States vis-à-vis third parties. Another reason is that such agreements met the Commission's interests in expanding its competences and the Council's interests in justifying its work, since most agreements – whether full or empty - create bilateral institutional arrangements such as joint Committees, Commissions, and Sub-Commissions that meet periodically to manage relations. In addition, this management is also useful for the EU in that it constitutes a basis for the establishment of its (unilateral) policies for developing cooperation. Although they are legally independent from the agreements, the fact that they are managed jointly contributes to the (mis)perception of third parties that the cooperation programmes owe their existence to the agreements, and are therefore negotiated, instead of unilaterally decided and implemented.[30]

---

[29] For this distinction and more details see Torrent, 1998, p.213-228. The differentiation is actually also pertinent to second-generation agreements. Among the full agreements, some were signed as pre-accession agreements to the EU, such as the ones with Estonia, Latvia, Lithuania and Slovenia. Others, such as with Czechoslovakia, Hungary and Poland, acknowledged the associate's intention to seek membership but did not include any contractual obligation in that respect. In this sense, it is a mistake to distinguish cooperation and association agreements with basis on the possibility of EU accession. The association agreements with Cyprus and Malta, or Chile and Mexico, make no reference to membership. See Phinnemore, 1999, pp.62-70.

[30] This point becomes particularly relevant in the case of Asian countries, which do not accept the democratic clause in bilateral agreements but are targets for development cooperation via NGOs. In this case, the EU support for democratization is against the national interest of the recipient country. See Lim, 1999, p.35.

Table 1: EU Bilateral (and Bi-Regional) Agreements

Type	Example (date of signature)	Legal commitments			
		Trade	Treatment of foreign companies	Capital movements	Financial protocol
Cooperation	Andean Community 1993	No	no	no	no
Cooperation	CACM 1993	No	no	no	no
Cooperation	Argentina 1990	No	no	no	no
Cooperation	Uruguay 1991	No	no	no	no
Cooperation	Brazil 1992	No	no	no	no
Cooperation	Paraguay 1992	No	no	no	no
Cooperation	Mercosur 1995	no	no	no	no
Association	Mercosur under negotiation since 1999	FTA goods and services	Probably yes	Probably yes	Probably no
Cooperation	Chile 1991, 1996	no	no	no	no
Association	Chile 2002	FTA goods & services	yes	yes	no
Cooperation	Mexico 1991	No	no	no	no
Association	Mexico 1997	FTA goods & services	yes	yes	no
' European'	CEEs	FTA asymmetrical calendar	National treatment	yes	Non quantified, mentions PHARE
Partnership & Coop (PCAs)	Russia 1994 Ukraine	MFN	National treatment	yes	Non quantified, mentions

	1994, Belarus 1995				TACIS
Euro-Med Association	Tunisia 1995, Egypt 2001, Lebanon 2002, etc	FTA asymmetrical calendar	confirm GATS obligations	FDI	Non quantified does not mention MEDA
Lome-Cotonou	ACP	Non-reciprocal preferences (WTO waiver)	Non discrimination	no	Quantified from EDF funds

Source: Based on Torrent, 1998, Ch.8 and updated by author.

In addition to developing relations with specific countries and sub-regions in Latin America, the Commission prepared a document concerning Latin America as a whole, entitled 'Prospects of a new association - European Union/Latin America in the 21st century' (COM (99) 105), providing an overview of bi-regional relations and proposing EU's main objectives for the 'First Summit of European Union-Latin American-Caribbean Heads of State and Government (EU-LAC Summit) to be held in Rio de Janeiro in June of that year.

During the First EU-LAC Summit, the 48 participant states signed the Declaration of Rio containing 69 points about the general principles that should guide the bi-regional relationship in the political, economic, and cultural spheres. The Declaration also created a bi-regional group, which should meet regularly, and contained an Action Priorities Plan establishing 48 priorities for implementing cooperation programmes. Negotiations for the conclusion of a trade liberalization agreement with Mercosur and with Chile were launched. A Second Summit of European Union-Latin American-Caribbean Heads of State and Government took place in Madrid in 2002, and a Third Summit is expected to be held in Guadalajara, Mexico in May 2003.[31]

2.2) Creation of the Southern Cone Common Market (Mercosur)

The process of integration that culminated with the creation of the Southern Cone Common Market (Mercosur) began with a rapprochement between Argentina and Brazil formalized in the 1985 Declaration of Iguaçu. Until then,

[31] About the Rio Summit see IRELA, 1999a and 1999b; Maior, 1999; Stuart, 1999; and about the Madrid Summit, see Gratius, 2002.

relations between the two countries had been of competition for political dominance of the region, consequence of a long historical tradition.[32] The process of regional integration can be seen mainly as the result of democratization and the need for economic restructuring in both countries. The process developed through a series of initiatives, such as the 1986 Program for Integration and Economic Cooperation, the 1988 Integration, Cooperation and Development Treaty, and the 1990 Act of Buenos Aires. The integration process was extended with an invitation to Paraguay and Uruguay to join in.[33]

On March 26, 1991, the four countries signed the Treaty of Asunción, formalizing their intention to create a common market after a transition period of four years. With the Protocol of Ouro Preto, signed on December 17, 1994, Mercosur became an international legal personality and its institutional structure was formalized. Chile and Bolivia became associate members of Mercosur on June 25, 1996 and December 17, 1996, respectively.[34] On July 24, 1998, Mercosur member states signed the Protocol of Ushuaia, conditioning membership to democratic principles and government, as well as a Political Declaration concerning the promotion of peace in the region, security cooperation, disarmament, and non-proliferation of nuclear weapons. On February 18, 2002, Mercosur gained a Permanent Court for Settlement of Disputes located in Asunción and created by the Protocol of Olivos.[35]

The institutional structure of Mercosur has inter-governmental character and consists of five institutions. The first is the Council of the Common Market (CMC), the superior and legislative organ, holder of the legal personality (although it may delegate authority to the Common Market Group to negotiate agreements with third parties). It is composed by the Foreign and Economic Ministers of member states. The Presidency of the Council rotates every six months. The second institution is the Common Market Group (CMG), which is the executive and technical organ, coordinated by the Ministers of Foreign Relations and Economy and the Presidents of Central Banks. It is comprised by four office holders and respective alternates from each country, and eleven sub-

---

[32] This dispute can be traced back to colonial times, but a more recent reference would be the end of the Paraguay War, in 1864, when Brazil lost its hegemony over the Southern Cone and Argentina consolidated its 'unification' and achieved significant economic development. Since then, both countries played a 'power politics' game, involving Chile, or support from the US or the UK to counterbalance each other, although they never reached the point of declaring war. For more, see Cervo & Rapoport, 1998.

[33] For a detailed description of the negotiations leading to the creation of Mercosur see Costa Vaz, 2002, Ch5 & & 6.

[34] The associate members participate in the political meetings and in the free trade area, but do not have to adopt the common external tariff. See Mello, 1997, p.83-92.

[35] For more about Mercosur see the Mercosur Home page: www.mercosur.org.uy, or : Brandao & Pereira, 1997, da Matta & Pena, (ogs), 1996, Brum 1995, Mello, 1997, Vigevani, 1998, Wehner, 1999.

groups working on specific areas.[36] The third institution of Mercosur is the Joint Parliamentary Commission, which has a consultative and deliberative character, consisting of 16 parliamentarians from each country. The fourth institution is the Foreign Trade Commission, subordinated to the CMG and coordinated by the Ministers of Foreign Relations. Finally, there is the Social and Economic Consultative Forum, which is composed by representatives of society, businesspersons, and workers. Apart from these five institutions, Mercosur has an Administrative Office in Montevideo, the depositary of the official documents.

Mercosur has made remarkable progress towards the liberalization of intra-regional trade flows, particularly through the elimination of barriers, and as a result, intra and extra trade in goods increased between 1990 and 1996 by 89% and 311% respectively.[37] However, it faced challenges to eliminate non-tariff barriers and to effectively enforce a common external trade policy. The common external tariff, which ranges from zero to 20%, also faces a long list of exceptions for sensitive products, such as motor vehicles and sugar. This means that in practical terms Mercosur is not yet a full customs union, despite its formal status since the 1st of January of 1995 (according to recent schedules, it should be fully implemented by 2006). By the end of the 1990s, Mercosur had faced a series of setbacks that may be considered a result of the macroeconomic instability of its member-states. The effects of the devaluation of the Brazilian currency, in 1999, and the Argentinean crisis, in 2001, led to a profound rethinking ("soul searching") of the whole integration project, even discussing whether Mercosur should really become a custom union, or if it would be best to limit it to a free trade area.[38]

Parallel to its specific characteristics, Mercosur may be seen as part of the new wave of regionalism, in which the creation of free trade areas or common markets are seen as a new strategy of insertion in the world economy. Instead of creating relatively closed blocks as a protection against competition from developed countries, as in the former regionalist approaches, the new regionalism is based in the concept of open regionalism, or building blocks, in which regional groupings is seen as a step towards multilateralism.[39] In this regard, Mercosur has engaged in negotiations and concluded agreements with other regions, such as the European Union and the Andean Community, as well as with individual countries,

---

36 The areas are: trade, border transport, technical norms, fiscal and monetary policies concerning trade, ground transport, maritime transport, industrial and technological policies, agricultural policy, energy policy, coordination of macroeconomic policies and labor, employment and social security matters.

37 For an analysis of the strengths and weaknesses of Mercosur's institutional framework see Torrent, 2002 and Malamud, 2003. For statistics, see EC-DG Trade, 1998, pp.2-3.

38 See Bouzas, 2002.

39 See Al-Agraa, 1997; Ethier, 1998; Fuentes, 1994; Heete at al, 1999; Mansfield, 1997 and 1999 Mattli, 1999 and Breslin et al, 2002.

such as Mexico, South Africa, and India, in addition to deeper relations with Chile and Bolivia.

By the end of 2000, Mercosur was involved in two major negotiation processes, one with the EU that started in 1999, and one with North and South American countries, with the exception of Cuba, since 1994, the Free Trade Area of the Americas (FTAA). [40] The importance of these negotiations is not only that they will establish the terms of Mercosur's relationship with the two most significant actors in the world's economy, but also that they will have an impact on additional developments of Mercosur itself. While the EU wishes Mercosur to continue evolving towards a customs union (the negotiations mandate for the Association Agreement explicitly mentions it), the US prefers it to become a FTA and ultimately dissolve into the FTAA.

2.3) EU foreign policy towards Mercosur

EU foreign policy for Mercosur evolved initially in the framework of Latin America policy, but progressively received a different treatment. On one hand, Mercosur is considered an emergent market together with Chile and Mexico, and on the other hand, it is seen as the most successful regional integration project, with special appeal to the European Union, who sees it as a receptive region in which to implement its "integration model." [41]

The first treaty the EU signed with Mercosur was the Inter-Institutional Cooperation Agreement between the European Communities and Mercosur on May 29, 1992. This agreement was intended mostly as a vehicle for technical assistance, personnel training, and institutional support for the integration process (Art.2), seen as the best strategy to promote social and economic development and political stability in the region.[42] The agreement created a Joint Consultative Committee with members from both the European Commission and Mercosur's Common Market Group to develop and intensify inter-institutional dialogue and to promote and insure the agreement's cooperation initiatives (Art.7). A number of cooperative programmes were implemented, such as the support to Mercosur's Administrative Secretariat and technical cooperation for customs regulations, as well as animal and vegetable health measures.

---

[40] The decision to establish a FTAA was taken by the Heads of State and Government of the 34 states of the region during the Summit of the Americas, which took place in Miami on December 1994, following the initiative of the then US President George H.W. Bush. The negotiations of the agreement were launched formally on April 1998, at the Second Summit of the Americas in Santiago, Chile. See Bouzas, 1999; Hirst, 1999; Jaguaribe, 1995; Mello, 1997; Schirm, 1997; Roett, 1999; Granell, 2002, Pastor, 1996; and the FTAA homepage http://www.ftaa-alca.org.

[41] About the idea of exporting the EU model see Torrent, 2002, pp.208-213.

[42] Grabendorf, 1999, p.103.

In October 1994, the European Commission prepared a detailed document entitled 'For a Strengthening of the EU Policy towards Mercosur' (COM (94) 428), in which it elaborated a long and a short-term strategy to guide foreign policy towards Mercosur. In its conclusions, the Commission declared that despite the achievements enabled by the Interinstitutional Agreement, the treaty was an insufficient instrument to promote the necessary strengthening of the EU's relations with Mercosur, and proposed an interregional cooperation framework agreement, which would, in a first stage, prepare the basis for bi-regional commercial liberalization and continue to support the integration process and, in a second stage, create a free trade zone. The two stages would be institutionalized by two independent agreements, although the second would be negotiated according to the principles stated in the first agreement. The European Council approved the Commission's strategy during the Summit in Essen, in December 1994, and, soon afterwards, signed, together with the Commission and the Mercosur member-states, a Solemn Joint Declaration officializing the intention to begin negotiations. In April 1995, the Council requested the COREPER to analyze the Commission's document, and in October, the Economic and Social Committee sent a reply adding new proposals and emphasizing the participation of several sectors of the civil society in the process of negotiation of the agreement (ESC Opinion 1176). The European Parliament also supported the Commission's proposal and added suggestions as well, such as including a political dialogue between members of the Joint Parliamentary Commission of the Mercosur and the European Parliament in the institutional provisions of the agreement (Resolution of 16-5-1995).

The Interregional Cooperation Agreement by and among the European Community and its Member States and Mercosur and its Member States was signed on December 15, 1995, becoming effective on July 1999. It is typically an empty third-generation agreement: very broad, containing 9 titles and 36 articles covering political, economic, and cultural aspects of bi-regional relations, but with no substantial commitments. On the positive side, the agreement established a forum for regular meetings at the ministerial level, with the establishment of a Cooperation Council to supervise the development of negotiations towards a second stage of the agreement. The Cooperation Council is composed by members of the European Commission, the Common Market Council, and the Common Market Group of Mercosur (Art.25), and assisted by a Joint Commission of Cooperation (Art.27) and a Commercial Sub-Commission (Art.29).[43]

During the 1st EU-LAC Summit in Rio de Janeiro, in June 1999, both sides decided to open negotiations intended to liberalize bilateral trade. One particular aspect of the negotiations between the EU and Mercosur is that it represents a

[43] For detailed analysis of the agreements, see Kinoshita, 2001, and Torrent, 1998, p.224-227.

negotiation between one block of developed countries and one of developing countries, in reciprocal terms. The concept of concluding reciprocal trade agreements between developing and developed countries is relatively new; it started with NAFTA, and the EU agreements with Mexico, Chile, and Mercosur. While the NAFTA is a mere trade liberalizing agreement, as will be the FTAA if and when concluded (although non-trade cooperation initiatives, such as aid and technical assistance, are taking place in parallel), the FTA promoted by the EU combine such initiatives with political and development cooperation commitments in one single undertaking that should contribute to compensating possible negative effects of the reciprocity among asymmetric partners. This represents a shift in the strategy of EU development policies and has been implemented with other developing countries as well, even ACP, as is becomes apparent in the new Cotonou Agreement.[44]

During the first Meeting of the EU-Mercosur Cooperation Council (on November 24, 1999) in which the High Representative Javier Solana and Trade Commissioner Chris Patten participated, among others, the structure, methodology, and calendar for the Association Agreement negotiations were defined. It was agreed that the results of the negotiations would constitute one single undertaking to be implemented as an indivisible whole and that, given its mixed character, it would be negotiated in parallel by the European Commission (covering its competences: trade and cooperation) and by the Member States (for their competences: investments and services). With regard to the structure of the negotiations, it was established that the following committees would be created: a Bi-regional Negotiations Committee to provide general oversight and management for negotiations related to trade and cooperation (with the ability to create Technical Groups to implement activities related to trade negotiations), a Cooperation Subcommittee to conduct negotiations on cooperation, and a Coordinating Secretariat comprised by representatives of the European Commission and of the Mercosur Presidency.

On the 6-7th of April 2000, during the First Meeting of the Bi-regional Negotiations Committee, in Buenos Aires, negotiations for the conclusion of the association agreement began. With regard to political dialogue, the conclusions of the meeting emphasized the importance of discussing topics such as conflict prevention, confidence and security building measures, promotion and protection of human rights, democracy and the rule of law, sustainable development taking into account the economic, social and environmental dimensions, and common actions against drug traffic, arms traffic, organized crime and international terrorism. Three subgroups were created to deal with economic, social, cultural, financial, and technical cooperation. Concerning trade negotiations, three

[44] See Devlin et al, 2002.

technical groups were created: trade in goods; trade in services and intellectual property; and government procurement, competition and dispute settlement.

The second round of negotiations took place in Brussels, on June 13-16, 2000. In this round, the EU negotiators presented the state of affairs regarding the EU agricultural policy and the enlargement process, while Mercosur negotiators presented the state of affairs regarding their integration process. The three trade-related technical groups exchanged information and discussed specific objectives. The subgroup on financial and technical cooperation, whose general objective is to offer European technical assistance to Mercosur with a view to reinforcing Mercosur's development and integration process and the integration between Mercosur and other countries in Latin America, established that cooperation should focus on three areas: modernization of the public administration, institutional cooperation (to reinforce the process of deepening regional integration, and providing support to the Administrative Secretary, the Parliamentary Joint Commission and the Economic and Social Consultative Forum of Mercosur), and regional cooperation (promoting trade and investment, encouraging land use planning and development of the communications infrastructure and environmental protection).

During the third round of negotiations, which took place in Brasilia on November 7-10, 2000, there were mainly exchanges of information and joint texts proposals on political dialogue and economic cooperation. Concerning trade, the technical groups held discussion sessions on agriculture, sanitary and phytho-sanitary rules, trade defense instruments, government procurement, etc. In the fourth round of negotiations, held on March 19-22, 2001, in Brussels, the trade representatives presented text proposals and working documents on several non-tariff issues, and the Commission launched a business facilitation initiative as an instrument for interaction with the business community, which could be implemented before the conclusion of the agreement.

During the fifth round of negotiations, which took place in Montevideo on July 2-6, 2001, the EU unilaterally presented a tariff offer on goods, covering 90,5% of its imports from Mercosur, and negotiation texts on goods, services, and government procurement. This initiative marked the beginning of a second stage in the negotiation process. Until then, the exchanges had a more fact-finding character. With the tariff offer in goods, the real negotiations actually started. A third stage would be the offer of preferential market access for services, government procurement and investment.

In reciprocity, at the sixth round, held in Brussels on October 29-31, 2001, Mercosur presented its tariff offer for goods, which, however, covered only 35% of its imports from the EU, besides negotiation texts on services and public procurement. A substantial progress on the cooperation chapter was made and joint texts on several fields, such as telecommunications, energy, and transport were agreed. During the seventh round, which took place in Buenos Aires on

April 8-11, 2002, the main topics discussed were the prospects for the Second EU-LAC Summit, the proposals regarding business facilitation measures of the EU-Mercosur Business Forum, and the increase of EIB funds to Latin America. Joint texts on the cooperation chapter, institutional framework, and political dialogue were prepared. In the eighth round of negotiations, which took place on November 11-14, 2002, in Brasilia, negotiating texts about intellectual property rights and settlement of disputes, discussion on methods and modalities for the negotiations about market access for goods (including agricultural) and services were concluded, and implementation of business facilitation measures was considered.

On the March 5, 2003, both parties exchanged a second offer on the liberalization of goods tariffs. The EU offer covered 91% of Mercosur exports, and Mercosur's 83,5%, a much better offer than the previous 35%, and above the 80% minimum required by the WTO to consider the EU-Mercosur agreements as a free trade area. [45] During the 9th round of negotiation, which took place on March 17-21, 2003, in Brussels, the tariff offers from the EU reached 91,5%, and from Mercosur 83,5%, and methods and modalities for negotiations on investment and government procurement were agreed.[46]

During the EU-Mercosur ministerial meeting held in Brussels in November, 2003, a calendar to conclude the negotiations was agreed, including five meetings of the Bi-regional Negotiations Committee (foreseen to take place until July, 2004) and two ministerial meetings. The first ministerial meeting should take place during the 3rd EU-LAC Summit in Guadalajara and the second, in October 2004. [47]

---

[45] Gazeta Mercantil, Editorial, 10/03/03; Daniel Ritter, Valor Economico, 10/03/03.

[46] Folha de Sao Paulo, Editorial, 22/03/03.

[47] For more details about the negotiation process, see DG External Relations Homepage, http://europa.eu.int/comm/external_relations/mercosur/ass_neg_text/index.html.

Chapter 3 - The dependent variable: the level of cooperation of EU foreign policy behavior towards the Southern Cone States

In order to define the dependent variable for this research, which is the level of cooperation of EU foreign policy behavior towards the Southern Cone States, as well as adequate indicators to analyze it, it is important to define what is deemed as foreign policy (section 3.1), EU foreign policy (section 3.3), and cooperative behavior (section 3.4), given that such concepts are subject to controversial debate in relevant literature. Each of these concepts is developed below, as well as the possibility of conceptualizing the EU as an international actor (section 3.2).

3.1) Foreign policy

As indicated in the terminology itself, foreign policy refers to policies directed to the outside. The identification of an 'outside' implies in establishing a borderline in relation to the inside, and therefore delineating a certain unit. Considering the modern international system, this unit has traditionally been the nation-state, given its distinctive position as the exclusive holder of territorial sovereignty and its endowment with international legal personality. Yet, the exclusivity of nation-states as initiator actors is not intrinsic in the definition of foreign policy.

This aspect of the definition of foreign policy, i.e., which actors are recognized as conducting a foreign policy, is particularly relevant when analyzing the European Union's foreign policy, since it is not a nation-state, as will be discussed in detail in the following section. The main objective of this section is to inquire how foreign policy can be studied independently of the type of actor who conducts it. A first step in that direction is to examine how it has been studied in the past or, in other words, to examine relevant foreign policy literature.

Although the behavior of political units in relation to the 'outside' has been studied for centuries, this has mostly been done from a historical perspective, or with analytical concepts such as *Realpolitik* or balance of power. It was only after the Second World War that scholars from the recently born discipline of International Relations began to engage in attempts to develop a systematic framework to study foreign policies. The most influential was the comparative foreign policy project (CFP) proposed by James Rosenau in 1966. The project must be seen in the context of the social sciences behavioral revolution, which sought to move away from non-cumulative descriptive case-studies and towards the construction of explanations using quantitative methods in comparative studies for theory building, but that was, however, not successful in producing a unified theory and therefore not able to incorporate many important factors that affect foreign policy behavior, as pointed out by critics.[48]

Less ambitious studies produced middle-range theories and focused on specific determinants of foreign policymaking, such as the role of the decision-making process (Snyder et al, 1954), bureaucratic politics (Graham Allison, 1971), group dynamics (Charles Hermann, 1978), public opinion (Cohen, 1973), and cognitive and psychological factors (Sprout & Sprout,1956; Axelrod, 1976).[49] Despite many advances in the study of foreign policies, a general skepticism developed against the subject with the so-called "structural turn" in IR theory, following the publication of the "Theory of International Politics" by Kenneth Waltz in 1979. The hegemony of structural approaches at the systemic level, especially in the American academy, first with Neorealism, but also with the development of Institutional Liberalism as in the work of Robert Keohane discredited the usefulness of unit-level approaches in explaining international politics.[50]

Although two sides of the same coin, the study of "action" by foreign policy approaches, and the study of "interaction" by international politics approaches imply methodological and meta-theoretical questions that are subject to great controversy in social sciences. On the one hand, this question may be seen in methological terms as advanced by David Singer as early as 1961, regarding at which level of analysis a study should be conducted. On the other hand, it may be seen as an ontological question, concerning which are the main forces in international politics: actors or structures, emphasizing the issue of purposiveness of behavior at any level of analysis. The relationship between the level of analysis and the ontological problem (or, the actor/structure debate) in IR has been extensively discussed in the last decade.[51]

The actor/structure debate brought to discussion the possibility of defining the behavior of international actors in non-intentional ways, and of using structural approaches to analyze foreign policies. Moreover, the development of synthetic approaches as exemplified by the structuration approach of Anthony Giddens opened up the floor to explore the possibility of combining both systemic and unit-level sources of behavior determination. Whereas the structuration approach relegated a passive role to the structures, in that they are defined as enabling and constraining the actor's behavior, "synthetic" approaches went a step further, claiming that there is no ontological unidirectional causality between

[48] See Neack et al, 1995; Linda Brandt, 1982.

[49] See Clarke & White, 1988 and Neack et al, 1995.

[50] See Carlsnaes, 2001, p.331-334; White, 2001, p.171-173.

[51] For the level of analysis and ontological questions, see Wendt, 1987, 1991 and 1992; Dessler, 1989; Hollis and Smith, 1991 and 1992; and Czempiel, 1996.

actors and structures, and that both are capable of influencing each other. These approaches transcend the actor/structure dichotomy, which is particularly welcome to the phenomena researched here insofar as some of the relevant approaches to cooperative behavior are, as seen in the previous section, systemic, while some are unit-level.[52]

3.2) International actorness of the EU

Apart from the above mentioned controversial issues regarding the study of foreign policies as such, an analysis of EU foreign policy needs to address the possibility of studying the EU as a unit in the international system, whose behavior and foreign policies may be analyzed separately from its member-states'. The definition of international actorness in the discipline of International Relations is based on assumptions concerning the nature of the international system, and vary with the different approaches, but remains closely related to the international legal personality in Public International Law.

In Public International Law, legal personality is defined as the potential ability to exercise certain rights and to fulfill certain obligations vis-à-vis other international legal persons. International institutions may also have an international legal personality, but this does not imply that the international legal personality of international organizations is equivalent to the one of states. On the contrary, whereas states are recognized as possessing the widest range of rights and duties (such as treaty-making power, enjoyment of privileges and immunities from national jurisdictions, capacity to embrace international claims and to protect its own personnel, locus stand before international tribunals, administration of territory, right of mission and recognition of states), those of international organizations are clearly circumscribed in terms of express powers – competences – laid down in their constituent instruments, or implied powers evolved from practice. The classic case is the United Nations, which were held to possess international legal personality by the International Court of Justice in its 1948 Advisory Opinion on the *Reparation of Injuries Suffered in the Service of the United Nations*.[53] However, the Court also pointed out that attributing such personality to the United Nations did not amount to declaring it a state or that its rights and duties were the same as those of a state; indeed, in its recent Advisory Opinion on the *Legality of the Use by a State of Nuclear Weapons in an Armed*

[52] The actor/structure debate has taken place in most Social Sciences' disciplines. For more details about synthetic approaches to Social Theory, see the works of Anthony Giddens and Juergen Habermas, or José Maurício Domingues. In the discipline of International Relations, see Wendt 1991, 1992; Hollis & Smith, 1991, 1992.

[53] ICJ Reports 1949, p.174.

Conflict, the Court reiterated the limited nature of an international organization's legal personality.[54]

The debate about EU's legal personality is often misunderstood. Although so far the EU itself has not been attributed explicit international legal personality, this does not necessarily mean that it does not, or cannot have, such personality. In fact, there is a debate in international and European law, in which one side, at least, claims that the denial of full legal personality is mostly due to the explicit unwillingness of member-states to confer independent rights and duties to the Union, as may be seen in the (unpublished) *travaux préparatoires* of the Maastricht negotiations. Nothing in the Treaties themselves, according to this view, precludes the assumption of such personality.[55]

Unlike the EU, the three original communities, the European Coal and Steel Community (ECSC), the European Atomic Energy Community (Euratom) and the European Economic Community (EEC) have provisions in their constituting treaties conferring them legal personality that allows them to conclude agreements with third parties in certain areas under provided competences, as indicated in Art.6/ECSC; Art.101 (1)/Euratom; and Art.210/EEC, respectively. With the Merger Treaty signed in 1965, the "executive" institutions of the three communities, that is, their Commissions and Council, were unified, but their legal personalities remained as before. With the Treaty of Maastricht, signed in 1992, the EEC was renamed European Community (EC) and the three communities came to be referred to as the first pillar, but they continued to have separate legal personalities. The Treaty of Amsterdam, signed in 1997, renumbered the EU and EC treaties without any changes in their legal personalities. With the Treaty of Nice, signed in 2001, the TEU and the EC Treaty were merged into one consolidated version, again without implications to the legal personalities of the respective entities. The ECSC expired on 23 July 2002, and its rights and obligations under the international agreements concluded were taken over by the European Community (EC).[56]

Another complicating issue affecting the definition of international actor for the EU is the complex distribution of competences between the community

[54] For more about the international legal abilities of international organizations see Kirgis, 1977, pp.7-29; Shaw, 1997, pp.909-915 & Brownlie, 1979, pp.677-704.

[55] Although some authors such as De Witte, 1998, assert that even in that case "the subjective intention to withhold legal personality does not exclude that legal personality may have been implicitly granted". Quoted in Wessel, 2000, p.521.

[56] In the case of ECSC Art.6 provides that the Community enjoys legal capacity as required to perform its functions, and is not explicitly empowered to conclude agreements, but it was interpreted as such, and the ECSC has in fact concluded many agreements. For details about its expiration, see Council Decision 2002/595/EC dated 7-19-2002. In the case of EEC/EC, there were many controversies about the limits of its competence, which have often been referred to the European Court of Justice. For more details, see MacLeod, Hendry & Hyett, 1996.

institutions and its member-states.[57] Before the Treaty of Maastricht, the distribution of competences was done primarily among European Communities, and could be exclusive or non-exclusive, and the residual competences of the member-states.[58] Aside from acting within the community institutions, the member-states were engaged in intensive pluri-lateral cooperative initiatives, the most important being the European Political Cooperation (EPC).[59]

The Treaty of Maastricht segmented even further the distribution of competences between community institutions and the member-states, notably by the institutionalization of the three-pillar structure. The first pillar includes the activities under the competence (exclusive or non-exclusive) of the Community, and the second and third pillars those under the competence of member-states, namely the Common Foreign and Security Policy (CFSP) and Judicial and Home Affairs (JHA). Apart from the three pillars, the member-states continued to retain competences over issues outside the EU system. However, some of them were effectively decided and managed from within the EU system, thus constituting an informal "fourth pillar."[60]

In International Relations, the debate on international actorness is not based directly on the concept of international legal personality, but rather on assumptions that vary according to the approach. Three main positions may be found with regard to the status of actorness in the EU. On one extreme, some scholars reject it entirely, as they reject the actorness of international organizations, claiming that nation-states are the only relevant units of the international system. This position is most commonly advanced by realists, for

[57] The final report of the Convention Working Group on Legal Personality suggested that the EU should be given a explicit legal personality, which would replace the Community one and possibly the EURATOM one, but that the distribution of competences between the EU and member-states and between the EU and the EC do not have to change necessarily. See CONV 305/02 - WG II 16, p.6, at the Convention Homepage: http://europa.eu.int/futurum/

[58] Under exclusive competence, only the Community may act, such as the case of the Common Commercial Policy, regulated by Art. 113/133. Under non-exclusive competence, member-states may act when the Community does not act (non-exclusive non-exercized competences). In some cases, they may continue to act in parallel to the Community even if the latter starts acting (such as a development policy or the conclusion of international association agreements Art. 238/310), and in some cases they lose the possibility to act. See Torrent, pp.39-40 and MacLeod, Hendry & Hyett, 1996.

[59] The EPC was created in 1970 as a forum where member-states could discuss and coordinate their position in foreign policy matters. It was institutionalized in 1986 by the Single European Act (SEA). About EPC and its evolution into CFSP, see : Allen, Rummel & Wessels (Eds), 1982; Allen & Pijpers (Eds), 1984; Hill, 1983, 1996); Holland, 1991; Nuttall, 1993; Ginsberg, 1989; Schoutheethe 1980, 1986; Regelsberger et al (Eds), 1997.

[60] As in the case of negotiating "mixed agreements" with Third Parties, i.e. agreements which cover issues under the competence of the Community as well as issues under the competence of member-states, such as the GATs and the Yaoundé/Lomé/Cotonou agreements, or under negotiation with Mercosur. See Torrent, Ch5.

whom the external behavior of the European Union should be analyzed as a zero-sum result of its member-states (Mearsheimer 1990, 2001; Bull, 1982).

Others scholars argue that the EU is not a political unit comparable to international organizations, nor will it become a state-like political unit either. These scholars claim that the European Union has a *sui generis* and evolving character, and therefore should be defined as a (so far) incomplete political unit of the international system. A complete international actor should be able to fulfill certain criteria, which is not (yet) the case with the EU. For some (Sjostedt, 1977), the criteria would include a community of interests, a decision-making system, a crisis management system, a system for management of interdependence, an implementation system, external communication channels, external representation, community resources, and a mobilization system. For others (Breterthon & Vogler, 1999), the requisites are a shared commitment to certain values and principles, ability to identify policy priorities, ability to negotiate with others, use of policy instruments and domestic legitimacy. Others (Hill 1993, 1996, 1998) identify as the major obstacle to EU unity the "gap" between expectations (from third parties) and EU's capacity to perform.

A third group of scholars supports the possibility of analyzing the EU as a political unit of the international system, given that, despite the fragmented foreign policy decision-making processes and lack of capabilities, the EU has developed a major "presence" in the contemporary global arena. Presence is defined by some authors as an actor who is an initiator, shaper, barrier, filter, facilitator and/or manager of policies regarding third parties (Allen & Smith, 1990, 1998), and by other authors as an actor who holds a clear international identity and produced significant impact upon other international actors (Whitman, 1994, 1997, 1998; Manners 1997; Ginsberg 2001; Smith K., 1999). This position is also held by realists who accept that the EU could be treated as an 'as if' international actor (Waltz, 2000; see also Kagan, 2002). [61]

This study assumes that the EU's actorness must be analyzed on an empirical case-by-case basis, rather than at the theoretical level. The case for EU's actorness seems to be stronger in the case of foreign policies where the Community holds exclusive competences and sufficient capabilities to manage and implement the policy in an issue-area in which the EU has a strong international presence, such as agricultural trade, than for policies under the "fourth pillar," such as FDI. Since the purpose of the present study is not to analyze the actorness of the EU, but to examine the level of cooperation of its foreign policy behavior, it seems to be sufficient to assume that the EU can be treated as a political unit of the international system, whose level of actorness at a particular point of time is more empirical than theoretical.

---

[61] For more references see Manners, 2000, p.28-29.

3.3) EU foreign policy

When referring to the EU, the label "foreign policy" is traditionally associated with security-military high politics, as the activities developed within the European Political Cooperation (EPC) and the Common Foreign and Security Policy (CFSP), while the activities developed within the Community are traditionally denominated "external relations." As stated above, however, the perspective adopted herein defines EU's foreign policy as encompassing both activities, since the two parameters of this differentiation (organizational structure of the policymaking system and categorization of issue-areas into high or low-politics, i.e., the degree of politicalization and sovereignty sensitivity) change with time and are considered an empirical matter.[62]

Another question that arises when analyzing the EU foreign policy refers to whether this can be done with foreign policy approaches designed to study nation-states. It is one matter to broaden the assumption that nation-states are exclusive foreign policy initiator actors, but it is quite another matter to apply foreign policy approaches developed to study nation-states to studies about the foreign policy of other types of actors, such as the European Union.[63]

This study assumes that, once the EU is considered an unit of the international system (with different levels of actorness, according to the policy area), approaches to the analysis of foreign policy, such as the Neorealist, Identity Constructivist, and Utilitarian Liberal foreign policy theories can be directly applied to study EU's foreign policy.

3.4) Cooperative behavior

International cooperation is one of the major topics addressed by the discipline of International Relations. There are, essentially, three main bodies of literature dealing with this subject: one regarding international negotiations, one regarding international regimes (and international organizations) and one regarding regional integration. An appropriate definition of cooperative behavior to be used in this work is the one proposed by Robert Keohane in the context of the literature of international regimes.

Cooperative behavior is defined by Keohane as a "process of policy coordination in which actors adjust their behavior to the actual or anticipated

---

[62] For more about this see section 4.1

[63] For an initial debate about the challenges posed by the development of European integration to the study of foreign policies, see Carlsnaes & Smith (Eds) 1994. Among others, the authors argue that the main theories for Foreign Policy Analysis have been developed in the US academic community, and to a large extent they reflect US views and concerns, therefore being at risk of becoming irrelevant to analyze European foreign policy (both at the EC/EU level and at the national states level), particularly as the process of integration develops further.

preferences of others".[64] Intergovernmental cooperation takes place when the policies actually followed by one government are regarded by its partners as facilitating the attainment of their own objectives, as a result of policy coordination. It is important to note that cooperation does not imply the absence of conflict; on the contrary, it is typically mixed with conflict, partially reflecting successful efforts to overcome conflict, whether actual or potential.

Therefore cooperation, as a proactive behavior, takes place only in situations where actors perceive that their policies are actually or potentially in conflict, not where there is harmony, i.e., situations where actors policies' automatically facilitate the attainment of a partner's goals. Discord, being the opposite of harmony, stimulates demands for policy adjustments, which can lead either to cooperation or to continued and possibly even intensified discord.

3.5) Indicators

The indicators of the level of cooperation of EU's behavior in foreign policy may be found in two distinct areas of EU foreign policy: in its unilateral foreign policies and in bilateral agreements concluded with the SCS. The precise indicators for each case study are detailed in Chapters 5 and 6, and briefly presented in the table below.

For the case study of foreign direct investment, the main indicators are the commitments and references to cooperation in bilateral agreements and programmes related to development policies, since the EU does not have a common FDI policy.

For the case of agricultural trade, the main indicators are the commitments and references to cooperation in bilateral agreements, the programmes related to development policies, and also the policies under common commercial and agricultural policy.

According to these indicators, the level of cooperation of EU foreign policy may be classified according to a scale consisting of four levels of cooperation: very low, low, medium and high.

Table 2: Indicators and level of cooperation of the EU foreign policy behavior

Indicators/Level of Cooperation	Very Low	Low	Medium	High
Number/budget of cooperation programmes in development policies	No programmes	More than before	More than before	More than before

[64] Keohane, 1984, pp.51-52.

Nature of cooperation programmes	-	Do not accommodate demands from recipient, but impose conditionalities against the will of recipient	Accommodate demands from recipient, but impose conditionalities against the will of recipient	Accommodate demands from recipient, and impose only conditionalities accepted by recipient
Commitments related to the issue area in bilateral agreements	No commitments, or commitments against the will of recipient	No commitments; but informal support of commitments favorable to recipient	Commitments favorable to both parts	Commitments favorable to recipient and unfavorable to the EU
Reference to cooperation in the issue area in bilateral agreements	No reference	General reference	Specific reference	Specific reference with financial protocol
Tariffs	-	Lower than before	Lower than before	Lower than before
Abusive use of CCP defensive instruments	Used	Less used than before	Less used than before	Less used than before
SGP concessions	No concessions	More than before	More than before	More than before

Chapter 4 - Research Design

This chapter describes the research design adopted to study the level of cooperation of the EU foreign policy behavior towards Southern Cone States. It describes first the methodology adopted (section 4.1) and then summarizes the selected approaches and their predictions regarding EU foreign policy behavior towards Southern Cone States (section 4.2).

4.1) Methodology

As mentioned earlier, this study seeks to answer two questions: whether or not the EU foreign policy behavior towards Mercosur has become more cooperative since the mid-to-end 1980s; and why change, if any, has occurred. The answer to the first question is addressed through a descriptive inference of the level of cooperation of EU foreign policy behavior towards Southern Cone States, performed with the help of general indicators developed in Chapter 3 and refined for each case study in Chapters 5 and 6.[65]

The answer to the second question, i.e., why the change (or non-change) occurred, is found by testing the hypotheses derived from selected theoretical approaches. However, since the main interest of this study is to provide a better understanding of the motivations of EU foreign policy towards Southern Cone States, i.e., it is a problem and not a method-oriented project, the research design does not offer the ideal conditions to produce a "strong" test of the approaches considered, therefore the conclusions cannot be generalized.

The hypotheses are tested in two steps. The first step follows the congruence procedure, according to which the explanatory power of a hypothesis may be assessed by the degree of consistency between predicted and observed values of the dependent variable, accompanied by an analysis of the covariance between the dependent and independent variable, i.e., whether the former has changed in the predicted direction. If it has not changed in the predicted direction, the hypothesis is falsified. However, since covariance does not imply causality, additional strategies must be adopted as well. A second step consists in the analysis of the causal mechanisms between the independent and dependent variables through process tracing. If causal mechanisms cannot be found, the covariance analysis should be at least complemented by an analysis of further observable implications of the hypothesis, as a second best option.[66]

---

[65] King et al, 1994, Chapter 2.

[66] About the congruence procedure and process tracing see Bennet & George, 1997; Van Evera, Ch.2; Rittberger 2001, pp.308-310. About multicausality (or equifinality), see King et al, 1994, p.87 & Bennet & George, 1997, p.5.

Information concerning the descriptive inference of the level of cooperation of EU foreign policy, as well as the selected hypothesis test, is based on primary and secondary sources. With regard to primary sources, EU documents, statements from EU officials and the general press were used, as well as a few interviews conducted in Brussels with officials responsible for the relations with Southern Cone States in the Council Secretariat and the Commission, and with an international relations consultant of the Green Party in the European Parliament.[67]

The selection of the time period to be analyzed took into consideration the following aspects: First of all, the alleged change of EU foreign policy towards Southern Cone States would have occurred in the mid-to-end 80s. Second, that cooperation is defined by long patterns of behavior and not by isolated acts or events and, therefore, the values of the dependent variable must be assessed within a certain time scope, for instance 5-year periods. As a result, the selected time periods are 1980-1985 and 1995-2000. The five years before and after the alleged change should be able to provide enough empirical evidence to test the hypothesis.

The criteria for selection of case studies were, in the first place, their relevance for the issue area identified as representative of a conflict between the EU and the SCSs. Second, the variance of the dependent variable (which should be the highest possible). Third, the variance of the tested independent variables (which should be the highest possible), and finally, the variance in the non-included potential independent variables (which should be the lowest possible).[68]

With regard to the representativeness of conflict, it is important to emphasize that one striking characteristic of the bilateral relationship between the EU and Southern Cone States is the asymmetry between the partners. This asymmetry has many facets: representation in international politics, recognition and assimilation of socio-cultural models, and level of economic development. In short, the asymmetry present in the bilateral relationship between the EU and the Southern Cone States is representative of the asymmetry between the "North and the South," the "First and Third World," or "developed and developing countries." Each facet of this asymmetry poses a different level of potential conflict for the relationship during each time period.

Within the analyzed time period, the asymmetry in the international politics representation did not cause any major conflicts between the parties, as it had previously happened in the context of the Non-Alignment Movement, at the UNCTAD creation, as a counterpoint to the GATT, or at the UNESCO crisis. In the early 80s, the SCSs seemed to accept the legitimacy of international institutions and engage in constructive criticism from within. Other actors of the

[67] The interviews were conducted under the condition of not revealing names.
[68] King et all, 1994, pp.139-150.

international politics rather than developing countries, such as the organized civil society, can be seen as the main critics of the asymmetric representation in international institutions. The main axe of the debate seems not to be the traditional North-South, but the civil society-private one. MNCs are accused of having hijacked the agenda of international organizations such as WTO or the aborted MAI to their advantage. Athough most of the MNCs are originally European or American (from the "north"), they are seen as independent actors who advance their interests independently of their home governments, and eventually against them.[69]

The risk of conflict between the EU and the Southern Cone States regarding socio-cultural matters has never been significant. The latter see themselves as sharing European culture and values. It can be said that there is no socio-cultural cleavage between the EU and Southern Cone States societies, such as, for instance, between "Western" and "fundamentalist Islamic" societies, which could be defined as a conflictive during the 1990s. Although Europe is seen as the birthplace of a hegemonic culture, and in that sense seen as the "hegemon," characterizing an asymmetric relationship, that culture is largely shared by the societies of Southern Cone States.[70]

The economic asymmetry between regions can be said to be the major cause of conflict between the European Union and Southern Cone States in the studied time period. This asymmetry is accused of being the cause of the less advanced stage of development of the Southern Cone States. The point here is not to evaluate the validity of this claim, but to acknowledge that the main source of conflict in the relationship between EU and Southern Cone States has been the need to coordinate policies that influence the accumulation of capital and economic development of the latter.

Within the economic area, two case studies seem to be particularly relevant: foreign direct investment (FDI) and agricultural trade. The EU policies in relation to FDI and agricultural trade directly affect the prospects for economic development of the Southern Cone States. Foreign direct investment has become the major source of capital inflows in developing countries during the period under consideration (vis-à-vis portfolio investment and aid resources), and is generally considered to be –potentially - the best form of foreign capital to promote economic growth. The conflict between the EU and the Southern Cone States during the period under consideration was not about the desirability of European FDI to the Southern Cone States, as in previous periods, but about the type of investment desirable. While European investors are interested in increasing profits and market share, the SCSs are interested in bringing the

[69] See the homepage of anti-globalization movement organizations such as ATTAC or Nologo: http://attac.org , http://www.nologo.org.
[70] See Huntington, 1993.

developmental potential of FDI to fruition. Conflict has arisen when both interests could not be simultaneously achieved.

Agricultural products are the main component of Southern Cone States' exports to the EU, and have a major impact on domestic accumulation of capital and economic development. Despite the liberal agenda pursued in the GATT/WTO, the agricultural sector of the EU remains highly protected. This discussion has polarized the EU and the Southern Cone States both in multilateral forums such as the WTO and in bilateral negotiations, going well beyond purely technical matters.

The criteria for selection of the specific approaches used in this study were criteria that: 1) offered testable hypotheses (in a positivist sense, and which could be applied to the congruence procedure method as outlined above)[71]; 2) offered hypotheses which made sense in the empirical case under consideration (special attention was given to the three motives found in secondary literature: balance against the US, accession of Portugal and Spain, process of democratization and regional integration of the Southern Cone States), and; 3) covered the three major groups of theoretical frameworks of the IR discipline (realism, constructivism and liberalism), thus minimizing potential independent variables left outside.

Moreover, although both selected case studies belong to the issue area of economics, the selection did not privilege approaches claimed to be best suited to explain economic issues, such as the Theory of Hegemonic Stability (Kindleberger, 1973, 1981; Gilpin 1971, 1981, 1984, 1991, 2000) [72] or IPE foreign economic policy approaches (Ikenberry 1986, 1988; Tooze, 1994) nor did it exclude approaches allegedly best suited to explain security matters, such as Neorealism (Waltz 1979) or Identity Constructivism (Wendt 1999).[73] A summary of selected approaches and their hypotheses follow.

---

[71] Positivism refers to epistemology as implied in scientific realism, a philosophy of science which assumes that the world exists independently from human beings, that all mature scientific theories typically refer to this same world, and that they do so even when the objects of science are unobservable. Wendt, 1999, p.85.

[72] The theory of hegemonic stability (THS) may be placed among the so-called Critical Approaches to International Political Economy (IPE), which questions the liberal emphasis on autonomous evolution and low level of policalization of conflicts emanating from the increasing international economic interdependence. Stability and cooperation are only possible if there is a hegemonic state supporting them. For the differences between Neorealism and THS, see Guzzini, 2001. For a summary of THS, see Hasenclever et al, 1997, pp.86-95. Other Critical IPE approaches (such as the work of Susan Strange and Robert Cox), although sharing the criticism of the excessively optimistic liberal view on international conflicts emanating from interdependence, maintain the opposite, that is, that states have lost their capacity to impact economic issues, which are driven mostly by multinational corporations, in line with neo-Marxist arguments.

[73] The assumption is that the division between high and low politics at the theoretical level is misleading and/or even normative. The degree of political sensitivity and security implications in certain specific issue-areas is more an empirical than a theoretical matter. Food and oil production, for instance, were at different times, and by different states, considered either as economic welfare

4.2) Hypotheses

4.2.1) Neorealism

According to Neorealism, when acting within the anarchic international system states try to insure their own survival and therefore seek to maintain and extend their autonomy from and their influence over other states. Their foreign policy behavior depends on their power position within the international system (independent variable), i.e., their share of certain capabilities such as gross national product (GNP), military forces, territory and population, and on the polarity of the system as a whole, given that it influences the maneuvering room of each state to use its capabilities. The better the power position of a state, the more autonomy for itself and the more influence over other states it will strive for. Autonomy and influence-seeking policies are therefore possible values for the dependent variable.

As regards the question of whether a state pursues autonomy or an influence-seeking policy, there are two main variants of neorealist approaches: classical Waltzianian neorealism, and that which has been defined by Rittberger *et al* as Modified Neorealism - or post-classical realism by Brooks. The main difference between the two approaches is that while the former holds that a state's foreign policy is based in worst-case scenarios always preferring autonomy rather than influence, the latter maintains that security pressure is an intervening variable, in which case states will attribute less importance to autonomy if they are exposed to low security pressure. In other words, the lower the security pressure a state is exposed to, the more willing it will be to sacrifice some autonomy in order to gain substantially more influence over other actors. [74]

Given the purpose of this study, it is important to specify under which conditions each of these two neorealist variants would foresee the existence, or an increase, of the cooperation level on the part of the EU towards Southern Cone States. According to the standard version of Neorealism, cooperation is seen as part of a strategy to make alliances against threatening dominant third states. When facing an increase in its power position, the EU would be expected to increase the cooperation with non-threatening secondary powers within the

---

issues belonging to low politics or as security issues belonging therefore to high politics. External investments may be considered a matter of *de facto* survival for developing states, where their sovereignty in managing internal economic policies is at stake (such as implied in the IMF-World Bank "conditionality").

[74]For a detailed analysis of Neorealism and its variants see Rittberger at at, 2002, Ch.3, especially pp.45-58.

international system, in order to counterbalance US hegemony in the Southern Cone. Although cooperation implies a certain degree of autonomy loss vis-à-vis the partner, it contributes to avoiding the threat of a far greater loss of autonomy resulting from the dominance of a powerful third country.[75]

Modified Neorealism foresees cooperation only in bilateral relationships towards weaker states as a means to increase the stronger state's influence over the weaker; in other words, the attempt to gain control over the behavior of another state through cooperation is only possible in relation to weaker states. Therefore, according to Modified Neorealism, when facing an increase of its power position, and when the security pressure faced by the EU from its major competitors is not very high (in which case the prediction would be different from classical Neorealism), the EU could promote a cooperative foreign policy towards Southern Cone States as part of a strategy to increase its general influence worldwide. Given its greater power, the EU would be expected to have more influence over cooperation initiatives, thus being able to impose certain modes of behavior (conditionality such as the democratic clause) or reinforce the existing asymmetrical interdependence to its advantage.

Hence, in principle, both variants of realism could be used to analyze the cooperative foreign policy behavior of the EU. However, as mentioned in Chapter 1, a frequently cited motive for the EU's foreign policy towards the Southern Cone States is the explicit attempt to counterbalance US hegemony in the region. Since one of the aims of the present study is to explore this rather loose statement, it opts to test the classical neorealist approach, and not the modified neorealist one, since the former explicitly addresses the role of the hegemonic power, i.e. the United States as a source of EU behavior.

Neorealist Hypothesis: As the EU evolves into a more powerful actor in the international system, it will promote a more cooperative foreign policy towards Southern Cone States, in order to counterbalance US hegemony in the region.

As a corollary, it is to be expected that EU's foreign policy will become more cooperative after the project of constituting a unified market in the Americas, as implied in the project of the Free Trade Area of the Americas (FTAA), was announced at the Americas Summit in 1994, and as the Southern Cone States engaged seriously in its negotiation.

Proceeding to the empirical analysis of the independent variable "EU power position", the polarity of the system and EU's relative power position is measured for both periods of observation.

[75] Rittberger at al, 2002, p.46.

As regards the polarity of the international system, during the period of 1980-1985 the United States and the Soviet Union were the two great powers in the context of the Cold War. The EU was an ally of the US and dependent on its strategic direction and military capabilities in order to insure its own security. The Southern Cone States were secondary regional powers under the sphere of influence of the US.

In the period of 1995 to 2000, the international system was characterized by a unipolar situation in which the US was defined as the "winner" of the Cold War and the hegemonic power. Despite this unipolarity, the EU gained maneuvering space to pursue its own interests. The EU did not depend so much on US military support, since the threat from the "east" had disappeared: it had developed a cooperative relationship with Russia, and engaged in the process of negotiation for the accession of most central and eastern European states (CEEs). According to Neorealism, in a unipolar situation, the major rising powers, such as the EU, face a strong incentive to counterbalance the hegemon by mobilizing its capabilities to match those of the hegemon, and /or by aggregating third party capabilities, such as the SCS, by establishing coalitions.[76]

Regarding the relative power position, the first thing to define is which states should be included in the reference group. According to Neorealism, the reference group consists of the state's major competitors. Although the major competitors of the EU are the United States, Japan, URSS/Russia and China, when the polarity of the international system is taken into consideration, it becomes unnecessary to include states other than the US, since in a unipolar system the EU as a great power would try to compete only with the hegemonic power. Moreover, insofar as the case study under consideration refers to the EU's behavior towards Southern Cone States, Japan, the USSR/Russia and China become negligible, since they have historically (and in the period under consideration) a very low engagement in Latin America in general, with the possible exception of Cuba. The relevant fact is that the major competitor of the EU for influence in Southern Cone States is by far the US. The reference group taken into consideration is, therefore, restricted to the US.

The capabilities considered in the relative power comparison are those traditionally pointed out by neorealists: gross national product (GNP), volume of exports, volume of military expenses, size of armed forces, population, territory, and also foreign direct investments, insofar as it can also be defined as a power capability and is one of the case studies in this research. An analysis of the tables below show that in all economic categories (GNP, volume of exports and FDI) the

[76] Note that while Waltzianinan Neorealism claims that the only predicted behavior of rising powers vis-à-vis the hegemon is to seek balance, other Realists such as Stephen Walt claim that sometimes they can bandwagon, i.e., join the stronger, even if rarely. On balancing and bandwagoning, see Waltz, 1979; Walt, 199; Ch.5 & Schweller, 1994, Ch.3.

EU clearly increased its power capabilities vis-à-vis the US, while in the military categories (military spending and armed forces) the US not only kept its primary position but increased the gap to other competitors. With regard to territory and population, the EU also increased its relative position, mainly due to the accession of Greece in 1981, Portugal and Spain in 1986 and Austria, Finland and Sweden in 1995.

It would be necessary to establish a hierarchy or a measurement for each power capability in order to conclude whether the sum of the losses and gains in capabilities was positive or negative. Such measurement is however not set out by realist approaches.[77] In the absence of specific rules of procedure, it is possible to claim that in the case of disputes between the EU and the US, economic power capabilities are more relevant than military power capabilities, given the improbability of use or the threat of use of military means in case of a conflict escalation. Based on this argument, it is possible to assert that the relative power position of the EU vis-à-vis its competitors, mainly the US, increased from 1980-1985 to 1995-2000.

To sum up, it can be said that the power position of the EU increased between the first period of observation of this study (1980-1985) and the second (1995-2000). This increase was due to the change in the polarity of the international system, from bipolar to unipolar, and the increased relative power position was measured in terms of relative power capabilities.

Table 3: Gross Domestic Product (GDP), current prices, current exchange rates (billions of US dollars)

	EU*	EU % OECD	US	US % OECD	OECD total
1980	2..954,6	35,5	2.771,5	33,3	8.331,4
1981	2.637,7	31,1	3.104,5	36,6	8.474,9
1982	2.538,7	30,6	3.228,6	38,9	8.309,5
1983	2.485,7	28,9	3.502,0	40,7	8.597,4
1984	2.367,2	26,3	3896,6	43,2	9.013,2
1985	2.440,7	25,8	4.174,9	44,1	9.474,3
1986	3.630,7	31,6	4.411,8	38,4	11.488,3
1987	4.493,0	33,7	4.698,9	35,2	13.344,5
1988	5.003,3	33,3	5.061,9	33,7	15.027,8
1989	5.079,3	32,4	5.439,7	34,7	15.667,1
1990	6.328,1	35,9	5.750,8	32,6	17.621,1
1991	6.603,4	35,4	5.930,7	31,8	18.632,1
1992	7.241,2	36,2	6.261,8	31,3	20.006,3

[77] Rittberger et al, 2002, p.43.

1993	6.528,5	32,3	6.582,9	32,5	20.233,1
1994	7.011,1	32,4	6.993,3	32,3	21.627,0
1995	8.622,1	36,4	7.338,4	31,0	23.674,2
1996	8.792,3	36,9	7.751,1	32,5	23.820,9
1997	8.265,4	35,3	8.256,5	35,2	23.432,5
1998	8.550,6	36,2	8.720,2	36,9	23.602,5
1999	8.562,8	34,4	9.212,8	37,0	24.877,0
2000	7.891,5	31,3	9.762,1	38,7	25.220,4

Source: compiled with data from the OECD homepage
(http://cs4-
hq.oecd.org/oecd/selected_view.asp?tableId=561&viewname=ANAPart2)
*EU - includes the member states for each year (Belgium, Denmark, France, Germany, Ireland, Italy, Luxemburg, Netherlands, UK until 1980; plus Greece after 1981; plus Portugal and Spain after 1986, and Austria, Finland and Sweden after 1995)

Table 4: Exports of goods, transaction f.o.b. prices, current exchange rates (millions of dollars)

	EU*	EU % World	US	US % World	World total
1980	660.775	32,6	225.566	11,1	2.028.000
1981	537.199	26,8	238.715	11,9	2.003.000
1982	590.288	31,5	216.442	11,5	1.875.000
1983	574.537	31,3	205.639	11,2	1.837.000
1984	585.754	30,1	223.976	11,5	1.994.000
1985	717.558	37,0	218.815	11,3	1.940.000
1986	795.746	37,5	227.158	10,7	2.121.000
1987	958.644	38,5	254.122	10,2	2.492.000
1988	1.063.478	37,5	322.427	11,4	2.833.000
1989	1.136.875	37,2	363.812	11,9	3.053.000
1990	1.383.419	40,7	393.592	11,6	3.395.000
1991	1.373.373	39,9	421.730	12,2	3.446.000
1992	1.458.640	39,7	448.163	13,0	3.667.000
1993	1.375.369	37,5	464.773	12,7	3.671.000
1994	1.562.367	37,2	512.627	12,2	4.203.000

1995	2.083.743	41,5	584.743	11,7	5.016.000
1996	2.181.902	67,4	625.073	19,3	3.237.000
1997	2.140.888	39,5	688.697	12,7	5.415.000
1998	2.231.378	41,8	682.138	12,8	5.342.000
1999	2.229.257	40,2	692.784	12,5	5.551.000
2000	2.307.178	36,9	692.784	11,1	6.252.000

Source: compiled with data from the WTO homepage (http//www.wto.org/english/res_e/satis_e/webpub_e.xls)

*EU - includes the member states for each year (Belgium, Denmark, France, Germany, Ireland, Italy, Luxemburg, Netherlands, and UK until 1980; plus Greece after 1981; plus Portugal and Spain after 1986, and Austria, Finland and Sweden after 1995)

Table 5: FDI Outflows (millions of dollars & % total world)

	1980	1985	1990	1995	2000
EU	23,812 (44)	26,084 (42)	121,344 (52)	159,713 (45)	968,019 (70)
USA	19,230 (36)	13,338 (22)	30,982 (13)	92,074 (26)	164,969 (12)
Total World	53,674	62,163	233,315	356,404	1,379,493

Source: Compiled with data from the UNCTAD Homepage (http//stats.unctad.org/fdi/eng/tableviewer/wdsview/print.asp)

Table 6: Defense expenditures as % of the gross domestic product, based on current prices

	Average 1980-1984	Average 1985-1989	Average 1990-1994	Average 1995-1999	2000 (estimative)
Belgium	3,2	2,8	2,0	1,5	1,4
Denmark	2,4	2,0	1,9	1,7	1,5
France	4,0	3,8	3,4	2,9	2,7
Germany	3,3	3,0	2,1	1,6	1,5
Greece	5,3	5,1	4,4	4,6	4,9
Italy	2,1	2,3	2,1	1,9	1,9
Luxemburg	1,0	1,0	0,9	0,8	0,7
Netherlands	3,0	2,8	2,3	1,8	1,6

Portugal	2,9	2,7	2,6	2,3	2,2
Spain	2,3	2,1	1,6	1,4	1,3
UK	5,2	4,5	3,8	2,8	2,4
US	5,6	6,0	4,7	3,3	3,0

Source: NATO's homepage, http://www.nato.int/docu/pr/2000/p00-107e.htm, table 3

Table 7: Armed forces, annual average strength, in thousands

	1980	1985	1990	1995	2000
Belgium	108	107	106	47	42
Denmark	33	29	31	27	25
France	575	563	550	504	395
Germany	490	495	545	352	323
Greece	186	201	201	213	205
Italy	474	504	493	435	382
Luxemburg	1	1	1	1	1
Netherlands	107	103	104	67	54
Portugal	88	102	87	78	73
Spain	356	314	263	210	160
UK	330	334	308	233	218
US	2.050	2.244	2.181	1.620	1.484

Source: NATO's homepage, http://www.nato.int/docu/pr/2000/p00-107e.htm, Table 6

Table 8: Neorealist independent variable: EU power position

	1980-1985	1995-2000
Polarity of the international system	Bipolar	Unipolar (US hegemony)
EU's relative power position (vs. US)	->	increased

4.2.2) Identity Constructivism[78]

This approach is a variant of the Constructivism developed by Alexander Wendt, maintaining that the interaction between actors depends on the knowledge structure of the international system. Knowledge has been defined as culture, or shared meaning, which is distinct from the concept of common knowledge. While the latter is a sum of individual beliefs, the former has a relation of supervenience with individual's beliefs and multiple possibilities of realizability. Culture cannot

[78] As labeled by Hasenclever et al., 1997, pp.186-192. For the approach itself, see Wendt, 1999.

exist or produce effects apart from the beliefs of individuals, but is not reducible to them.[79] Depending on how 'others' are conceptualized, as enemies, rivals or friends, three distinct macro-level knowledge structures, or cultures, develop: Hobbesian, Lockean or Kantian, respectively.

The Hobbesian culture is characterized by four tendencies: 1) permanence of an endemic and unlimited state of war, i.e., a self-help system in which survival depends on military power; 2) a high death rate of actors, due to elimination of the unfit; 3) unsuccessful balancing behavior, leading to the dominance of the strongest actor; 4) impossibility of non-alignment or neutrality. The Lockean culture is characterized by: 1) a situation in which warfare is simultaneously accepted and constrained, i.e., the right to life and liberty (sovereignty) of Others is recognized, although not the right to settle disputes without violence, which is limited only by 'Just War standards'; 2) a low death rate of actors; 3) a successful balancing behavior (although not essential for survival), 4) the possibility of non-alignment and neutrality. Finally, the Kantian culture is characterized by: 1) a *de facto* rule of law, in which disputes are settled without war or the threat of it; 2) members fight as a team if the security of any member is threatened by a third party; 3) types of power other than the military, such as discursive, institutional and economic, are more salient.

According to Wendt, each of these three cultures may be internalized by the actors in three different degrees, which can be seen as answers as to why the actors comply with the norms of the culture in which they are embedded. The first degree of internalization is the most superficial, meaning that states comply because they are forced to (coercion) do so. States have no choice but to follow the norms of the culture; thus, their behavior is externally driven, not internally. In the second degree of internalization, states comply because of self-interest (price). They do have an alternative, but decide to follow the norms for instrumental reasons, because they think they can advance some exogenously given interest. In the third degree of internalization, states comply because they want to; they see the norms as legitimate. Their behavior is even more internally driven than the second degree, since norms construct their identities and interests; therefore, the level of compliance is the highest.[80]

In adapting Identity-Constructivism to analyze the behavior of a unit of the international system, the systemic variable 'knowledge distribution' is transformed into the variable 'knowledge position', or role position.[81] Structural change, or cultural change, occurs when actors redefine who they are and what they want. Changes in foreign policies vis-à-vis third countries occur with

---

[79] Wendt, 1999, p.161.

[80] Ibid, pp.266-78.

[81] Much the same as it was done in the case of Neorealism. For more about this procedure, see Baumann, Rittberger & Wagner 1998, p.3. & Rittberger & Schimmelfennig 1997, pg.10.

changes in the role position attributed to them (independent variable). In Wendts' original formulation, the possible values for role position would be enemy, rival or friend. These roles are symmetrical because they were defined for the issue-area of security (high politics) and equal states.

The present study develops further role position sub-types (within each of the three cultures) in order to analyze the relationship between non-equal states as well as other issue-areas.

The types of role-position attributed by the EU to the SCSs and its respective expected behavior are: 1) conquered/colonized - enmity regarding economic issues would imply in non respect for sovereignty, in the attempt to obtain economic advantages; the level of cooperation would be inexistent; 2) neglected - rivalry regarding economic issues would imply respect for sovereignty, but exploration of the Other in self advantage, without any attempt to avoid conflicts. The third country would be politically neglected, and cooperation would be very low or low. Given this unequal relationship, the negligence on the part of EU towards Southern Cone States is perceived as more problematic than the opposite; 3) benign client - friendship regarding economic issues would imply in the attempt to incorporate the Other's demands and minimize or solve conflicts; higher levels of cooperation are expected to occur. In the case of economic friendship between unequal partners, the relationship assumes a paternalistic character, in which the third country is seen as a benign client.

It must be emphasized that although cooperation is a typical behavior among friends, enemies or rivals may also cooperate. The difference is that, in the case of enemies or rivals, either the cooperation will be short-lived or its practice will transform the actors themselves into friends, in a process of collective identity formation. Cooperation among enemies and rivals is not only atypical and transitory, but also of a lower quality; it occurs only to the extent that it is instrumental to attain other interests (in the case of rivals) or to the extent that states feel coerced to do so (in the case of enemies). A high level of cooperation is only expected to occur between friends.

Identity Constructivism states that roles are objective, collectively constituted positions that give meaning to subjective self-images of the states (role identities). While the latter comes and goes as states adopt or disregard beliefs, the former persists as long as states fill them. For that reason, the methodology to find out role positions must not take into consideration self-declared EU beliefs about itself (as in a discourse analysis approach of how the EU defines the SCS) but rather the systemic determinants of the role position.

These determinants are what Wendt calls "master variables." Three of them, namely interdependence, common fate and homogenization are active or efficient causes of collective identity formation, while the fourth, self-restraint, is an enabling or permissive cause of collective identity formation. All four variables may be present in a given case, and the more they are present the more likely collective identity formation will occur. Still, one single efficient cause, combined with self-restraint, is enough to trigger the process. The importance of the variable self-restraint is that it enables states to overcome the fear of being engulfed, physically or psychically, by the other. In order to engage in a cooperative behavior, actors must trust that their needs will be respected and that they will not be sacrificed to the group.[82]

Identity Constructivist hypothesis: As the role position the EU attributes to the SCS changes from neglected to benign client, the level of cooperation of the EU foreign policy will increase.

Table 9: Level of cooperation according to role position

Level of cooperation	Enemy (conquered)	Rival (neglected)	Friend (benign client)
Null	X		
Very low		X	
Low		X	
Medium			X
High			X

Proceeding to the analysis of the independent variable in the periods of 1980-85 and 1995-2000, the four master variables and the role position of the SCS vis-à-vis the EU are analyzed below.

Although self-restraint is a crucial variable, it can be said that when dealing with weaker partners it becomes less relevant. Stronger actors do not have the fear of engaging in cooperative behavior with weaker ones, because they are backed by their asymmetrical power. In the case of an analysis of the level of cooperation of EU foreign policy towards Southern Cone States, it is possible to consider as independent variables only the three active master variables, i.e., homogenization, interdependence and common fate.

The variable common fate is defined as the extent to which individual survival, fitness or welfare of each partner depends on what happens to the group as a whole. Although common fate can refer to something good, in international politics it is typically constituted by an external threat, which can be social (a military attack from a third party) or material (ozone depletion). Common fate differs from interdependence in that it is constituted by an external actor or fact, and not by the interaction between the partners. Regarding the period from 1980 to 2000, it can be said that the EU and the SCSs did not share any strong common fate.[83]

[82] Wendt, 1999, pp.343-344 and 358.
[83] Ibid, pp.349-353.

Regarding the level of homogenization, Wendt differentiates between two senses of alikeness: corporate identities and type identity. The former refers to the extent to which partners are isomorphic with respect to basic institutional form, function and causal powers. In that regard, it can be said that with the development of the process of integration among the Southern Cone States, the degree of alikeness with the EU increased. The process of integration started formally with the *rapprochement* between Brazil and Argentina in 1985, gained institutional form in 1991 with the creation of Mercosur, and obtained additional strength with the inclusion of Chile and Bolivia as associate members in 1996 and 1997, respectively.

The alikeness in type identity refers to type variation within a given corporate identity, such as how political authority is organized, and its control over economic matters. During the first period of observation, all Southern Cone States were governed by military dictatorships; the first democratic governments of Brazil, Argentina, Paraguay and Uruguay were installed in 1985, 1983, 1989 and 1985 respectively. Although the situation in Paraguay is considered more unstable, given the two attempts of military coups in 1996 and 1999, the political stability of the region was strengthened with the inclusion of a 'democratic clause' in the Treaty of Asunción of 1991. Regarding the control of the political authority over economic matters, in Southern Cone States a direct state control over enterprises prevailed until the end of the 80s. Argentina, Brazil and Uruguay started a process of economic liberalization and privatization with the governments of Carlos Menem, Collor de Mello and Luis Lacalle, respectively, all elected in 1989, and Paraguay with the government of Juan Carlos Wasmosy, elected in 1993.

Considering the three factors analyzed corporate identity, organization of political authority, and political control over economic matters, it can be said that the degree of isomorphism or alikeness between the EU and the Southern Cone States, increased from the first to the second period of observation.[84]

The variable interdependence is defined as a situation in which the outcome of an interaction for one actor depends on the choices made by the other actor, and has two aspects, as identified by Keohane and Nye: sensitivity and vulnerability. The former measures the degree to which changes in one actor's circumstances affect the other actors and the latter measures the costs an actor would incur by ending a relationship. When either one is highly asymmetric, which is the case between the EU and Southern Cone States for both variables, the relationship is of dependence and not interdependence. Although the increase of dependence does not favor cooperation in the same way as interdependence, it can

[84] Ibid, pp.353-357.

still be said that it does favor unilateral cooperation from the stronger partner, in the sense that it diminishes even more the fear of the other.[85]

Finally, it can be said that in the first period of observation, none of the three efficient master variables: common fate, homogenization, and dependence were very high, suggesting that no process of collective identity was in place, and that the role position attributed by the EU to the SCS was the "neglected" position.

In the second period of observation, the level of homogenization between both regions increased. With the processes of integration, democratization and economic liberalization the SCSs became more alike the EU in all of the most important aspects of homogeneity: corporate identity, organization of political authority and political control over economic matters. A trend towards a process of collective identity formation took place, although only in its initial stages; the role position may be said to have evolved in the direction of a "benign client," although not fully consolidated.

Table 10: Identity Constructivist independent variable

	1980-85	1995-2000
Role position	Neglected	Benign client

4.2.3) Utilitarian Liberalism[86]

a)Summary of the approach and hypothesis

According to Utilitarian Liberalism, foreign policy is a 'net gain-seeking policy' (dependent variable) determined by the interests of the societies involved (independent variable). The term societal groups includes all organized societal actors involved in the foreign policy decision-making process; i.e. not only societal actors in the narrower sense, such as private actors (companies, business and labor interest groups, etc.) but also societal actors in the wider sense, such as political and administrative actors.

All actors are conceived as rational utility maximizers, they all strive for gains, which may be material (income) or immaterial (power), in order to safeguard their survival. As a result of the interaction of domestic actors in the process of interest intermediation, they create policy networks with a given

[85] Ibid, pp.344-349.

[86] The Utilitarian Liberalist approach follows the model developed in Bienen, Freund & Rittberger, 1999, and Freund & Rittberger et al, 2001.

structure. Each actor's capability to assert its preferences in the process of foreign policymaking is determined considering their relative dominance within the policy network.[87]

The analysis of a foreign policy network is done in three steps: first, the organized private and political administrative actors involved in the policy network are identified, then, their foreign policy preferences are ascertained; and, finally, those actors who are capable of dominating foreign policy decision-making are identified on the basis of the network structure.

The organized actors are those who show evidence of interaction in the form of communication (hearings, consultations, exchange of information) and/or coordination or cooperation (division of labor, exchange arrangements, bargaining processes) in a policy field or in relation to a certain policy. [88] The preferences of organized actors may be informed by a theoretically deductive method that assumes that these actors choose their preferences in order to maximize their income or power.[89]

With regard to the types of societal actors, Utilitarian Liberalism differentiates between actors from the political administrative system and private actors. The former encompasses political actors (which are democratically elected, such as the Prime Ministers and Presidents), administrative actors (which are appointed by the political actors to perform political tasks, such as Executive organs) and political-administrative actors (which are also appointed by the political actors to perform political tasks such as administrative actors, but which require a broader political support, such as Ministers). Private actors are subdivided into companies, economic pressure groups (issue-area associations such as manufacturing, farming, trade associations), and political advocacy groups (non-profit issue-area oriented private organizations such as NGOs, etc).

The most dominant actor is determined by an analysis of the pertinent policy network. The assertiveness of actors in policy networks is determined by the level of actors' mobilization and the independence of political and political-administrative from private actors. The most assertive private and PAS actors must be identified, and then the independence of the latter from the former. Regarding the mobilization of private actors, it is possible to distinguish the level of situational mobilization (how intense an actor's preferences are), which increases the more a policy affects its basic interests; and the level of structural

---

[87] Policy networks are defined as a set of relationships among organized private and political administrative system actors resulting from their interaction in the form of coordination, cooperation and communication with a view to the formulation and implementation of policy. Freund & Rittberger et al, 2001, p.75.

[88] Rittberger et al, 2001, p.10.

[89] If it is not possible, or only possible to a limited extent, to determine actors' preferences deductively, help can be sought in the empirical-inductive method, in particular the method of questioning experts. Ibid, p.12.

mobilization, which increases the higher the actor scores in the four following dimensions: level of representation (the more individuals and legal entities affected by the respective policy it represents); the representation of individuals and legal entities concentrated in that actor (the less the actor has to compete with other organized private actors for the same members); level of hierarchy (the better he is in the position of making binding decisions for its members); and capacity for generating technical and political information.

The mobilization of political and political-administrative actors is also determined by the level of situational mobilization and the level of structural mobilization. The former is defined in the same terms as in the case of private actors, and the latter is determined by the formal competences of the actor in the policy area and its formal and informal powers in the decision-making process.

Finally, according to Utilitarian Liberalism, as a last step once dominant interests in the policy network have been identified, the strength of the dependent variable 'net gain-seeking foreign policy' must be evaluated. This strength depends on the degree of strength of societal interests, which can be analyzed according to the following indicators: 1) strong societal interests exist if the dominant actor in a monopolistic network has highly pronounced preferences or if the majority of dominant actors in a pluralist or corporatist network have highly pronounced preferences for the same option of foreign policy action; 2) medium-strength societal interests exist if the dominant actor in a monopolistic network has low-intensity preferences or if the majority of assertive actors in a pluralist or corporatist network have low-intensity preferences for the same option of foreign policy action; 3) weak societal interests exist if the dominant actor in a monopolistic network is not mobilized situationally or if there is no majority of actors with the same preferences of at least low intensity in a pluralist or corporatist network. Only in the first two cases will utilitarian liberalism allow any statements about foreign policy. In the last case, when there are only weak societal interests, the foreign policy is not determined by societal interests, since society is then indifferent to the various options of foreign policy action.[90]

To sum up, in the utilitarian liberal view, foreign policy is determined by the interests of those societal groups that are able to dominate the foreign policy decision-making process. Foreign policy changes are, consequently, a function of changes in the preferences of dominant actors, or of changes in the composition of the set of dominant actors in each foreign policy network. Changes towards cooperative policies are expected to happen when it becomes the interest of the dominant actors in the EU foreign policymaking network.

[90] Bienen, Freund & Rittberger, 1999, pp.20-21.

Utilitarian-Liberalist Hypothesis: As the configuration of the EU societal interests' changes towards favoring cooperation with Southern Cone States, foreign policy becomes cooperative.

The empirical analysis of the independent variable 'EU dominant domestic interests' is carried out separately for each case study in Chapter 5 & 6. A few general features of the EU political system and policymaking are examined below in order to provide a general background for case studies. However, it should be emphasized that the use of Utilitarian Liberalism to study EU's foreign policy is in conformity with the trend that uses approaches from Comparative Politics to analyze EU policymaking. Scholars have claimed that approaches such as pluralism, corporativism, and new-institutionalism (in its rationalist, sociological and historical version) are better suited to explain EU politics than the previously predominant approaches, such as (neo) functionalism and (liberal) intergovernmentalism (Risse, 1996; Hix, 1994; Caporaso, 1997; Kleistra, 2001). The use of policy networks was also introduced in the EU studies as a new paradigm to study European governance (Börzel, 1997; Heritier, 1996). While most empirical studies conducted so far have focused on EU domestic policies, this study develops an empirical analysis of EU policies towards third countries.

b) EU societal actors

In the case of the EU, the political actors are considered to be the European Parliament, whose members are directly elected at the European level, which is the European Council, whose participants, i.e., member-states' Heads of State or Government are nationally elected, and the Ministerial Councils, whose participants, i.e., member-states representatives at ministerial level, are accountable to their national parliaments. The main administrative actors are considered the European Commission, the European Investment Bank (EIB), the European Central Bank (ECB), the Economic and Social Committee (ESC), the Committee of the Regions (CoR), the Court of Auditors and the EUROPOL. The COREPER (COREPER 1, 2 and Special Committee on Agriculture) and the subcommittees, such as the Committee 133, are considered as political-administrative actors. A brief description of these actors and their points of connection with private interest groups follow below.

With regard to private actors, the economic and political advocacy pressure groups taken into consideration are the ones lobbying in Brussels, since the preferences of those lobbying in national capitals are incorporated to the member-states preferences, and therefore to European and Ministerial Councils. Companies include both the EU member-states' national companies and EU multinationals or joint ventures, but only when lobbying individually in Brussels, outside the sectorial economic pressure groups. In the case of EU foreign policy towards Southern Cone States, it seems that most companies do not try to exert influence individually, but rather by participation in organizations such as the European Round Table of Industrialists (ERT) or the Mercosur-European Union Business Forum (MEBF). Although their participation in the policy network occurs separately for each case study, it can be said that both organizations are very active in the issue area of economic policies. Other pressure groups particularly involved in EU foreign policy towards Latin America in general are NGOs working in the development and human rights areas such as the International Cooperation for Development and Solidarity (CIDSE), and the Working Group on European Union-Mercosur negotiations (WG/EU-Me). The main EU societal actors and their presumed basic interests are listed in the following table.

Table 11: Main EU societal actors

Type	• Actors	• Interests
Political (EU level)	• European Parliament	• extend policymaking power (re-election at EU level, competences within the EU) • increase financial means (EC budget)
Political (national level)	• European and Ministerial Councils	• extend policymaking power (re-election at national level, competences within the EU) • increase financial means provided that net national contribution does not increase
Administrative	• European Commission • European Investment Bank (EIB) • European Central Bank (ECB) • Economic and Social Committee (ESC) • Committee of the Regions (CoR) • Court of Auditors	• extend policymaking power (competences) • increase financial means (EC budget)

	• EUROPOL	
Companies	• European companies	• increase financial means (profits)
Economic Pressure Groups	• European Round Table of Industrialists (ERT) • Mercosur EU Business Forum (MEBF) • sectorial lobbies (COPA/COGECA)	• increase financial means (membership contribution, consultancy fees) • fulfill organizational purpose (influence content of policy outcome)
Political Advocacy Groups	• International Cooperation for Development and Solidarity (CIDSE) • Working Group EUMercosur	• increase financial means (membership contribution, donation, consultancy fees) • fulfill organizational purpose (influence content of policy outcome)

Source: adapted from Rittberger 2001, p.86-87 & 89.

Although the role of each societal actor in the policy networks of FDI and agricultural trade are seen in Chapters 5 and 6, the general activities of two of them, the MEBF, and the Working Group EU-Mercosur, are briefly described here since they are particularly involved in both networks.

The Mercosur-European Union Business Forum (MEBF) was launched in February of 1999, in Rio de Janeiro, with the objective of pursuing the enhancement of trade and business relations between the two regions, as stated in its founding document, the Rio Declaration. The idea was that entrepreneurs of each region should together identify barriers to trade, services and investment, and prepare joint recommendations to policy decision-makers on how to reduce or eliminate such restrictions, speaking to governments with one voice on issues where business consensus has been reached. MEBF has been particularly active in the negotiations of the Interregional Association Agreement, started in November of 1999. The recommendations are approved in plenary sessions, after being prepared by three working groups: (Trade) Market Access, Investment/Privatization, and Services. The second plenary meeting of the MEBF took place in Mainz, in November 1999, concluded with the Mainz Statement; and the third in Madrid in May/2002 during the second EU-Latin America and Caribbean Summit (EU-LAC Summit), and closed with the signature of the

Madrid Declaration. The contents of these documents in what regards FDI and agricultural trade are seen in Chapter 5&6.

The Commission has welcomed the founding of MEBF, as well as the activities proposed by it, as stated in the official reaction to the MEBF Rio Declaration, in which its signatory, Commissioner Manuel Marin, explained how he viewed the possibilities for implementing MEBF's recommendations. An example of close consultation between the Commission and the MEBF was the EU-Mercosur Action Plan on Business Facilitation, launched during the second EU-LAC Summit in Madrid. The document was based, to a large extent, on the list of business facilitation measures prepared by the MEBF, originally presented to the negotiators of the Association Agreement in Sept/2001, and reformulated in a final proposal by means of the Buenos Aires Statement on Business Facilitation. Commissioner Pascal Lamy congratulated MEBF for its involvement: "At your conference in December last year in Buenos Aires you surprised us all by an unprecedented consensus amongst the business from both sides and a very comprehensive set of some 62 concrete business measures for customs, standards and e-commerce(...) today we are on the verge of announcing an agreement with Mercosur on a Business Facilitation Action Plan, which apart from the areas you proposed to us at your Buenos Aires conference, include sanitary and phytosanitary measures for which Mercosur has demonstrated great interest." The parts of the initiative regarding FDI and agricultural trade are treated in Chapters 5 and 6.[91]

An expression of the growing importance of MEBF is the increase in attendance from about 100 to 200 businesspersons between the Rio and the Madrid meetings, and from one representative from the Commission (Industry Commissioner Martin Bangemann) to as much as the Vice President of the European Commission, Loyola de Palacio, the European Commissioners Pascal Lamy, Erkki Liikanen, Chris Patten and Pedro Solbes, and the President of the Delegation of the European Parliament for the Latin American Countries and the Mercosur, Rolf Linkohr. The size and level of detail of the declarations also support the perception of a growing importance: while the Rio Declaration was a 10-page document with rather general recommendations, the Madrid Declaration has 42 pages and very specific recommendations at the level of particular instruments and economic fields.

The Working Group on EU-Mercosur negotiations (WG/EU-Me) was created by academics of the Mercosur Chaire of the Institut d'Etudes Politiques de Paris (Science Po) as a follow up initiative to a seminar organized jointly with the University of Sao Paulo (USP), in May 1999, on "Political and economic stakes of EU-Mercosur negotiation and the agricultural deadlock". The main objective was to have a permanent consultative group set in a neutral and independent

[91] MEBF, 2001a, pp.4-5; MEBF 2001b, p.15; Lamy, 2002 (speech 15-05-2002)

academic framework to discuss, monitor, and make recommendations in the negotiation processes in which the EU and Mercosur are engaged at the interregional (Association Agreement) and multilateral levels (WTO), serving as an interface between negotiators, firms and civil society. It is organized around a core of about 30 international experts who meet periodically in workshops and conferences, and produce specialized papers and annual reports concerning the negotiations. The experts have established links with the Commission and participate in conferences organized with the civil society to discuss the EU-Mercosur and EU-Chile association negotiations, the first of which in October/2000 and the second, in February/2002.[92]

c) Assertiveness of EU actors

Helen Wallace identifies five main types of EU policy processes, which aggregate patterns of competences and decision-making powers for different issue-areas, and imply different patterns of assertiveness for EU actors. Although this classification by no means replaces a proper empirical analysis for particular case studies, it provides a helpful overview of the general patterns of policymaking in the EU.[93]

The first variant of the EU policy process is what the author calls the community method, which constitutes a form of supranational policymaking, in which powers are transferred from the national to the EU level. The main characteristics of this community method are: a strong Commission role in policy design, policy-brokering and policy-execution; an empowering role for the Council of Ministers through strategic bargaining and package deals; an engagement of national agencies as subordinated operational arms of the agreed common regime; a distancing from the process of elected representatives at the national level, and limited opportunities for the Parliament to influence policy; an

---

[92] The core group of experts are: Jorge Balbis,Uruguay; Klaus Bodemer,Germany; Roberto Bouzas,Argentina; Jean-Christophe Bureau, France; German Calfat,Belgium; Daniel Chudnovsky, Agentina; Patricio Contreras,OEA; Robert Devlin,IADB; Antoni Estevadeordal,IADB; Renato Flores Jr.,Brazil; Christian Freres,Spain; Paolo Giodano, IADB; Paolo Guerrieri, Italy; Marcos Jank,Brazil; Ekaterina Krivonos, IADB; Andres Lopez, Argentina; Patrick Messerlin, France; Pedro da Motta Veiga, Brazil; Alejandro Nin,Uruguay; Peter Nunnenkamp,Germany; Sheila Page, UK; Felix Pena, Argentina; Marta Reis Castilho,Brazil; Jose Luis Rhi-Sausi,Italy; Maryse Robert;OEA; Pierre Sauve, OECD; Karsten Steinfatt,OEA; Sherry Stephenson,OEA; Jose Tavares de Araujo Jr.,OEA; Vera Thorstensen, Brazil; Ramon Torrent, Spain; Marcel Vaillant,Uruguay; Alfredo Valladao,France; Alvaro Vasconcelos,Portugal; Soledad Zignago,France. For more information and download of reports, see homepage: http://chairemercosur.sciences-po.fr/. For details about the Conferences organized by the Commission see http://www.europa.eu.int/comm/external_relations/mercosur/conf/obj.htm

[93] Wallace, 2001, pp.28-35. Other authors such as Neil Nugent also explore the variations in EU policy processes, see Nugent, 1999, pp.351-358.

occasional, but defining, intrusion by the ECJ to reinforce the legal authority of Community regimes; and resorting to policy on a collective basis, as an expression of sustained solidarity. Although this method was considered for a long time "the" emerging process of policymaking in the EU, its empirical validity was questioned, and alternative methods were identified. Still, it is generally considered as descriptive of policymaking structure for policies such as the Common Agricultural Policy (CAP).

The second method is the EU regulatory model, characterized by: the Commission as the architect and defender of regulatory objectives and rules, increasingly by reference to economic criteria; the Council as a forum for agreeing on minimum standards and direction (mostly upwards towards higher standards), to be complemented by mutual recognition of national preferences and controls, operated differentially in individual countries; the ECJ as the means of ensuring that rules are applied reasonably and evenly, backed by national courts in local application, and enabling individual entrepreneurs to have access to redress in case of non-application or discrimination; the EP as one among several means for prompting consideration of non-economic factors (environmental, regional, social etc) with increasing impact as legislative powers grow; and extensive opportunities for private economic and social interest groups to be consulted and influence policies. The regulatory model has been applied to the development of single market and policymaking in the areas of competition policies, social policy, environmental domain, and in several business and development foreign policies concerning third countries. Wallace argues that the regulatory model replaced the community method as the predominant policy paradigm, and its successful implementation had instigated its promotion as a model for the development of broader global regulation.

The third variant is multi-level governance. This method describes the structure of policymaking in distributive policy, such as policies based on structural funds. With the development of distributive policies, the monopoly of national central governments over contacts with the EU policymaking level was broken, and regional and local authorities became actively engaged in the policymaking process. The main characteristics of the multi-level governance model are: the Commission as the deviser of partnership programmes with local and regional authorities, and the use of financial incentives to gain attention; member governments in the Council under pressure from local and regional authorities, agreeing to an enlarging and redistributive budget; members of the EP as a source of territorial politics pressure in the regions; empowerment of local and regional authorities, which gained an official forum of representation in the Committee of the Regions in 1993; increased allocation of funds from the EC budget to "cohesion".

The fourth variant is policy coordination and benchmarking (also called the OECD technique), characterized by: the Commission as developer of networks of experts or epistemic communities; the involvement of independent experts as promoters of ideas and techniques; the convening of high-level groups in the Council to brainstorm rather than to negotiate; dialogue with specialist committees in the EP. The object of this method is not to establish a single common framework but rather to share experience and to encourage the spread of best practices. Examples of issue areas in which it seems to operate well are education and employment policies.

The last variant of EU policy process proposed by Wallace is intensive transgovernmentalism, in the sense of a strong commitment to achieve cooperation between member-states in areas that remained to a large extent under their competence, such as the Common Foreign and Security Policy (CFSP), and its predecessors, the European Political Cooperation (EPC) and the Justice and Home Affairs (JHA) policies. This method is characterized by an active involvement of the European Council in setting the overall direction of policy; the predominance of the Council of Ministers in consolidating cooperation; the limited or marginal role of the Commission; the exclusion of the EP and the ECJ from the circle of involvement; the involvement of a distinct circle of key national policymakers; the adoption of special arrangements for managing cooperation; the opaqueness of the process for national parliaments and the general public; and the capacity to deliver substantive joint policy.

d) Independence of EU PAS actors from private actors

Although subjected to variations according to particular issue area and case study, a common ground in the literature of private interest group representation in the EU is that the Commission is seen as the main institutional target in attempts to influence policy outcomes. Two main reasons are pointed out, the first being the fact that the Commission is constantly understaffed and overloaded with work, which makes it particularly dependent on private actors offering information and expertise – a drafting official in the Commission has been defined as "a very lonely person with a blank piece of paper in front of him, wondering what to put on it".[94] Often companies, industrial associations or other interest groups have more expertise in an issue area than the Commission, which sometimes even asks an interest group to prepare a report on its behalf. The second reason is the exclusive power of initiative of the Commission, combined with the perception that it is in the early stages of initiatives that most influence can be exerted. [95]

[94] Hull (1993, p.83) cited in Greenwood, 1997, p.18.

[95] About private interest groups representation in the EU in general, see Greenwoood 1996, 1997; Bowen 2002; Hix,1999, Ch7. Other references include: Cowles, 1994; Gorges, 1996; Mazey & Richardson (eds), 1993; Kirchner, 1981;; McLaughlin & Greenwood, 1995; McLaughin, Maloney

Other "bargaining chips" of private interest groups vis-à-vis the Commission, apart from information and expertise, are: a) economic muscle – some big companies and sectorial groups, such as for instance the pharmaceutical industry, have so much resources and influence in key economic indices, such as employments or exports, that they cannot be ignored; c) status – the Commission, for instance, is particularly keen on high-prestige high-technology industrial domains such as information technology, biotechnology etc, and these exert a special appeal; d) power of implementation – groups as farmers are powerful actors because they own significant land resources, and if they refuse to implement a policy it will probably fail. Other groups such as pharmaceutical companies can offer help in implementation through self-regulation, which is attractive for the Commission because it diminishes its overload; e) non-competitive and efficient organization format – the Commission prefers to have a "one-stop-shop" European group based in Brussels representing all the interests within the category.[96]

Next to the Commission, the Parliament is the second most important institutional target for interest groups in the EU. With regard to external relations, the formal powers of the EP in foreign policy decision-making, both regarding the bilateral agreements and developmental policy are quite limited, but it has managed to participate in the determination of policies via informal channels. In the Treaties of Paris and Rome, the then Common Assembly had a very restricted consultative role in the conclusion of association agreements under Art.238/EEC. With the establishment of the Luns (in 1964) and Westerterp (in 1973) procedures, it was accorded the right to hold a debate prior to the opening of association negotiations and trade agreement with 3rd countries, and the right to be informed by the Commission and the Council on the progress of the negotiations and on the content of the agreements before their conclusion. In 1982, the two procedures, referred to as the Luns-Westerterp procedure, were extended to the negotiations for any international agreements, including accession treaties. Some of the EP's suggestions, in fact, came to constitute one of the main characteristics of the international agreements with third countries, namely the so-called democratic clause. It also got closely involved in the implementation of such agreements, by the inclusion of clauses about inter-parliamentary dialogues between partners. Another tool used by the EP is the question procedure (Art.140/EEC), by which the Commission has to reply orally or in writing to questions put to it. The Council was not bound by this provision, but agreed to reply as well. The Single European Act (SEA) introduced the assent procedure under which the EP came to have a formal final say on the conclusion of

---

& Jordan, 1993; Maloney et al, 1995; Sargent, 1987, 1987; Streeck & Schmitter 1985, 1991; Traxler & Schmitter, 1994; Tsinsizelis, 1990; Van Schendelen, 1993, 1994).

[96] See Greenwood, 1997, pp.18-20 & 33-43; Bouwen, 2002; Nugent, 1999, Ch.6.

association (Art.238/EEC) and accession agreements (Art.237/EEC). The EP decision, if reached by an absolute majority, became fully binding, which represented a turning point for the EP, in its struggle for power in EU foreign policy. Another innovation of the SEA was the inclusion of the EP as an associate in the also then formalized European Political Cooperation (Art.30.4 SEA), meaning that the Presidency had to inform the EP about the issues being discussed, taking its view into consideration. The Treaty of Maastricht expanded the assent procedure (reached by absolute majority) to a wide range of treaties with third countries, but the value of this measure was weakened by allowing the Council to suspend any agreements to which the EP had assented without prior consent. Another new measure was that the EP could reject the annual budget and amend non-compulsory expenditures, impelling and even determining financial priorities in the context of external relations and the financing of aid projects. Regarding the CFSP, the EP was accorded the right to be consulted about its main aspects and basic choices (Art.J.7/TEU) but the vagueness of these terms implied that the application of the consultation mechanism was open to wide interpretation. Under the Treaty of Amsterdam, the right of information was extended to any decision in the field of external trade policy, and the right of consultation to international agreements (Art.300/TEU), but the latter only after the Council has reached a decision, which entails that the involvement in the formulation and negotiation stages of international agreements remains marginal.[97]

The most important mechanisms for interest groups to engage with the European Parliament are the committee systems, rapporteurs, and intergroups. Proposals from the Commission and initiatives from the EP itself are considered first in the standing committees of the Parliament. Each has a secretariat of about five officials, who are usually targeted by interest groups. Rapporteurs are MEPs appointed by Committees to prepare the Parliament's response to Commission proposals and to those measures taken within the Parliament itself. When an appointment is made, a shadow rapporteur is appointed by each political group to monitor the process on behalf of the interests of that party. Because of the centrality of their involvement with a particular initiative, they are key targets for interest groups as well. Intergroups are unofficial groupings of MEPs clustered around particular areas where members have particular interests. They began to emerge after the first direct election to the Parliament in 1979, and do not receive official resources, which has provided an opportunity for interest groups to provide them with financial and secretarial resources. The semi-anarchic existence of intergroups means that they do rather different things (their area of interest vary from Social Economy to Friends of Music, from Ageing to Cuba, etc) and offer

[97] About the powers of the EP in the EU foreign policy, see Weiler, 1980 and Viola, 2000.

quite different avenues of influence to interest groups, but are recognized as having a considerable effect on the working methods of the EP, in particular during the plenary sessions in Strasbourg. [98]

The third institutional target for private interest groups in the EU is the Council of Ministers, which, as the final point of decision-making, makes it a target for last-minute interest representation; at this later point in the decision-making cycle, it becomes more difficult to exert influence because issues have already been shaped, and interventions may require seeking changes to entrenched positions rather than seeking to shape problems into policy initiatives. The main access to decision-making in the European Council is through the "national route". Interest groups need to work through their usual channels of national representation, but also through the ways in which national governments coordinate their machinery for working on the EU level. More centralized member-states tend to have better coordination, but this may mean that their COREPER representatives (COREPER 1, COREPER 2 and the Special Committee on Agriculture) are given little room for bargaining, and such delegations may therefore be less available to private interest groups. Although it is often easier to establish contact with officials from the Commission than with national administration officials, the "national route" is pursued by many interest groups. For instance, despite the measures at the EU level aimed at producing competition on equal terms and removing national favoritism, the interest of some large companies (national champions) and domestic governments are extremely intertwined. Representation at the national level is also more available to those interest groups lacking the resources to take the Brussels route, such a small firms and public interests. [99]

The Economic and Social Committee (ESC), the Committee of the Regions (CoR), the European Investment Bank (EIC) and the Court of Auditors have also been traditionally targeted by private interest groups. Other institutions such as the European Monetary Institute (EMI), the European Central Bank (ECB) and the EUROPOL are, however, by nature likely to be more insulated from the pressures of private interest groups. The most relevant for this study are the following.

The Economic and Social Committee (ESC) is a consultative institution, created by the Treaty of Rome to provide input from outside interests, but with the exception of particular cases, its profile has been considered relatively low. It is a consultative body and it is made up of 222 members from representative organizations, nominated by national governments and appointed by the Council of the European Union for a renewable 4-year term of office. The members are divided into three broad categories: employers, workers and other interests, and,

[98] See Greenwood, 1997, pp.43-48 and Nugent, 1999, Ch.9.
[99] See Greenwood, 1997, pp.31-33 and Nugent, 1999, Ch.7 &8.

historically, the most active interests groups have been the trade unions (such as the European Trade Union Confederation – ETUC) and the associations of professions (such as SEPLIS, representing the liberal professions; EUROCADRES, representing salaried, unionized professional and managerial staff; and CEC, representing independent organizations of managerial staff primarily in industry and commerce) and their main task is to issue opinions on specific matters to the Council, the Commission and the European Parliament, when requested, or by its own initiative. Every two years the ESC members elect a bureau made up of 24 members, a president, and 2 vice presidents chosen from each of the three groups in rotation. It also has a number of specialist sections covering the functional range of EU competences, and works in a similar manner to the EP, with rapporteurs and plenary meetings (ten times a year) in which opinions are adopted by simple majority.[100] Like the ESC, the Committee of the Regions (CoR) was also designed for the input of specific interests and has only advisory powers, but its political profile has been much higher, since it was created by the Treaty of Maastricht in 1991. The Treaties oblige the Commission and Council to consult the CoR whenever new proposals are made in areas that have repercussions at regional or local level. The Maastricht Treaty established 5 such areas - economic and social cohesion, trans-European infrastructure networks, health, education and culture. The Amsterdam Treaty added another five areas to the list - employment policy, social policy, environment, vocational training, and transport - that now covers much of the scope of the EU's activity. Outside these areas, the Commission, Council and European Parliament have the option to consult the CoR on issues where they see important regional or local implications to a proposal, and the latter may also draw up an opinion on its own initiative. CoR's work is based in three main principles: a) subsidiariness, which was written into the Treaties at the same time as the creation of the CoR, and means that decisions within the EU should be made at the closest possible level to the citizen, i.e. the EU, therefore, should not take on tasks which are better suited to national, regional or local administrations; b) proximity, by which all levels of government should aim to be 'close to the citizens', in particular by organizing their work in a transparent fashion, so people know who is in charge of what and how to make their views heard; and c) partnership – by which sound European governance means European, national, regional and local government working together. With respect to its organizational structure, the CoR has 222 members and the same number of alternate members, appointed for a four-year term by the Council, acting on proposals from the member states. Each country chooses its members in its own way, but the delegations all reflect the political, geographical and regional/local balance in the member state. The members are elected members

---

[100] See Greenwood, 1997, p.49, 133-136 & 159; Nugent, 1999, pp.279-285 and ESC Homepage (http://www.esc.eu.int/).

of or key actors in local or regional authorities in their home region. The Committee organizes its work through six specialist Commissions, made up of CoR members, who examine the details of proposals on which the CoR is consulted, and draw up a draft opinion, which highlights where there is agreement with the European Commission's proposals, and where changes are needed. The draft opinion is then discussed during the plenary sessions that take place five times per year. If a majority approves it, the draft is adopted as the opinion of the Committee of the Regions and sent to the Commission, Parliament and Council. The CoR also adopts resolutions on topical political issues.[101]

The European Investment Bank (EIB) was created by the Treaty of Rome as the financing institution of the EU. Its responsibilities and functions are referred in several articles of the TEC; Art.267 is especially important because it sets out the task of the EIB as contributing, on a non-profit basis, to the development of the common market. Around 90% of its loans are from projects within the member-states, and the remaining for projects in third countries. It has its own legal personality and financial autonomy, as it funds most of its operations by borrowing on the capital markets rather than by drawing on the Community budget. The EIB's management and control structures reflect this independence and allow it to take lending and borrowing decisions solely on the basis of projects' merits and the best opportunities available at financial markets, but it must also take into consideration the objectives of the EU developmental policy. Its governing body includes: a) a Board of Governors - consisting of Ministers nominated by each of the Member States, usually Ministers of Finance, Economic Affairs or the Treasury who, among others, lay down general directives on credit policy and authorize the Bank activities outside the Union; b) a Board of Directors - consisting of 25 Directors and 13 Alternates appointed by the Board of Governors (24 Directors and 12 Alternates nominated by member-states and one of each nominated by the Commission). It meets once a month and its main tasks are, among others, to ensure that the Bank is managed in accordance with the European Treaties, the EIB's Statute and the directives laid down by the Governors and to approve the granting of loans; and, c) a Management Committee - which is the Bank's full-time executive body that oversees day-to-day business. It recommends decisions to Directors, notably borrowing and lending decisions, ensuring that these are implemented. Its members are appointed by the Governors, on a proposal from the Board of Directors, for a period of six years. Regarding its organizational structure, the EIB had a number of directorates and departments, among them, of particular interest to this research, a department responsible for lending operations in 3rd countries, with an official responsible for each world region. The EIB has increasingly found itself a target of interest groups from the

[101] See Greenwood, 1997, Ch.9; Nugent, 1999, pp.285-289; and CoR homepage (http://www.cor.eu.int/).

areas related to industry and infrastructure, as well as environmental groups, who have been active in pressing the EIB to ensure compliance with environmental criteria in funded projects.[102]

[102]See Greenwood, 1997, p.49; Nugent, 1999, pp.289-293; and EIB Homepage (http://www.eib.org/).

Chapter 5 - Case Study 1: Foreign direct investment

5.1) Case description and dependent variable

Foreign direct investment (FDI) is one of the major sources of capital that may be used to promote economic development. In countries such as the Southern Cone States, which have a low level of domestic savings, external capital is of central importance. According to economic theory, private investment flows will seek locations in which companies expect to increase either profitability or market share. While some countries manage to attain a desirable level and quality of foreign investment without governmental intervention, that is not the case with most developing countries (Section 5.1.1). Despite the fact that absolute FDI flows to developing countries increased significantly since the late 1980s, it is still a fact that in most cases these flows were not enough or, even worse, were not able to have the expected effect on economic development (Section 5.1.2). The need for governments to intervene in private FDI flows has been discussed in many forums, but the modalities and limits remain a major conflict between the developing and developed countries in general, and the EU and the Southern Cone States in particular. At the multilateral level, attempts to constitute an international FDI regime to address this conflict have so far failed (Section 5.1.3). At the bilateral level, the EU has signed agreements on FDI (though without assuming legal commitments on account of its lack of competence) and, as part of its developmental policy, it has created specific instruments to promote European FDI to developing countries, including Southern Cone States (Section 5.1.4). Although the efficacy and efficiency of these instruments may be questioned, it can still be said that the EU has been trying to increase the developmental quality of European FDI to the Southern Cone States, and that the level of cooperation regarding FDI as indicated in its foreign policy has increased from 1980-1985 to 1995-2000 (Section 5.1.5).

5.1.1) Role of FDI in economic development

Economic development presupposes capital, and the major sources of capital (for a nation-state) are domestic savings and external capital. Whether domestic savings are enough to promote a desired level of investment and economic growth for a given country depends on many factors, but for the purpose of this research it is enough to say that this was not the case in the Southern Cone States in the period analyzed, i.e. 1980-2000, and that these countries depended on external capital inflows in order to promote economic development.[103]

External capital can take the form of portfolio or direct investments.[104] The advantages of FDI over portfolio capital are subject to controversy, with regard to both its economic basis, and the political implications of foreign control of strategic activities. In most Latin American countries, until the early 1980s, there was much political distrust towards FDI and multinationals, but it lost prominence, not by coincidence, with the advent of the external debts crisis, which had been financed by portfolio capital.[105] As regards economic grounds, the alleged advantages of direct investments are longer term maturation and lower volatility, immediate transformation into investment (not linked to consumption or speculative purposes), and the fact that it facilitates the transfer of technology, therefore contributing, in theory, not only to the accumulation of capital but also to an increase in efficiency of the economic system of production.[106]

The traditional economic factors considered as determinants of FDI location are economic stability, size of domestic market, possession of natural resources, and the presence of cheap labor. While these factors remain relevant, they are of diminishing importance, particularly for the most dynamic and technologically advanced industries. The new determinants of location reflect

---

[103] Fishlow, 1992, p.136; Martins Lima, 1994, p.235; Santagostino, 1997, p.35. Economic development is defined in pure economic terms, i.e., as economic growth, not including social indicators

[104] Foreign direct investment (FDI) occurs when an investor based in one country (the home country) acquires an asset in another country (the host country) *with the intent to manage that asset.* The management dimension is what distinguishes FDI from portfolio investment in foreign stocks, bonds and other financial instruments. In most instances, both the investor and the asset managed from abroad are business firms. In such cases, the investor is typically referred to as the "parent firm" and the asset as the "affiliate" or "subsidiary". There are three main categories of FDI: a) Equity capital, the value of the MNC's investment in shares of an enterprise in a foreign country. An equity capital stake of 10 per cent or more of the ordinary shares or voting power in an incorporated enterprise, or its equivalent in an unincorporated enterprise, is normally considered as a threshold for asset control. This category includes *mergers and acquisitions* and "*greenfield*" investments (the creation of new facilities); b) Reinvested earnings, the MNC's share of affiliate earnings not distributed as dividends or remitted to the MNC. Such retained profits by affiliates are supposed to be reinvested in the affiliate. This can represent up to 60 per cent of outward FDI in countries such as the United States and the United Kingdom; c) Other capital refers to short or long-term borrowing and lending of funds between the MNC and the affiliate.

[105] The political distrust is alleged to be based in past imperialist, neoimperialist and "gun boat diplomacy" policies practiced by the US and European countries, in which MNCs were an instrument of dominance of national governments in detriment of political and economic interests of developing countries. On this matter, see Graham, 2000, pp.167-173 and Krasner, 1978. For a good recent edited volume about Latin America external debt crisis see KAS 1999 with papers from Eliana Cardoso, Reinaldo Goncalves and Paulo Nogueira Batista Jr., among others.

[106] For the debate and the economic grounds about FDI advantages in general and vis-à-vis portfolio investments to promote economic development see: UNCTAD 1999; Petrochilos 1989; OECD 1990; Gomes-Casseres & Yoffie 1993, Lim, 2001.

domestic FDI and regulatory regimes, existence of favorable infrastructure and synergies derived from the presence of other firms in the same industry or companies offering complementary products and services. Developing countries, and among them the Southern Cone States, are in clear disadvantage vis-à-vis developed countries in terms of these new determinants of FDI. The desirability and necessity of attracting FDI above the level provided by private capital flows has led these countries to adopt certain policies, such as the (unilateral) liberalization of the rules regulating the entrance and conditions of permanence of FDI, and offering incentives such as tax concessions, exemptions from import duties and subsidies to foreign firms. During the period of 1990-1998 over 135 countries reduced regulatory restrictions on FDI. For major changes in the Southern Cone States, see Table 1.[107] These countries also moved away from the so-called Calvo Doctrine, which advanced the inclusion of a clause in FDI agreements in which the foreign investor agreed to waive all rights to diplomatic protection afforded him by his own country under international law, and any conflict had to be solved through the legal remedies available in the host state.[108]

Despite the unilateral liberalization, and active promotion of FDI, a closer look at Latin American aggregates, which reflect the same trends of Southern Cone States', show that investment and economic growth rates did not follow capital inflows (see Table 1). The main reasons pointed out for the lack of success of FDI in generating economic growth are that most FDI was done via privatization programmes and therefore did not expand economic capacity, having merely shifted the control of existing companies from domestic to foreign; most FDI went to services (not the manufacturing sector), and therefore did not contribute to increase exports nor to improve the quality of the services, given the lack of good local regulatory systems and competition law. Both countries and provinces within countries engaged in fiscal wars to compete for FDI and were, therefore, unable to increase their tax revenues. Finally, the major FDI sources

[107] See UNCTAD, World Investment Report 1999. Another possible determination for FDI location is the perception of a protectionist threat; big firms fearing protectionism from countries which could put in risk its exports decide to produce directly in that country as a means to secure its markets. This fact seems to be one of the motivations for the massive Japanese FDI in the US during the 1980s, but would be less relevant in developing countries as FDI determinant. See Bhagwati, 1991.

[108] The Calvo Doctrine is named for an Argentinean diplomat and jurist, Carlos Calvo, and evolved from a treatise written by him in 1896 addressing the Latin American countries' outcry for protection as a result of diplomatic and military interventions in these countries by foreign investors in the 19th Century, stemming from European colonialism. The doctrine contends that, if these countries acceded to the international legal concepts, they would be at the mercy of the powerful states and this would be injurious to the weaker nations, thus, and unjustifiable inequality between national and foreigners would be established. The doctrine is a clear desincentive to FDI in what it increases the risks for the foreign investor. Baker, 1999, pp.90-91.

were mergers and acquisitions, and in many cases local employees were replaced by foreigners.[109]

Table 12: Latin America Macroeconomic indicators (%GDP)

	1976-81	1983-90	1991-94	1995-96
Net capital inflows	4.9	1.2	4.9	4.9
Variation in reserves	1.0	0.2	1.5	1.9
Current accounts deficit	3.9	1.0	3.4	3.0
Gross capital formation	24.0	16.7	17.9	18.0
Savings	20.1	15.7	14.5	15.0
Real annual growth	5.5	1.6	3.6	1.9

Source: French-Davis & Reisen, 1998, p.13.

Therefore, the empirical evidence of the 1990s qualified the thesis asserting the almost unconditional benefits of FDI with regard to development. After two decades of research about the impact of FDI on economic growth in developing countries, it was recognized that FDI is not monolithic, and its benefits vary from one sector and country to another. Whether positive or negative aspects of FDI will prevail depends on the policies adopted by the host country, the investing company's code of conduct, the financial institutions that support it, and the international policy context. In other words, not only quantity of FDI matters, but quality as well. Governments have thus developed policies aiming at improving the quality of FDI, the first wave of which became known as second-generation FDI policies, with liberalization and the strengthening of standards of treatment for foreign investors being considered the first generation of such policies.[110]

---

[109] For more details and empirical examples see: UNCTAD 2002; UNCTAD 2001a; UNCTAD 2001b; UNCTAD 2001c; Uthoff & Titelman 1998; Wallace 1990; Barbosa 1995; Barry 1999. For specific case studies regarding the concession of tax exemption and subsidies to General Motors and Ford in Brazil, see Hanson, 2001 and Nodari, 2002.

[110] International organizations such as the UN and OECD have stimulated debate about the impact of FDI on economic growth, among other subjects, through the organization of major international conferences with academics and policymakers such as the "OECD Global Forum on FDI", from which the Inaugural Conference took place in Mexico City in November 2001, the First Conference in Paris in February 2002, and the Second in Shanghai in December 2002; the "UN Financing for Development", in March 2002, in Monterrey, Mexico, and the UN World Summit on sustainable Development in Johannesburg in September 2002, and; the "ECLAC FDI Policies in Latin America", in January 2002 in Santiago. In the UN, matters related to foreign direct investment were carried out until 1992 by the United Nations Centre on Transnational Corporations, from 1992 to 1993, by the Transnational Corporations and Management Division of the UN Department of Economic and Social Development, and since 1993 by the UN Conference on Trade and Development (UNCTAD). UNCTAD stated that its purpose is to further the understanding of the nature of transnational corporations and their contribution to development, and to create an enabling environment for international investment and enterprise development.

Second-generation (governmental) policies on FDI addressed such issues as the marketing of countries as possible locations for FDI and the setting up of national investment promotion agencies (IPAs). In 2000, more than 164 national IPAs and well over 250 sub-national agencies were in operation. IPAs are typically financed by the public sector although they try to supplement their income with services revenues, private sponsorships and aid from international institutions. In the case of developing countries, international assistance has been of great importance, especially in the first years after their establishment. Most IPAs were created under the ministry of economic, finance or foreign affairs or the president/ prime minister's office (approximately 60%), some as autonomous public bodies (20%), some as private agencies (8%) and some as joint private-public enterprises (3%). In the case of sub-national IPAs, which are frequent in developed countries, such as Italy (with 20 offices) and Germany (16), they are often independent organizations and not subsidiaries of the national agencies, although the latter try to perform a coordinating role to avoid unnecessary competition.[111] Pursuing a similar purpose on the global level, high-level IPA officials founded, in a meeting under the auspices of UNCTAD in 1995, the World Association of Investment Promotion Agencies (WAIPA). According to its statute, WAIPAs main goals are to promote and develop understanding and cooperation amongst IPAs, to strengthen information-gathering systems and information exchange amongst IPAs, to share country and regional experiences in attracting investment, to help IPAs gain access to technical assistance and training through WAIPA sponsored events or by way of referrals to relevant international or multilateral agencies, and to assist IPAs in advising their respective governments on the formulation of appropriate investment promotion policies and strategies.[112]

Third-generation FDI promotion policies are more complex and target foreign investors at the level of industries and firms, to meet their specific location needs at the activity and cluster level, in light of a country's developmental priorities. A foreign affiliate, like any other firm, has three options for obtaining inputs in a host country: import them, produce them locally in-house, or buy them from a local supplier. For developing countries, the formation of the so-called 'backward linkages' with foreign affiliates, i.e. a network of domestic suppliers, has crucial importance, since it contributes to the upgrading of the technological capabilities of domestic enterprises and to embed foreign affiliates more firmly in their economies. The extent to which foreign affiliates forge linkages with domestic suppliers is determined by the balance of costs and

---

Furthermore, the UN Economic Commission for Latin America and Caribbean (ECLAC) also deals with FDI issues in Latin America and Caribbean.

[111] See UNCTAD, 2001, The World of Investment Promotion at a Glance.

[112] See WAIPA homepage: www.waipa.org

benefits, as well as differences in company-level perceptions and strategies. The lack of efficient local suppliers, lack of information about potential suppliers and misperceptions from foreign affiliates are the main obstacles to the creation of backward linkages. Host governments can play a central role in providing information and supporting local firms to meet minimum requirements, as long as the policy instruments do not go against existing multilateral rules.[113] Examples of third-generation measures are, for instance, supplier audits, provision of advice on subcontracting deals, sponsoring of fairs, exhibitions and conferences, organization of meetings and visits to plants, introduction of technology transfer as a performance requirement, incentive for research and development cooperation, promotion of suppliers associations, collaboration with private sector training programmes, provision of legal protection against unfair contractual arrangements, encouragement and guarantee of recovery of past-due payments, and concession of fiscal benefits to companies that provide long-term resources to suppliers.[114]

Table 13: FDI promotion policies in the Southern Cone States (measure, date of adoption or creation)

	1st generation (liberalization & incentives)	2nd generation (creation of IPAs)
Argentina	Law 21.382/93; Decree 1.853/93	-Agencia de Desarrollo de Inversion [115]
Brazil	CVM Normative Instruction 130/90; BC Communication 2.099/90; INPI Resolution 22/91; BC Letter 216/91; BC Resolution 1.832/91; revocation of BC Instruction 85/81; Law 8.383/91; Decree 368/91; BC Resolution 1.894/92; BC Letter 2.266/92; BC Letter 2.282/92; INPI Resolution 35/92; BC Letter 2.313/92; SRF Normative Instruction 12/92; INPI Normative Instruction 120/93; Law 9.249/95; Constitution Amendment nr.6/95, Arts.171 & 176; Decree 2.452/88; Law 9.440/97; Law	-Investe Brazil, 2002[117]

[113] For more about multilateral rules on FDI, see section 5.1.1.3.
[114] For a detailed overview see UNCTAD, World Investment Report 2001, and on third-generation measures, p.22.
[115] Barry in OECD 1988, FDI policy and promotion in LA, p.53-56.

	9.449/97; Decree 20.725/97; Interministerial Measure 1/96 and 3/97 [116]	
Paraguay	Law 60/90; Law 117/91; Decree 19/89; Decree 27/90, Decree 6.361/90	- Proparaguay, 1991[118]
Uruguay	Law 16.906, 1988	-Instituto de Promocion de Inversiones y Exportaciones, 1996[119]

Source: compiled by the author.

5.1.2) FDI flows and trends

By the end of the 1970s, the annual outflow of FDI from OECD countries to all destinations (including to one another) doubled from approximately US$ 25 billions in the beginning of the decade to nearly US$60 billions. After declining sharply in the early 1980s, it began once again to increase. From 1986 to 1989 annual FDI flows increased at a phenomenal rate, multiplying four times. FDI flows to Latin America followed the global trend. In the early 1980s these countries faced a shortage of foreign private capital and most inflows were governmental or multilateral loans as part of rescheduling arrangements for their external debt (following the high level of capital inflow of the 1970s, predominantly in the form of portfolio investment as commercial bank loans). In the early 1990s, there was a resurgence of capital inflows in the form of FDI. This increase in FDI flows was driven by the operations of multinational and transnational corporations (MNCs & TNCs) with their affiliates abroad, and by

---

[116] The important thing to note about Brazilian legislation regarding FDI is that from the creation of a specific legislation with Law 4.131/62 and Decree 55.762/65 until the 1990s, the trend was towards the creation of restrictions to FDI, and afterwards, specially during the government of President Collor de Mello, the trend inverted towards the elimination of restrictions. Legislation includes a constitutional legal basis, specific statutes or laws, and regulatory legal acts from agencies responsible for FDI, such as the Securities Commission (CVM), the Central Bank (BC) and the National Institute for Industrial Production (INPI). For details see Barreto Filho, 1999, p.130-133 and IDB, 1997 Chapter on Brazil.

[117] See homepage: www.investebrasil.org.br. The structure of the national agency Investe Brasil was largely inspired in the Instituto de Desenvolvimento Industrial de Minas Gerais (INDI), a regional agency from the state of Minas Gerais created in 1968 to promote economic and industrial development. INDI is also a Brazilian member of WAIPA, besides Investe Brasil. About INDI, see homepage: www.indi.gov.br.

[118] See homepage: www.proparaguay.gov.py

[119] See homepage: www.uruguayxxi.gub.uy

cross-border mergers and acquisitions, having been considered as the major component in the process of economic globalization.

As regards the major sources of global FDI outflows, developed countries account for more than three-quarters of the total world average during the relevant period, with the EU becoming the leading group, rising from a share of 44% of total world outflows in 1980 to 70% in 2000. The United States ranks second, although with decreasing participation, from 36% of the total in 1980 to 12% in 2000, followed by Japan (see Table 3). It is interesting to note that until the mid-1970s the US was the major source of FDI outflows, with a share of total stocks of 55% in 1967, and 52% in 1971. [120]

Table 14: FDI Outflows (millions of dollars & % total world)

	1980	1985	1990	1995	2000
EU	23,812 (44)	26,084 (42)	121,344 (52)	159,713 (45)	968,019 (70)
USA	19,230 (36)	13,338 (22)	30,982 (13)	92,074 (26)	164,969 (12)
Japan	2,385 (4)	6,452 (10)	48,024 (21)	22,630 (6)	31,558 (2)
Total World	53,674	62,163	233,315	356,404	1,379,493

Source: Compiled with data from UNCTAD Homepage

With regard to global FDI inflows, there was an upward trend favoring developing countries that peaked in 1994 with a share of 41% of total world inflows, but returned to its original share of approximately 15% in 2000. Latin America lost ground along these two decades, from 14% of total world inflows in 1980 to 6% in 2000, and the Southern Cone States as well, although in a smaller scale; from 5% to 3% in the same period (see Table 4).[121]

Table 15: FDI Inflows (millions of dollars & % total world)

	1980	1985	1990	1995	2000
Developed c.	46,530 (85)	42,693 (74)	164,575 (81)	203,311 (62)	1,227,476 (82)
Developing c.	8,380 (15)	14,873 (26)	37,567 (19)	112,537 (34)	237,894 (16)
LA & Carib.	7,485 (14)	7,278 (12)	10,282 (5)	30,866 (9)	95,405 (6)
SCSs.	2,908 (5)	2,346 (4)	2,938 (1)	10,270 (3)	44,312 (3)
Total World	54.945	57.596	202.782	330.516	1.491.934

Source: Compiled with data from UNCTAD Homepage

[120] Gilpin, p.13

[121] See World Bank, *Global Development Finance*, 1999& UNCTAD, *World Investment Report 2001*.

Considering FDI flows to Latin America and the Caribbean, the United States remained the major source country from 1980 to 1994, having increased this advantage in the 1990s. The EU ranked second and Japan third (see Table 10). The same trend may be observed when only Mercosur member-states are taken into account. However, in the second half of the 1990s this trend was reversed, especially due to the extraordinary increase in the Spanish outflows to these countries.

Table 16: Major sources of FDI to Latin America & the Caribbean (net flows, annual average in millions of US dollars & % total)

	1980-1984	1985-1989	1990-1994
EU	1.176 (41%)	1.265 (54%)	1.952 (22%)
US	1.263 (44%)	941 (40%)	6.732 (74%)
Japan	435 (15%)	149 (6%)	386 (4%)
Total	2.874 (100%)	2.355 (100%)	9.070 (100%)

Source: IRELA, 1996, p.95.

Table 17: Major sources of FDI to Southern Cone States (net flows, annual average in millions of US dollars & % total)

	1980-1984	1985-1989	1990-1994
EU	812 (47%)	846 (44%)	962 (24%)
US	678 (39%)	893 (46%)	2.918 (72%)
Japan	233 (14%)	194 (10%)	154 (4%)
Total	1.723(100%)	1.933 (100%)	4.034(100%)

Source: IRELA, 1996, p.108.

Since the beginning of the 1990s, but especially after 1994, Spain has had an extraordinary increase in its FDI outflows to Latin America. Spanish companies participated in many privatization programmes, such as in the telecommunications sector in which the Telefónica de Espana bought privatized companies in Brazil, Argentina and Peru; and the participation of Spanish banks in mergers and acquisitions, such as the purchase of Banespa (Brazil) by BSCH for US$3.6 billion, Serfin (Mexico) by BSCH for US$1.6 billion and Bancomer (Mexico) by BBVA for US$1.9 billion. Other examples of significant acquisitions by Spanish companies are the purchase of YPF in Argentina by Repsol, and of Endesa and Enersis in Chile by Endesa Espana. In 1994, Spain became the main European country investing in Latin America, and ranked second world-wide after the United States. For example, from 1992 to 1999 Spain accumulated inflows in Argentina that represented 31.8% of the Argentinean total (US ranked 2nd with 21.1% and Netherlands 3rd with 7.3%), and 20.8% in Brazil from 1996 to 2000 (US ranked 1st with 23.7%, and the Netherlands 3rd with 9.3%), coming from a participation of 5.6 and 0.6% of stocks in 1992 and 1995 respectively.[122]

Table 18: Spanish FDI (% of total net investments)

	1980-1985	1986-1991	1992-1995
Latin America	23.53	4.89	28.34
Argentina	-0.8	1.37	5.29
Brazil	2.4	0.24	0.77
Paraguay	1.13	0.04	0.13
Uruguay	2.33	0.25	0.41
Chile	9.79	0.89	0.85
Mexico	3.13	1.12	2.2
Peru	0.87	0.01	16.07

Source: OECD, 1996, p.29.

One last interesting remark is that when stocks of FDI, rather than flows, are analyzed, the EU assumes the first position both in Argentina and Brazil. This indicates that the EU was the major investor in these countries for a certain period prior to 1980. In Brazil, Germany stands out as the major source, and in Argentina, Italy, as can be see in the following tables.

Table 19: FDI in Brazil (stock in Dec. of the year in billions of dollars & %)

	1980	1990	2000
USA	5.0 (29%)	10.4 (28%)	35.4 (22%)
EU*	6.2 (35%)	14.1 (38%)	69.1 (43%)
Spain	0.1	0.1	21.8
Netherlands	0.4	0.9	11.2
France	0.7	2.0	9.9
Portugal	-	0.1	7.7
Germany	2,4	5,6	7,5
UK	1,1	2,5	3,8
Italy	0,5	1,2	2,9

[122] About Spanish FDI in Latin America, see OECD, 1997, p.28; CEPAL, 2000; Giordano & Santiso, 1999; Santiso, 1996; Nunnenkamp, 2001, p.19-20.

Belgium	0,6	1,1	2,2
Sweden	0,4	0,6	2,1
Japan	1,7	3,8	4,1
Switzerland	1,8	3,5	3,9
Canada	0,6	2,2	2,9
Off-shore	1,2	1,8	21,7
Other	1,0	1,5	23,8
Total	17,5	37,3	160,9

Source: adapted from Banco Central do Brasil in IIKH, 2002, p.184.
* Sum of member-states listed below

Table 20: FDI in Argentina (stock in Dec. of the year in billions of dollars & %)

	1980	1990	2000
USA	2,1 (40%)	3,7 (42%)	54,7 (38%)
EU*	2,0 (38%)	2,9 (33%)	64,0 (45%)
Spain	0,1	0,1	33,1
France	0,4	0,6	10,7
Italy	0,5	0,8	7,8
UK	0,3	0,3	5,8
Germany	0,3	0,7	3,8
Netherlands	0,4	0,4	2,8
Brazil	0,1	0,1	2,2
Chile	-	-	8,9
Australia	-	-	1,8
Switzerland	0,5	0,5	2,0
Other	0,4	2,2	3,7
Total	5,3	8,8	143,2

Source: adapted from Ministerio de Economia, in IIKH, 2002, p.185.
* Sum of the listed above

5.1.3) International cooperation regarding FDI

The development of international FDI rules at the multilateral level started after WW II in the context of the establishment of the Bretton Woods system. Before that, FDI was regulated predominantly by national law with a restrictive bias, and a few bilateral initiatives (see below). In its beginning, the main impulse towards the development of a multilateral regime for FDI came from the US, at that time the largest exporter of capital, although without success. The Havana Charter for the establishment of the International Trade Organization (ITO) contained provisions about investment in its Arts.11 & 12, but not the General Agreement on Tariffs and Trade (GATT), signed in 1947. The question of investment was reviewed in the context of the 1955 GATT review conference, held when it became clear that the Havana Charter would not become effective due to the insufficient number of signatory countries and the refusal of the American Congress to ratify it. The Resolution on International Investment for Economic Development signed at the Conference recognized that an increased flow of capital to countries in need of foreign investment and, in particular, to developing countries, would facilitate the objectives of the General Agreement, and urged contracting parties to take part in negotiations for the conclusion of bilateral and multilateral agreements on FDI-related issues, even though these had only recommendatory status. In the Tokyo Round negotiations in the 70s, rules on subsidies, technical standards and government procurement were negotiated, and although the focus was on their impact upon trade in goods, the rules were relevant to the competitive conditions faced by foreign investors.[123]

A more directly relevant development in the GATT regarding FDI came during the Uruguay Round, concluded in 1994. The Ministerial Declaration that launched the negotiations in 1986 included a request for examination of the restrictive and distorting effects of investment measures on trade. After difficult negotiations which polarized both developed and developing countries, an agreement was reached about Trade Related Investment Measures (TRIMs) with a compromise between the prohibition of performance and domestic-content requirements for investments related to trade in goods (Art.1) (as advanced by developed countries) and the granting of special treatment to developing countries for the concession of national treatment (Art.4) and the periods for implementation of the new rules (Art.5). Art.9 provides a review of the agreement.[124]

Although less directly, the General Agreement on Trade in Services (GATs), also had an impact upon FDI, which might, given the growing importance and volume of trade in services, become even more significant in the long-term than TRIMs. The GATT rules only create obligations for governments concerning the treatment of foreign goods, not being concerned with the treatment of foreign persons, whether legal or natural, operating in their territories, a central issue for FDI. GATS, however, in establishing obligations regarding the treatment of services, recognizes that the supply of several services to a market is difficult or impossible without the physical presence of the service supplier. Trade in services is therefore closely linked to FDI in that foreign firms offering service products often need a commercial presence in that country, a topic dealt with under the FDI rules about establishment and permanence. In GATS, signatory countries must offer to foreign companies MFN treatment, the right of market

[123] WTO, 1996, p.35; Barreto Filho, 1999, pp.94-98; Moran, 2000.

[124] The TRIMs agreement covers two types of performance requirements; local content requirements and trade balancing requirements. Graham, 2000, p.61.

entry (Art.16) and national treatment (Art.17), though the latter not as a general principle but only in specific sectors.

Two other agreements finalized in the Uruguay Round also refer to FDI. The first is the Trade Related Aspects of Intellectual Property (TRIPs) agreement, since the definition of investment explicitly includes intellectual property. With its provisions on minimum standards, domestic enforcement procedures and dispute settlement, the agreement is directly relevant to the legal environment affecting FDI. The second is the Agreement on Subsidies and Countervailing Measures (ASCM). Although it refers to trade in goods, which by definition occurs only after investments have been made and, therefore, is not easily applied to FDI, the agreement forbids incentives such as grants, subsidized credits, tax exemptions, preferential access to government contracts, monopoly position and closure of the market to further entry.[125]

Still within the context of the Breton Woods organizations, there were also debates in the UN General Assembly in the 1960s and 1970s, instigated by developing countries and their promotion of the New International Economic Order (NIEO). The purpose here was to maximize the contribution of MNCs to the economic development of host countries; yet the proposal had a protective character and was, therefore, not supported by the US and other developed countries. The most relevant point was the attempt to create a Code of Conduct for Transnational Corporations, for which negotiations started in 1977, only to be officially suspended in 1992 with the justification of a revision need due to changed international circumstances.[126] As regards the settlement of disputes, UNCITRAL developed arbitration rules that can be used by other arbitration institutions regarding disputes between two governmental parties.[127] Other examples from the UN system are the two codes negotiated in the framework of UNCTAD, one on Restrictive Business Practices, which was adopted on a non-binding basis in 1980, and one on technology transfer, never adopted. The weakness of these codes has also been attributed to the lack of support by developed countries. Some developing countries and NGOs propose that the negotiations of a multilateral agreement should take place in a UN framework, and not in WTO or OECD, given that the main objective of such an agreement should be to increase the developmental potential of FDI, and not liberalization *per se*, but so far there are no concrete proposals in that respect.[128]

Under the World Bank Group, three agencies were created to deal with FDI. The first is the International Finance Corporation (IFC), established in 1955

---

[125] About FDI and the Uruguay Round, see WTO, 1996, pp.35-40 & Barreto Filho 1999, Ch.9

[126] Barreto Filho, 1999, p.63.

[127] Baker, 1999, p.42.

[128] See the debate in the report from the Civil Society Consultation on Trade and Investment meeting, organized by the European Commission, DG Trade, dated 04-28-1999 (http://europa.eu.int/comm/trade/miti/invest/csdmti.html accessed on 02-10-2001.

to provide loans and, later, equity investments in private sector projects in developing countries that are members of the World Bank, without government guarantees. In 1985, the IFC created a Foreign Investment Advisory Service (FIAS) to assist governments in the creation of improved conditions to attract FDI.[129] The second agency is the International Centre for the Settlement of Investment Disputes (ICSID), established in 1966 to assist in the arbitration or conciliation of investment disputes arising between foreign private investors and host state governments when both the investor's home country and the host government have signed the Convention. One predecessor of ICSID was the Permanent Court of Arbitration (PCA), an intergovernmental body established by the Hague Conventions of 1899 and 1907, which established its Rules of Arbitration and Conciliation for Settlement of International disputes between state and non-state parties. However, this is a bureau for the management of a panel of international arbitrators rather than a court.[130] The ICSID, despite some problems, has been recognized as one of the pre-eminent arbitration institutions by the international investment community, particularly the community involved in FDI projects in LDCs, also providing assistance in the formulation of treaties and laws regarding FDI in developing countries. In the EU and Southern Cone States, only Brazil did not sign the Convention, Argentina signed it in 1992 (effective in 1994), Paraguay in 1981 (1983) and Uruguay in 1992 (2000). Other major non-signatory countries are Mexico, Canada and India. [131]

The third World Bank Group agency dealing with FDI is the Multilateral Investment Guarantee Agency (MIGA). It was created in 1985 to provide political risk insurance (guarantees) to investors, lenders, services provision such as research and technical assistance to member-states, mediation of investment disputes etc. In 1992, the agency formulated a legal framework commissioned by the Development Council of the World Bank and IMF regarding guidelines on the treatment of FDI. MIGA Guidelines were different from the ones negotiated at the UN General Assembly in that they did not include rules of good conduct for foreign investors, and did not intend to represent a codification of customary international law with regard to the treatment of FDI, but rather to formulate generally acceptable international standards to support the objective of promoting

---

[129] See homepage from IFC: www.ifc.org and FIAS: www.fias.net . FIAS developed projects in the Southern Cone States such as: Argentina, assistance of the creation of IPA in 1994; Brazil, proposal for the creation of IPA in 1996, study about FDI environment with emphasis on export-oriented FDI and administrative costs to FDI in 2001; Paraguay, support in the development of legal policy and institutional changes in 1993, support to the Cabinet to prepare a Investment Policy Statement in 1994, support to develop a strategy and business plan for the IPA in 1995 and support to the new IPA in 1996; Uruguay, study of the investment climate in 1991. See FIAS-ICC projects in Latin America at the homepage.

[130] See for Baker, 1999, p.42 and for PCS its homepage: http://www.pca-cpa.org/

[131]Fore more about the history and records of ICSID see Baker, 1999, Chs.3-6; Homepage: www.worldbank.org/icsid.

FDI. All EU and Southern Cone States signed the MIGA Convention and Guidelines, and among major non-signatories, we find only Mexico.[132]

Apart from the international organizations of the Breton Woods System, the Organization for Economic Cooperation and Development (OECD) has also developed international rules regarding international investments. In 1961, its member-states signed two codes related to the right of establishment of foreign-controlled enterprises, the Codes of Liberalization of Capital Movements and Current Invisible Operations. In 1976, member-states signed the Declaration on International Investment and Multinational Enterprises, which consists of four instruments, namely , the Guidelines for Multinational Enterprises, concerning the behavior of MNCs, as well as one regarding the treatment accorded to foreign-controlled enterprises, including new investments by already established enterprises (National Treatment); one regarding Conflicting Requirements; and one regarding Incentives and Disincentives. The National Treatment Instrument sets out the principle that, as indicated in the name, foreign-controlled enterprises operating in member countries should be accorded no less favorable treatment than that accorded to domestic enterprises in similar situations, however it contains a long list of country exceptions. The attempts to upgrade the National Treatment Instrument into a binding agreement in 1991 failed due to disagreements among negotiating parties. The Declaration has been reviewed in 1979, 1984, 1991 and 2000. In 1991, three new countries, Argentina, Brazil and Chile acceded to it, and in 2000, Estonia, Lithuania and Slovenia, followed suit. By the end of 2002 Israel, Latvia, Singapore and Venezuela were in process of accession negotiations as well. [133]

In the early 90s, the OECD engaged in a major effort to create a wider agreement about FDI, assuming that the existence of a broader range of issues would facilitate negotiations by increasing the probability of each party to obtain something to their satisfaction. After three years of preparations, negotiations were launched in 1995 for the conclusion of a Multilateral Agreement on Investment (MAI). The main features of the proposed agreement would be the application of national treatment and MFN to the establishment and subsequent treatment of investment, the creation of certain standards for investor protection regarding expropriation and compensations, the prohibition of performance requirements, and the establishment of a dispute settlement procedure for governments and private investors regarding violations under the MAI. It did not address investment incentives such as subsidies, nor tax policies, would have had

---

[132] See Baker, 1999, Chs.7-11; Barreto Filho, 1999, Ch7; WTO, 1996, p.33-34; MIGA Homepage www.miga.org.

[133] The two major problems concerned the opposition of some members, particularly France and Canada, to the inclusion of cultural industries, and the skepticism of the US delegation in obtaining support from the Congress. See Graham, 2000, p.20-21. Fore more about the Declaration and its instruments see OECD, 1991.

a broad list of general exceptions and country-specific reservations and, according to specialists, would have actually merely codified the *status quo* of the practice of FDI regulation in OECD member-states, not advancing much in terms of liberalization. Still, negotiations did fail, being suspended in late 1998.[134]

The main reasons for the failure of MAI were disagreements among the negotiating parties, which were deadlocked among other reasons by the lack of involvement of higher-ranking political officials, as well as external opposition, most notably from the anti-globalization movement. It seems that the background of the disagreements and opposition was, essentially, a lack of clear and solid information about the costs and benefits of the agreement and of each particular provision. FDI became a polemic issue due to on a superficial knowledge of the matter, both in terms of technical issues and domestic demands. To address this problem the OECD refocused its efforts on the dissemination of information about FDI, with initiatives such as the OECD Global Forum on International Investment advanced by the Centre for Cooperation with Non-Members. If a new round of negotiations were to be launched in the future, it would be expected to take place within the WTO and not the OECD, and would therefore include developing countries.[135]

One last issue concerning international cooperation regarding FDI at the multilateral level are the agencies created to deal with the settlement of disputes between private parties, i.e., between a private foreign investor and a private local company, individual or institution, and not, therefore, between a private party and the host government, in which case the PCA, UNCITRAL, ICSID and MIGA would be the appropriate agencies. The first international agreements addressing the settlement of international disputes in the case of two private parties, and covering also issues regarding FDI, were the Treaty of International Procedural Law, signed in Montevideo in 1888, which was however only ratified by four countries; the Geneva Protocol on Arbitration Clauses from 1923, in which "each of the contracting states recognizes the validity of an agreement whether relating to existing or future differences between the parties subject respectively to the jurisdiction of different contracting states by which the parties to a contract agree to submit to arbitration all or any differences that may arise in connection with such contract relating to commercial matters or to other matters capable of settlement by arbitration, whether or not the arbitration is to take place in a country to whose jurisdiction none of the parties is subject" (Art.1); and the Geneva Convention on the Execution of Foreign Awards of 1927. To deal with

[134] Graham, 2000, p.2-3.

[135] Although Japan, South Korea and specially the European Commission have manifested their preference to use the WTO/GATT as a forum rather than OECD as early as the 1990s, the consensus was that it would be easier to negotiate first among developed countries which have similar demands and then expand it to developing countries, which in light of the failure of MAI turned out to be quite ironic. Graham, 2000, pp.190-191 & Walter, 2000.

these cases a number of arbitration agencies were created, the most important being the American Arbitration Association (AAA), the Korean Commercial Arbitration Board (KCAB), the Japan Commercial Arbitration Association (JCAA) and the International Chamber of Commerce (ICC). The ICC was established in 1919 to promote international commerce and, in 1923, created an international arbitration system, covering also FDI-related matters. It also accepted cases with governmental agencies.[136]

As mentioned earlier, in parallel to the developments at the multilateral level, a number of bilateral and regional agreements concerning FDI have been signed. Regarding the Bilateral Investment Treaties (BITs), the first ones were promoted by the United States after the WW I, as provisions in the "Treaties of Friendship, Trade, and Navigations." After WW II, the US signed specific agreements regarding FDI, such as the "Establishment Conventions." In the late 1950s, Germany started promoting BITs, signing the first in 1959 with Pakistan, and developing the broadest network of BITs so far.[137] The number of BITs proliferated especially in the 1990s, reaching 1.857 in 2000. Although these treaties remain quite standardized, they are able to reflect in their provisions the differing positions and approaches of the many countries that have concluded such agreements. The first ones were typically between one country exporting capital (a developed country) and one importing capital (a developing country) at the initiative of the developed country in order to secure legal protection and guarantees for the investment in its companies. The developing country would sign a BIT to promote a favorable climate to attract foreign investors, but usually demand the inclusion of protection of its own economy. This pattern has changed since the late 1980s and especially the 1990s, as developing countries and economies in transition began to sign BITS between themselves with the dual purpose of protecting their outward investment and attracting inward investment as well, including sometimes market access (right of establishment) instead of merely protection (post-establishment treatment).

The main principles and provisions of BITs are the same as national FDI regulations. They deal with the scope and definition of investment (which in most cases include tangible and intangible assets, direct as well as portfolio investments and existing as well as new investments) and investor (natural persons, national or permanent residents; and/or legal persons, or companies), national and most-favored-nation treatment in relation to the right of establishment and/or post-establishment, guarantees and compensation in respect to expropriation and compensation for war and civil disturbances, guarantees of free transfer of funds and repatriation of capital and profits, subrogation on insurance claims, mechanisms for the settlement of disputes state to state and investor to state. In

---

[136] For more about these agencies see Baker, 1999, pp.31-38.
[137] Barreto Filho, 1999, pp.44-46.

addition, they might include provisions regarding transparency of national laws, performance requirements, entry and residence of foreign personnel, general exceptions, etc. [138]

Latin American countries have not signed BITS until the late 1980s, but by 2000 have concluded as much as 300. Argentina is signatory of 53 BITS, with the first one signed in 1993. Brazil has signed 14, the first in 1994, Paraguay 23, 20 of each after 1993, and Uruguay 24, of each 18 after 1990 (for the ones signed with EU member states, see table 10). These numbers however hide some peculiarities. In the case of Brazil, for instance, none of these agreements became effective because they were not ratified by Congress. It has been alleged that these agreements were signed under pressure to attract investments but that they were unconstitutional by conceding more advantages to foreign firms than to national ones, namely by allowing controversies to be solved by private arbiters abroad, or expropriations to be paid in cash instead of government bonds. Even if this is, essentially, a technically legal problem, the motives behind non-ratification are clearly political, showing a change of perspective about the limits of liberalization.[139]

Table 21: BITs signed between the Southern Cone States and EU member states until 01-01-2000 (year of signature/ date of effectiveness)

	Argentina	Brazil	Paraguay	Uruguay
Austria	1992/95	-	1993/99	-
Belgium/Luxem burg	1990/94	1999/-	1992/-	1991/-
Denmark	1992/95	1995/-	1993/-	-
France	1991/93	1995/-	1978/80	1993/97
Finland	1993/96	1995/-	-	-
Germany	1991/93	1995/-	1993/98	1987/90
Greece	1999/-	-	-	-
Italy	1990/93	1995/-	1999/-	1990/98
Ireland	-	-	-	-
Netherlands	1992/94	1998/-	1992/94	1988/91
Portugal	1994/96	1994/-	1999/2001	-
Spain	1991/92	-	1993/96	1992/94
Sweden	1991/92	-	-	-
UK	1990/93	1994/-	1981/92	1991/97

Source: Adapted from UNCTAD 2000, Bilateral Investment Treaties

[138] See UNCTAD, 2000, Bilateral Investment Treaties 1959—1999; Robert at al, 2002.

[139] See Estado de Sao Paulo, 27-12-2002.

At the regional level, most countries participating in regional free trade agreements such as the North American Free Trade Area (NAFTA), the Asia-Pacific Economic Cooperation (APEC), the Andean Community (CAN), the Caribbean Community (CARICOM), and the Common Market of the South (MERCOSUR) have included provisions on intra and extra FDI (see table 11).[140] The provisional draft for the Free Trade Area of the Americas (FTAA) also provides a very detailed chapter on investments including national treatment (Art.2) and MFN clause (Art.3) with a list of exceptions (Art.4), prohibition of certain performance requirements (Art.7), provisions about key personnel (Art.8), state-to-state and investor-to-state dispute settlement mechanisms (Art.14 & 15), commitments not to relax labor (Art.18) environmental (Art.19) laws to attract investment, etc..[141]

The case of the EU is examined in the next section. Mercosur has three instruments regarding FDI which have been established by Decisions of the Common Market Council (CMC): The Colonia Protocol (CMC/Decision No.11/93 from 17/01/1994) and the Montevideo Protocol (CMC/Decision No.13/97 from 15/12/1997) for intra-zone originated FDI, and the Buenos Aires Protocol for extra-zone originated FDI (CMC/Decision No.11/94 from 05/08/1994). These protocols have not yet become effective until April/2003 (because they were not yet ratified by the member states). Despite this fact, the main provisions of the Buenos Aires Protocol, which is the relevant one in terms of FDI relations with the EU, are seen below.

The Buenos Aires Protocol adopts a broad definition of investment, including intellectual property, copyright, patents and publicly awarded concessions, including those conferred to natural resources exploration and exploitation (Art.2A1), and also a broad definition of investor, including permanent residents in third countries and legal persons registered elsewhere, owned or controlled by persons registered and domiciled in signatory and third countries (Art.2A2). As regards the right of establishment, the application of national treatment and MFN is left to the discretion of member states. As far as post-establishment treatment is concerned, it gives national treatment, non-discrimination and MFN (except for privileges deriving from participation in FTAs, common customs or similar regional agreements or international tax conventions) and encompasses coverage for political risks and permission for free transfer of funds including benefits, dividends, royalties, etc. (Art.C,D&E). The protocol also establishes a dispute settlement mechanism by which state-to-state differences are dealt with through diplomatic action and alternative international arbitration and investor-to-state disputes are treated through friendly consultation,

[140] For more details about the provisions see WTO, 1996, pp.27-31 or Barreto Filho, Chs.8&10.

[141] For the text of the second draft see FTAA homepage: www.ftaa-alca.org (accessed on 17-01-2003).

intervention of host courts or international *ad hoc* or institutional arbitration (Art.2G,H,I). Despite this quite liberal approach, favoring FDI, the Buenos Aires Protocol does not mention performance requirements or commitments concerning personnel.[142]

Mercosur has signed agreements on FDI matters with the EU (which are looked at in detail in the next section), as well as with Chile, Bolivia and the United States, though they are just cooperation agreements, and do not include any legal commitments. The most recent one, dated 06-19-1991, was signed by the four member-states, because Mercosur still did not have legal personality, and provided for cooperation only on information exchange. The agreements with Chile and Bolivia, signed on 06-25-1996, are broad and contemplate incorporation as associated members of Mercosur. Both contain references as to their objectives (Art.1) with regard to the promotion and protection of reciprocal investments but without specific commitments. The agreement with Chile contains in addition on the article about investments (Art.41) in which both parts confirm that the bilateral treaties between Chile and Mercosur member-states will remain effective.

Table 22: International rules regarding FDI

Year of Sign.	Instrument	Type*
1888	Treaty of International Procedural Law (Montevideo)	ML
1923	Geneva Protocol on Arbitration Clauses	ML
1927	Geneva Convention on the Execution of Foreign Awards	ML
1955	UN General Assembly Resolution on International Investment for Economic Development	ML
1957	Treaty Establishing the European Community	RE
1957	Agreement on Arab Economic Unity	RE
1958	New York Convention on Recognition and Enforcement of Foreign Arbitral Awards	ML
1961	OECD Code of Liberalization of Capital Movements	PL
1961	OECD Code of Liberalization of Current Invisible Operations	PL
1962	PCA Rules of Arbitration and Conciliation for Settlement of International Disputes	ML
1962	UN General Assembly Resolution 1803: Permanent Sovereignty over Natural Resources	ML

[142] Colombi & Podrez, 1996; Chaire Mercosur, 2002, p.17; Robert at al, 2002, p.270.

1965	Common Convention on Investments in the States of the Customs and Economic Union of Central Africa	RS
1966	UNCITRAL	ML
1966	IBRD Convention establishing the International Centre for Settlement of Investment Disputes (ICSID)	ML
1969	Agreement on Andean Pact	RE
1970	Agreement on Investment and Free Movement of Arab Capital among Arab Countries	RS
1970	Decision No. 24 of the Commission of the Cartagena Agreement: Common Regulations Governing Foreign Capital Movement, Trademarks, Patents, Licenses and Royalties	RS
1971	Convention Establishing the Inter-Arab Investment Guarantee Corporation	RS
1972	Joint Convention on the Freedom of Movement of Persons and the Right of Establishment in Central African Customs and Economic Union	RS
1973	Agreement on the Harmonization of Fiscal Incentives to Industry	RS
1973	Treaty establishing the Caribbean Community	RE
1974	UN General Assembly Resolution 3201: Declaration on the Establishment of a New International Economic Order	ML
1974	UN General Assembly Resolution 3202: Programme of Action on the Establishment of a New International Economic Order	ML
1974	UN General Assembly Resolution 3281: Charter of Economic Rights and Duties of States	ML
1975	The Multinational Companies Code in the Custom and Economic Union of Central Africa	RS
1976	OECD Declaration on International Investment and Multinational Enterprise	PL
1977	ILO Tripartite Declaration of Principles Concerning Multinational Enterprises and Social Policy	ML
1979	Draft International Agreement on Illicit Payments (not adopted by the UN General Assembly)	ML
1980	Unified Agreement for the Investment of Arab Capital in the Arab States	RS

1980	Treaty Establishing the Latin American Integration Association	RE
1980	UN General Assembly Resolution 35/63: The Set of Multilaterally Agreed Equitable Principles and Rules for the Control of Restrictive Business Practices	ML
1981	Agreement on Promotion, Protection and Guarantee of Investment among the Member States of the Organization of the Islamic Conference	PL
1983	Treaty Establishing the Economic Community of Central African States	RE
1983	Draft United Nations Code of Conduct on Transnational Corporations (not adopted by the UN General Assembly)	ML
1985	IBRD Convention Establishing the Multilateral Investment Guarantee Agency (MIGA)	ML
1985	UN General Assembly Resolution 89/248: Guideline for Consumer Protection	ML
1985	Draft International Code of Conduct on the Transfer of Technology (not adopted by the UN General Assembly)	ML
1986	ILO Procedure for the Examination of Disputes Concerning the Application of the Tripartite Declaration of Principles Concerning Multinational Enterprises and Social Policy by Means of Interpretation of its Provision	ML
1987	Community Investment Code of the Economic Community of the Great Lakes	RS
1987	Agreement for the Establishment of a Regime for CARICOM Enterprises	RS
1987	Revised Basic Agreement on ASEAN Industrial Joint Enterprises	RS
1987	Agreement Among the Governments of Brunei Darussalam, the Republic of Indonesia, Malaysia, the Republic of the Philippines, the Republic of Singapore and the Kingdom of Thailand for the Promotion an Protection of Investments	RS
1989	Fourth ACP-EEC Convention of Lomé	PL
1990	Charter on a Regime of Multinational Industrial Enterprises (MIEs) in the Preferential Trade Area for Eastern and Southern African States	RS
1990	Resolution Adopted by the Conference Strengthening the Implementation the Set of Multilaterally Agreed Equitable	ML

	Principles and Rules for the Control of Restrictive Business Practices (adopted as UN General Assembly Resolution 35/63)	
1991	Decision No.291 of the Commission of the Cartagena Agreement: Common Code for the Treatment of Foreign Capital and on Trademarks, Patents and Royalties	RS
1991	Decision No. 292 of the Commission of the Cartagena Agreement: Uniform Code on Andean Multinational Enterprises	RS
1992	North American Free Trade Agreement (NAFTA)	RE
1992	MIGA Guidelines on the Treatment of Foreign direct investment	ML
1993	Treaty Establishing the Common Market for Eastern and Southern Africa	RE
1994	Mercosur Colonia Protocol	RS
1994	Mercosur Buenos Aires Protocol	RS
1994	APEC Non-binding Investment Principles	PL
1994	Final Act of the European Energy Charter Conference, the Energy Charter Treaty, Decisions with Respect to the Energy and Annexes to the Energy Charter Treaty	PL
1994	WTO TRIMs	ML
1994	WTO GATs	ML
1994	WTO TRIPs	ML
1994	WTO ASCM	ML
1997	Mercosur Montevideo Protocol	RS

Source: compiled from WTO, 1996, p.27-29 & 32-33.
*RS=regional separated instrument, RE= regional instrument embedded in broader framework, PL=plurilateral instrument, ML=multilateral

5.1.4) FDI in EU foreign policy, or non-existent FDI policy

The EU does not have one single regime for FDI towards third parties. Instead, it treats separately the three main aspects of FDI, namely, movement of capital, right of establishment and post establishment regime.

Movement of capital - both intra member-states and with third parties - is regulated by Ch.4/TEU (Arts.56-60). Art.56 prohibits restrictions to exchanges of capital between member-states and third parties, but loses strength due to Art.57, which allows member-states to preserve certain restrictions present on 31-12-1993, and to Art.58, which allows them to introduce new restrictions for reasons of fiscal control, public order, public security, administrative information or prudential supervision. The TEU also establishes that the Community has a non-exclusive competence in general matters concerning movements of capital (Art.57); it is, however, exclusive with regard to measures that would represent a retrocession in the liberalization of movements of capital, in particular regarding the adoption of safeguards up to the limit of 6 months. The Council shall decide by QMV in the first and third case and by unanimity in the second. Art.60 creates a special regime regarding sanctions, by which the Community can act, but if not, the member-states can do it individually under certain restrictions. In sum, regarding the external competences of the EU in the case of movements of capital, it is possible to say that a) in cases of liberalization, given that the Community competences as nonexclusive, the member-states retain their competences as long as the Community does not exercise its own; b) in cases of standstill, the member-states retain their competences if referring to measures addressed in Art.58, and the Community has exclusive competence if it concerns a retrocession in liberalization or safeguards; c) member-states remain with competences regarding most specific aspects of movements of capital, subject to reserves on the part of the Community in its non-exclusive competence.[143]

The second aspect of the EU legislation regarding FDI, the right of establishment, is covered by Ch.2/TEU (Arts.43-48), but only regarding intra member-states. The Community can in theory exercise external competences derived from its internal responsibilities (implied competences) but this has not been the case so far regarding the right of establishment. The right of establishment remains in practice, therefore, under the competence of member-states.[144]

The third aspect of the EU legislation about FDI, the post-establishment regime (treatment of foreign companies), is covered by different provisions regarding each economic sector, such as transports, or regime of enterprises, and fiscal matters, both for intra member-states and third parties' companies. Regarding the conclusion of bilateral agreements with third parties, the Community can accept commitments about treatment of companies under

[143] Torrent, 1998, pp.85-87.

[144] Torrent, 1998, pp.88-90 & 108-110.

Art.238/310. In the case not covered by this Art., such as the multilateral negotiations under WTO, the competences for each case must be analyzed individually. [145]

As a result from this rather complex combination of competences, when the EU engages in multilateral negotiations regarding FDI, such as was the case during the negotiations for the GATS and TRIMs and the failed negotiations for the OECD MAI, or in agreements with 3rd parties containing FDI related matters, such as was the case of the CEEs under the European Agreements and the former Soviet States, which contained provisions about the right of establishment of companies, the Community and the member-states will work as indicated in the description of the "fourth pillar": i.e. each of them will negotiate the portions of the agreements under their competence, but within the EU system. In other words, although member-states negotiate individually in their own name, they do it in the intergovernmental forum of the EU, i.e., the Council, and the concluded agreements are managed by institutions from the EU system, mostly the Commission. [146]

Among the agreements signed with Southern Cone States, none contained specific commitments regarding FDI; they only mentioned the intent of developing cooperation regarding the promotion of EU FDI, seen in detail below.

5.1.4.1) Bilateral agreements

As seen in the previous section, the competence for FDI issues remains to a large extent with the EU Member-states and, consequently, the negotiations regarding FDI commitments with Southern Cone States remain mostly at the bilateral level, as indicated by the BITs signed between EU member-states and Southern Cone States. However, EU's mixed agreements with third parties could contain FDI commitments. These agreements can also contain references to cooperation on FDI matters. The contents about FDI in the EU agreements with the SCS are seen in detail below.

The bilateral agreements between the EU and individual Southern Cone States were signed by the EEC/EC, which does not have the competence to negotiate FDI provisions (or Euratom, but these are not included, given the peculiarities of atomic power foreign policy). The first and second-generation agreements also do not contain any reference to cooperation.[147] It is worth

[145] Torrent, 1998, pp.90-93.

[146] Torrent, 1998, pp.111-112 & 146-147.

[147] What characterize First Generation Agreements are their conventional bilateral and technical structure and their reference to possible reciprocal cooperation. In practical terms, however, these treaties only extended the Most Favored Nation (MFN) status to its signatories. The second-generation agreements reaffirmed the MFN clause and declared the intention to increase commercial and economic cooperation. Third-generation agreements are broader in scope and

mentioning that in the EEC-Argentina agreement of 1971, Argentina stated its desire for an increase in European investments, as a means to economic development, as a unilateral declaration (nr.9). The third-generation agreements state the intention to promote cooperation regarding FDI, such as: Art.6 of EEC-Argentine of 1990: "the contracting parties agree to cooperate in particular to encourage joint ventures, especially for diversification of Argentine exports and the assimilation of technology..."; Art.3.2 of EEC-Brazil of 1982: "as means to (promote economic cooperation), the contracting parties shall endeavor inter alia to facilitate and promote by appropriate means: (a) broad and harmonious cooperation between their respective industries, in particular in the form of joint ventures; (...)(f) favorable conditions for the expansion of investment on a basis of advantage for both parties"; Art.7(b) of EEC-Uruguay of 1992: "(the contracting parties agree) to improve the favorable climate for mutual investment between the Community member-states and Uruguay, particularly through agreements for the promotion and protection of such investment based on the principles of non-discrimination and reciprocity". Texts contained in the other treaties are quite similar.

The 1992 bi-regional agreement between EU and Mercosur does not contain any commitment about FDI (it was signed by the EC), nor does it mention cooperation in that regard, given that its major objective was to promote technical assistance to the integration process. The 1995 agreement of was signed by both the EC and member-states, and could contain FDI commitments (in the fourth pillar format, such as the agreements with CEEs) but it does not. Nevertheless, it provides for cooperation in Arts.11 & 12. Note that in Art.12-2b (emphasis added) it is explicitly stated that specific commitments should be done at the bilateral basis among EU and Mercosur member-states. Art.11 reads as follows: "(cooperation in business) shall focus in particular on:(1a) increasing the flow of trade, investment, industrial cooperation projects and the transfer of technology...(1c) identifying barriers to industrial cooperation between the Parties and eliminating such barriers using measures which promote compliance with competition rules and foster the tailoring of those rules to the needs of the market, giving due attention to the involvement and consultation of operators, (1d) stimulating cooperation between the Parties' economic operators, especially small and medium-sized enterprises;...(3b) suitable initiatives to back cooperation between small and medium-sized enterprises, such as the promotion of joint ventures, the establishment of information networks, encouraging the opening of

include political conditionality regarding democracy, environment and human rights by means of the so-called democracy clause, and can be renegotiated with total flexibility as stated in the so-called 'evolutive clause'. See Lamothe, 1996; Calderón, 1996; García, 1996;CEPAL, 1999; COM(95) 216.

trade offices, the transfer of specialist know-how, subcontracting, applied research, licensing and franchising, (3c) promoting initiatives to increase cooperation between Mercosur economic operators and European associations, with the aim of establishing dialogue between networks". Art.12 addresses the promotion of investment and states that: "1. Within the bounds of their spheres of competence, the Parties shall promote an attractive and stable climate for greater mutually beneficial investment; 2. Such cooperation shall encompass measures including the following:(a) promoting regular exchanges of information, the identification and dissemination of information on legislation and investment opportunities; (b) promoting the development of a legal environment which is conductive to investment between the Parties, particularly, where applicable, *through the conclusion between interested Community Member States and Mercosur Party States of bilateral agreements for the promotion and protection of investment and bilateral agreements to prevent double taxation;* (c) promoting joint ventures, particularly between small and medium-sized enterprises."

The association agreement under negotiation since 1999 is not yet concluded, and is not included in the analysis, although it is supposed to include commitments about FDI.

Table 23: FDI matters in the EU-Southern Cone States Agreements (year of signature and signatory on the EU side)

	Effective in 1980 (1st generation)	2nd generation	3rd generation
Argentina	1971 (EEC) - nothing	-	1990 (EEC) no commit; coop Art.4 (1&2), Art.6
Brazil	1973 (EEC) - nothing	1980 (EEC) - no commit, coop Art.3 (2a, 2f)	1992 (EEC) no commit; coop Art 3(1d, 1e, 3b), Art.8, Art.9, Art.10(1)
Paraguay	-	-	1992 (EEC) no commit; coop Art 2(3c), Art.5(1),Art.7
Uruguay	1973 - nothing	-	1991 (EEC) no commit; coop Art.3 (1d, 1e, 3b, 3c, 3e) Art.5(1); Art.7
Mercosur*	-	-	a-1992 (ECs) nothing b-1995 (EC+MS) no

			commit., coop Art.11; Art.12 c- Association agr. under negotiation, probably will include commitments(EC+ MS)

Source: compiled by author

*the Agreement of 1992 was signed by Mercosur, the one of 1995 by Mercosur and its member-states and the one under negotiation should be signed by Mercosur and its member-states as well.

5.1.4.2) EU development policy

Apart from the negotiation of specific commitments, the EU has addressed the issue of FDI in the context of its developmental policy. It has created a number of instruments to promote European FDI towards developing countries in general, and the SCS in particular. Before reviewing these instruments in detail, the general features of the EU developmental policy are described, in order to contextualize the strategy adopted towards the SCSs.

5.1.4.2.1) General features

The origins of the EU developmental policy can be traced back to the Schuman Plan. In the Declaration of May 9, 1950, Robert Schumann mentions among the main tasks of a united Europe the development of the African continent.[148] When the Treaty of Rome was signed in 1957, France, Belgium, Italy and the Netherlands still had responsibility for dependent overseas countries and territories. An arrangement was then made for their association with the Community as indicated in Art.131-135 (Arts.182-188 TEC), and the European Development Fund (EDF) was set up to supply such countries with financial aid. In 1963, eighteen former and mainly francophone colonies reached an agreement under the Yaoundé Convention to continue the relationship set out in the Treaty of Rome. The Yaoundé Convention, conceived in the context of Cold War decolonization, reflected recognition of the importance of offering to recently independent associated countries benefits over and above those available to the Soviet bloc. With the accession of the United Kingdom, the Yaoundé Convention was replaced by the Lomé Convention, in 1975, which incorporated the

[148] The reference to cooperation with Africa was a request by deputy René Mayer. See Bitsch, 2001, p.65.

Commonwealth member countries from Caribbean and Pacific. The new group of countries were no longer denominated "associated" but continued to receive special aid and trade preferences. The Lomé Convention was renegotiated every five years thereafter until Lomé IV in 1990, which was renegotiated for ten years including a mid-term review in 1995 and has been extended to cover an increasing number of ACP partners. It was replaced in June 2000 by the new Cotonou Agreement.

Although the ACP countries have remained the main priority of the EU development policy, a wider perspective was defined in the Paris Summit of 1972, when the EU decided to address its developmental policy not only to its former colonies, but also to the "Third World" in general.[149] In 1974, the Community announced a cooperation policy for non-associated countries (Asian and Latin American – ALA) as distinct from ACP and Mediterranean countries and, in 1976, for the first time financial and technical cooperation with ALA countries were included in the EC budget for development, although limited to the instrument of GSP, at the initiative of the European Parliament. In the late 1970s and beginning 1980s cooperation agreements – the so-called second generation - were signed with many developing countries such as in 1977 with the Mediterranean countries, in 1980 with ASEAN and Brazil, in 1983 with the Andean Pact and CACM. After the end of the Cold War, the EU included the former communist countries in its developmental policy. In 1989, the PHARE programme was created to provide aid to Poland and Hungary, and was extended in 1990 to all Central and Eastern European countries (CEEs). In 1991, a similar programme (Tacis) was created to address the New Independent States of the former Soviet Union (NIS). The nature of the cooperation with CEEs was developed in a special relationship, given it geopolitical importance; between 1991 and 1993 each party signed association agreements with the EU, which aimed not only at promoting bilateral cooperation but at preparing these countries to become EU members themselves. The commitment to the new wave of enlargement was announced at the Luxemburg Summit of December 1997 and

[149] Note that the terminology Third World is not used anymore. The most important contemporary classifications are the following: a) from the UN: based on a number of social and economic criteria; b) from the World Bank, based on the gross national income per capita in the year 2000: high income (US$9.266 or more), upper middle (2.996-9.265), lower middle (756-2.995) and low income (755 or less) – the last three being addressed as developing countries; c) from the IMF: based on subjective factors developed "with the objective of facilitating analysis by providing a reasonably meaningful organization of data", in 2001: advanced economies (subdivided in major advanced economies (the seven largest in terms of GDP, referred as the G-7), European Union Countries (EU-15), Euro Area (12) and Newly Industrialized Asian Economies), developing countries (125 countries broken down by region: Africa – Sub-Sahara and North, Asia, Europe, Middle East and Turkey, Western Hemisphere, other developing countries such as the Heavily Indebted Poor Countries – see the next footnote), countries in transition (subdivided in Central and Eastern Europe, and Commonwealth of Independent States and Mongolia).

started officially with the beginning of the accession process with the candidate countries of Bulgaria, Cyprus, Czech Republic, Estonia, Hungary, Latvia, Lithuania, Malta, Poland, Romania, Slovak Republic, Slovenia, and Turkey in March 1998.[150] It is interesting to note that the EU developmental policy towards CEEs and enlargement were clearly supported by the US government. The Bush administration in fact encouraged the EU to take the international lead in providing assistance for the democratic transitions and market reforms in the CEEs. The idea was that the PHARE program, together with Western multilateral aid, performed the same tasks as the Marshall Plan after the Second War, but under the coordination and main responsibility of the EU. The EU has actually managed aid resources from the G-7 and G-24, together with its own, since the 1990s.[151]

Although it can be said that the scope of the EU developmental policy has been broadened from only the member-states' former colonies to the developing countries in general, with special emphasis on the CEEs since the 1990s, it can be observed that the traditional instruments for development cooperation, i.e., aid and trade concessions, have been reserved to the poorest countries, while new instruments involving the private sector have been used in the most advanced developing countries. The latter approach has been clearly taken to address Latin American countries, among them the Southern Cone States, as stated for instance in Regulation 443/92, which addresses the cooperation with Asia and Latin America countries (ALA). In this regulation, the EU distinguishes what it denominates "development cooperation" from "economic cooperation." While the former focuses purely on the recipient, the latter focuses on mutual interests from both the recipient and the EU economic and corporative actors. As stressed in an evaluation report about the regulation, prepared by an independent consultant company, the definition of mutual interests must involve a reciprocal (two-way) direct and measurable flow of benefits in order not to render redundant the concept of economic cooperation vis-à-vis development cooperation.

Although this measurement is extremely difficult to be done, and the differentiation between economic cooperation and development cooperation is not clear at all, one major distinction is the already mentioned role of the private sector. Whereas in development cooperation the EU acts more as a donor of resources, directly or indirectly, through instruments such as the SGP, Stabex and Sysmim, and whereas the target country is a relatively passive recipient, the EU tries to act as a partner in economic cooperation, in which not only the target country has a larger role but also business corporations and associations as well. The specific objectives of economic cooperation with Latin American (and Asian)

[150] Considering that cooperation with CEE gained a very specific treatment, it will not be further developed here.
[151] See Ginsberg, 2001, pp.220-222

countries, based on the Regulation's wording, are creating a more favorable environment for investment and development and enhancing the role of businessmen, technology, and know-how from all member-states. According to the evaluation report, the essence of this strategy has been to raise the profile of the EU - as distinct from its member-states - within Latin American (and Asian) countries, and to enhance the influence of the EU, both politically and economically, particularly as a more effective counterweight to the influence of the US and Japan. [152]

After the trend towards broadening the emphasis on CEEs and NIS, the EU development policy has been redirected to prioritize poorest countries, as stated in the Council Declaration on the Development Policy of the European Union of 10/12/2000, in which it states that "the principal aim of the Community's development policy is to reduce poverty, with a view to its eventual eradication, (and that) the resources available for development aid will be allocated in accordance with their impact on the reduction of poverty. The least developed countries (LDCs) should be given priority." Other developing countries have been addressed via economic cooperation, which has been included in the third (and fourth) generation agreements together with trade liberalization and political cooperation. Even the ACP countries have been progressively allocated to this new source of cooperation, as stated in the Cotonou Agreement that replaced the Lome Conventions. It is interesting to note that given the great differentiation in the development strategy directed to LDCs and other developing countries, the criteria used to define which countries are LDCs or not has been subject to controversy.[153]

Concerning the legal basis, it was only with the Maastricht Treaty on the European Union that development cooperation gained a specific legislation, under Articles 177 to 181. It is defined as of exclusive competence of the Community, its main goals are to foster the sustainable economic and social development of the developing countries, in particularly the most disadvantaged among them; their smooth and gradual integration into the world economy; and their campaign against poverty. It should also contribute to the consolidation of democracy and the rule of law and to the respect of human rights and fundamental freedoms. A

---

[152] See Nordic Consulting Groups A/S, 2001.

[153] The least developed countries (LDCs) are used as a synonym for the Heavily Indebted Poor Countries (HIPCs) as defined by the IMF and World Bank, to be the targets of the Debt Relief initiative. The criteria to be considered a HIPC are to face an unsustainable debt burden beyond available debt-relief mechanisms; and to have a track record of reform and sound policies thought IMF and World Bank supported programs. For more details see for example: Debt Relief under the Heavily Indebted Poor Countries Initiative Fact Sheet in the IMF Homepage. For a strong criticism of this criteria see Press Release ECOSOC/5880 of 16/12/1999, in which the Economic and Social Council of the EU recommends a reviewed identification criteria for the least developed countries list.

salient feature of the Maastricht Treaty is the incentive for member-states to use the EU framework in their individual development policies in order to try to make them more coherent and better coordinated, among themselves and in Community's programmes, but respecting the principle of subsidiariness, i.e., that in areas of non-exclusive competence, the Community takes action only insofar as the objectives of the proposed action cannot be sufficiently achieved by the member-states.[154]

Apart from this specific legal basis, another primary legal basis regarding the development policy (which was used as an axis for development cooperation before the TEU) are the articles referring to the conclusion of international agreements with 3rd countries which may contain development cooperation instruments such as: Art.133, which regards the common commercial policy and therefore tariff concessions under the SGP; Art. 300, which is the basis of international cooperation agreements; Art.308, which allows the Community to develop financial and technical aid; Art.310, which refers to the conclusion of international association agreements. Regarding the EU secondary law, the most important points on development cooperation with Latin America are the already mentioned Regulations EC 442/81 and EC 443/92.[155]

The main instruments for the development policy are: 1) Programme Aid (support to structural adjustments in the balance of payments, in kind or in foreign currency - most go to ACP, some to Mediterranean, since 1992, and commodity compensation schemes such as Stabex to agricultural exports and Sysmin to the mining sector – most to ACP, with some exceptions from 1987 to 1991; 2) Food Aid – it was the first development policy instrument introduced outside cooperation agreements signed with the ACP, and created in 1967. It was originally managed according to the rules of the Common Agriculture Policy (CAP), but after many reforms, in 1982, 1986, 1987 and 1996, was gradually integrated to the development policy, as of 1996 a portion of the allocations were re-denominated food security, and as of 1992 food aid for humanitarian purposes was transferred to ECHO;[156] 3) Humanitarian Aid - emergency relief to victims of natural disasters, wars, refugees, rehabilitation, reconstruction, etc., and most go to CEE and ACP; 4) Aid to NGOs – may be done through contracting (where the NGO is contracted to implement Commission-designed projects and programmes) or co-financing (where the Commission provides financing for up to 50% of the total for a NGO project, for a maximum of 5 years); most go to ACP and LA,

---

[154] OECD, 1996, pp.12-13.

[155] The secondary EU legislation consists of: regulations – general legislative measures binding and take effect directly in the national legal order without need for national implementing measures; directives – binding but require implementing national law; decisions- binding measures to individuals, or MS, conclusions, communications, declarations, recommendations, resolutions, opinions – rules of conduct, without legally binding force.

[156] More details are seen in Chapter 6.

Brazil was the major recipient in the period of 1986-1998; 5) Project Aid: 5.1) Natural Resources Productive Sectors(rural development and agriculture, forestry, fisheries); 5.2) Other Productive Sectors (industry, mining & construction – most to ACP, trade, tourism, investment promotion - fastest growing sub-sector due to ECIP scheme); 5.3) Economic infrastructure & services (transport, communications, energy, banking, business – most to ACP, CEE & NIS); 5.4) Social infrastructure & services (education, health, population, water, other); 5.5) Governance & civil society; 5.6) multi-sector-crosscutting (environment, women in development, rural development).[157]

Other instruments are the so-called 'horizontal programmes', managed by the Europe Aid Agency such as: Al-Invest (facilitates the contact between European and Latin American small and medium-sized companies, but without providing finance or guarantees); ALFA (promotes cooperation in higher education between both regions); URB-AL (establishes direct links between European and Latin American cities); ALURE (encourages the optimal and most rational use of energy, replaced Synergy programme); ALIS (promotes the benefits of using information technologies and tries to bridge the gap of the digital divide); and ATLAS (facilitates and encourages economic cooperation through a network of Chambers of Commerce and Industry).

In regard to the financing of development cooperation projects there are three sources, the first is the Community budget, which is allocated according to a geographical (Mediterranean basin, Asia and Latin America and southern Africa) or a thematic approach (among which the most important are food aid, humanitarian aid and cooperation with NGO's). The second financing source is the European Development Fund (EDF), which is fed by contributions from Member-States, calculated according to a specific distribution key and allocated to the ACP countries. The third financing source is the European Investment Bank (EIB), which uses either its own resources or risk capital, and grants loans to countries upon approval of the Council or Commission. Since the 1980s, the relative weight of the EDF has fallen from an average of 57% in 1986-88, when the EC Budget provided only 36%, to an average of 17% in 1996-1998, when the EC Budget became the major source of EU development cooperation financing, with an average of 75% of the total. The EIB remained a third source with about 7% during the last two decades. This shift is attributed to the start of initiatives designed for the CEEs (Phare) and the New Independent States (Tacis), in the 1990s, financed by the EC Budget.[158]

The evolution of EU development cooperation in presented in the tables below, where it may be seen that the proportion of aid to the CEEs and NIS rose from next to nothing to almost 30% and 10%, respectively, from 1986 to 1998.

[157] See Cox & Chapman, 1999 & OECD, 1996.
[158] Cox,1999,p.4.

This increase was almost totally compensated by the decrease of aid to the ACP, which decreased by almost half, from approximately 60% to about 30%. Aid to Latin America showed a minor increase of approximately 2%.

Table 24: Regional Distribution of EC External Cooperation (commitments in % total)

Region	1986	1990	1995	1998
ACP	44,7	41,9	35,4	33,1
South Africa	0,3	0,9	1,7	1,5
Asia	5,5	9,8	9,5	7,2
Latin America	6,3	6,8	6,6	5,6
Med & Mid.East	15,7	11,9	11,8	15,9
CEEs	-	21,0	19,7	18,4
NIS	0	0,2	11,2	12,1
Non-allocable	27,6	7,7	4,1	6,2

Source: Cox, 1999, p.4.

When seen in the context of total world development cooperation, it may be observed that the EU, including the bilateral aid from member-states, is the single largest donor for the periods considered below.

Table 25: Major World Aid donors (share of total aid %)

Donor	Average 1986-1991	Average 1992-1997
US	20,5	17,0
Japan	17,9	18,5
Canada	4,7	3,6
EC	6,6	10,0
France	12,7	13,2
Germany	12,0	14,9
Italy	6,7	4,4
UK	5,3	5,5
Netherlands	4,7	4,7

Source: Cox, 1999, p.121.

Table 26: External Cooperation to Latin America (US$ mi)

	1994	1995	1996	1997	1998	%(1994-98)
EU Member-States	1.696	1.911	2.112	1.394	1.590	36.2
EU (EC)	288	413	418	822	424	9.2
Europe (EU+MSs)	1.984	2.325	2.530	1.716	2.014	46.4

US	986	736	344	544	492	13.6
Japan	808	1.102	938	659	508	17.6
Other*	688	823	930	769	853	17.4

Source: IRELA, 2000
* Including multilateral donors

The decision-making procedure is the following: the Commission prepares proposals and sends them to the Development) Council, which adopts regulations and directives, after Maastricht by QMV. It is interesting to note that although the European Parliament does not play a direct formal role in the decision-making of the developmental policy, it does act via budgetary powers. The Commission produces a preliminary draft of the EC Budget and then sends it to the Council which, acting by QMV, makes amendments and then establishes the draft budget. The Parliament can propose modifications to non-compulsory expenditures, which must be adopted by a majority of the members of Parliament. Parliament may also act through the majority of its members and three-fifths of the votes cast, rejecting the budget as a whole. Should it do so, the procedure must begin again from the start, based on a new draft.[159]

Table 27: Decision-making actors of the EU Development Policy

Actor	Competence
European Commission	-Formal monopoly of policy initiation - Setting of Agenda
EU Member-States	-(Development) Council -EDF committee and other management committees -Financial contribution to the EDF
(Development) Council	-Formal power to issue resolutions and regulations
European Parliament	-Control of Commission's budget -Introduction of special budget lines to support policies

Source: Cox, 1999, p.23.

The organizational structure of management of the development policy within the Commission has suffered many alterations since its inception. Until 1985, it was managed by a single Directorate-General Development. Responsibility for managing aid to Asia, Latin America, and the Mediterranean was transferred in 1985 to a separate DG that, in the early 1990s, merged with DGI (foreign policy). The original DG Development, which became DG VIII,

[159] Cox, pp.22-23.

remained responsible for relations with the ACP countries and food aid. DG I covered North-South relations, Eastern Europe and Former Soviet Union. In 1992, a separate office was created to deal with humanitarian assistance, the European Community Humanitarian Office (ECHO). In 1993, DG IA was created to deal with the political aspects of external relations, while DG I kept control over trade relations and North-South issues. This situation changed again in 1995, when DG IB was set up to deal with relations with Asia, Latin America and the Southern and Eastern Mediterranean. In 1998, a Common Service for External Relations (SCR) was created to deal with the technical, financial, and legal aspects of implementing the aid and cooperation programmes, and with audits and evaluation.

In 1999, there was a major reform in which the DG Development became responsible for ACP, South Africa, non-emergency food aid and NGO co-financing. The DG External Relations became responsible for NIS, Mediterranean, Middle East, Latin America and most Asian developing countries, human rights and democratization. DG Enlargement was created to be responsible for pre-accession countries, including the PHARE programme. Other DGs are also involved in the performance of development policies such as the Economic and Financial Affairs DG (responsible for economic monitoring, dialogue with third countries and macro financial assistance), and Eurostat (technical support to the design, implementation, monitoring and evaluation of statistical cooperation programmes and statistical components of more generic programmes).

In 2001 the Europe Aid Cooperation Office was created as a department of the Commission on the basis of the existing Common Service for External Relations office, to be responsible for the implementation of the Commission's external assistance instruments managed by the DG External Relations services, which are financed from the EC Budget and the European Development Fund, with the exception of pre-accession instruments, humanitarian aid, macro finance assistance, Common Foreign and Security Policy actions, and the Rapid Reaction Facility. Europe Aid is supervised by a Board comprising the Commissioners for External Relations, the Chairman for Development and Humanitarian Aid, and the Chief Executive for Enlargement, Trade, and Economic and Monetary Affairs, as members that meet regularly to approve the annual programmes, reports and budgetary programmes.

In regard to other EU institutions involved in the management of the development policy, the European Court of Auditors may be mentioned, as responsible for verifying that the accounting rules have been complied with in the Commission's expenditures, as well as increasingly concerning itself with broader issues related to effectiveness, relevance and impact, and the European Investment Bank (EIB), which is described in detail in the next section.[160]

5.1.4.2.2) FDI policy instruments

The EU has created a number of instruments to address the promotion of FDI towards developing countries. Regarding Southern Cone States, the most important are the loans and guarantees from the European Investment Bank (EIB), and the support from horizontal programmes such as the European Community Investment Partners (ECIP), Al-Invest, Business Cooperation Network (BC-Net) and the Business Cooperation Centre (BCC), also known by the French acronym BRE (Bureau de Rapprochement d'Enterprises). The sectorial programmes Synergy/ALURE (energy) and ALIS (information technology) also involve cooperation in FDI.[161] Although part of the EU (unilateral) development policy, these instruments are often mentioned in the bilateral and bi-regional agreements with the Southern Cone States in relevant cooperation articles (see section above). Each of them is described in detail below.

a) European Investment Bank (EIB)

EIB's main task is to grant medium- and long-term loans and guarantees for investment projects within the European Union. However, it also assists non-member countries whose development the Union wishes to foster, and participates in implementing the Union's development aid and cooperation policies. The Bank's operations take the form of loans out of its own resources, generally accompanied by interest subsidies financed by the EC budget. It may also manage, under mandate, risk capital funds provided by budgetary resources. The major part of the financing goes to large projects with State guarantees (where the minimum EIB contribution is 20 million EURO), but it also provides long-term risk-capital funds for smaller projects through on-lending lines with local banks. The final contribution to individual investments or projects often consists of equity investment loans on a cost plus basis, with guarantees. The EIB is progressively shifting from global on lending to providing support to investment funds. It selects as partners the banks or other financial institutions that can deal in equity and equity-linked products, and channels financing through partner institutions.

[160] About the reforms in the management structure of the dev. policy see Cox, 1999, p.19-20 and EU homepage: www.europa.eu.int/comm/external_relations/reform/intro/europeaid_en.htm
[161] ALIS is not included in the analysis because it was initiated in 2002.

The EIB received a mandate to operate in Latin America in 1993.[162] Its financing projects in Mercosur member states, from 1996 to 2000, may be seen in the following table.

Table 28: EIB financing projects in Mercosur member-states

Year	Country	Project	Beneficiary	Loan (millions of EUROs)
1994	Argentina	Modernization of natural gas distribution network	Gas Natural Ban	46.0
1995	Argentina	water	Aguas Argentinas	70,0
1995	Argentina	water	Ailinco	6,0
1995	Paraguay	water	Asuncion Sewage	17,0
1996	Argentina	roads in Mercosur network	Argentina Rep	45.0
1997	Brazil	construction of cement producing facilities	Cia Minas Oeste de Cimento	32.5
1997	Brazil	construction of optical fiber plant	Pirelli Cabos SA	22.0
1997	Uruguay	eucalyptus plantation	Eufores SA	10.0
1998	Argentina	water supply services	Aguas Cordobesas SA	36.8
1998	Brazil	motor vehicle manufacturing	Mercedes Benz do Brasil SA	70.0
1998	Brazil	gas pipeline with Bolivia	Transp Bras Gaseoduto Bolivia-Br SA	55.0
1999	Brazil	small ventures financing	ABN Amro Bank & BBA	59.0
1999	Brazil	mobile telephone network	Celular CRT SA	57.7
1999	Brazil	tire manufacturing	Pirelli Pneus SA	37.0
2000	Argentina	construction of gas pipeline	Metrogas SA	51.7
2000	Argentina	conversion of gas power station to combined cycle plant	Pluspetrol Energy SA	57.8
2000	Argentina	water supply and sewage systems	Servicios de Aguas de	20.4

[162] See EIB Homepage, and for the mandate the online paper: Financing in Asia & LA at www.eib.eu.int/pub/divers/ala_en.pdf

			Missiones SA	
2000	Argentina	glass container production	Rayen Cura SA	17.1
2000	Brazil	mobile telephone network	Telebahia celular SA	40.0
2000	Brazil	mobile telephone network	Telesergipecelular SA	15.0
2000	Brazil	mobile telephone network	Telpecelular SA	58.5
2000	Brazil	motor vehicle manufacturing	Volkswagen do Brasil LTDA	91.5
2001	Argentina	Construction of electric power central	Central Dock Sud	77,3
2001	Argentina	Fabrication of biote de vitesse	Volkswagen Argentina	46,6
2001	Brazil	energy	Light Power Distribution	33,6
2001	Brazil	energy	Comgas	46,8
2001	Brazil	industry	Vega do Sul Galvanization	58,0
2001	Brazil	forestry	Veracel Forestry	32,7
2002	Brazil	energy	Coelce Power Distribution	54,6

Source: compiled by author based with data from EIB Homepage http://eib.eu.int/loans/cbcneuoo.html

Table 29: EIB loans to EU non-member states (millions of Euros)

Year	Total	Southern Cone states	%
2000	5.389,0	352,0	6,53
1999	4.035,0	153,7	3,81
1998	4.410,0	161,8	3,67
1997	3.244,0	64,5	1,99
1996	2.294,0	45,0	1,96
1995	-	93,0	-
1994	-	46,0	-
1993	-	0	0

Source: compiled by author based on data from EIB Homepage http://eib.eu.int/loans/cbcneuoo.html

b) European Community Investment Partners (ECIP)

The ECIP programme was conceived in 1988 at the initiative of the Commission, with the support of the European Parliament for the mutual interest and advantage of the developing countries in Asia, Latin America and the Mediterranean, and of European industry wishing to invest in them, by encouraging the creation of joint ventures among small and medium enterprises (SMEs) in an attempt to improve the developmental quality of private FDI. Larger companies can also participate if their projects are particularly interesting for the development of the host countries, but multinationals are strictly excluded.

The programme was extended to South Africa, giving rise to the JOP programme for Phare and Tacis countries. It was the first programme launched by the Commission to specifically support FDI in third countries, although only countries signatories of cooperation or association agreements with the EU were eligible to benefit from ECIP. It was originally established as a pilot project, defined based on Article 205 of the Treaty of Rome (concerning implementation of the EC budget – Art.274 of the consolidated version, and the European Parliament provided the necessary credits from within its margin of maneuvering (Non-Obligatory Spending). The pilot project ran for three years (1988-1991), receiving in 1992 a legal and budgetary basis with Regulation EEC 319/92 dated Feb 3, 1992. The latter was modified by Regulation EEC 213/96 of 29 Jan 1996. The programme was considered a success and was extended twice, for the periods of 1992-94 and 1995-99. However, as of 1996 it became progressively more bureaucratic and heavier, due to its "labor intensive" characteristic and the insufficient number of staff available to work in it. Therefore, instead of renewing the programme again in 1999, the Commission merely demanded a 2-year extension to finance the management costs for closure and winding down of the existing projects portfolio.[163] Although recognizing the programme's success, the Commission alleged, based on their own reports and independent evaluations, that further assessment was needed in order to redefine overall policy priorities and optimize the synergy with other investment promotion and financing programmes of the EU.[164]

The principal characteristics of ECIP were: a) responding exclusively to initiatives coming from enterprises (demand-driven); not granting quotas to particular regions or industry sectors; conceding five types of financing: Facility 1 - grants up to 100.000 EUR for identification of potential joint venture partners; Facility 2 – interest-free loans of up to 250.000 EUR for feasibility studies or pilot projects; Facility 3 - equity (holdings or loans) of up to 1 million EUR in joint ventures; Facility 4 – interest-free loans or grants of up to 250.000 EUR for

[163] COM(1999) 726.

[164] See the commissions' Progress Reports in COM (1998)752, for the years 1995 to 1997, COM(2000)135 for 1998 and COM (2000) 439 for 1999. For evaluations, see Touche Ross 1990; SEMA Group 1994; and Deloitte & Touche 1999 and Lamigeon, 1999.

training costs in joint ventures; Facility 1B - grants of up to 200.000 EUR for the preparation of BOO/BOOT schemes; b) enterprise accessibility via a network of financial institutions (development and commercial banks). The Commission used to provide advances to the ECIP financial institutions who in turn, and after a green light from the Commission, allocated these funds to the final beneficiaries; c) covering all the phases of putting a joint-venture in place: partner search; feasibility studies by the enterprise (interest-free advances reimbursable by the enterprise in case of success, or converted into grant in case of non-success); participation in the equity capital of the joint-venture; grants for small and medium enterprises, and interest-free reimbursable advances for larger enterprises to finance training in case of technology transfer.[165] The Commission emphasized facilities 1 and 2, i.e., promotion and preparation of joint ventures.

c) Program of Business Cooperation and Promotion of Investments (AL- Invest)

The AL-Invest project was considered operational in 1995, after a two-year pilot phase, and in 2000 was renewed for four years. The main purpose of the programme is to facilitate the contact between European and Latin American businesses; unlike the ECIP programme, it does not limit the risk involved and provide financial instruments or support for the identified common projects.

The Programme operates with the following mechanisms: a) a network of Eurocentres - Latin American organizations, called 'economic operators', chosen by the Commission as focal points for the rest of the interested companies, which form a network working in contact with the Delegations of the European Commission in Latin America, and are responsible for the promotion and organization of activities taking place within the Al-Invest programme, providing support in the search for business partners, furthering partnership opportunities, etc.; b) a network of Coopecos - European organizations, such as Chambers of Commerce, Federation of Industries, Development Agencies, and Consultant Companies that support industrial cooperation and investment promotion in Latin America. They cooperate with the Al-Invest programme by informing businesses, increasing awareness of cooperation opportunities, putting them in contact with corresponding Latin American networks, etc; c) sectorial meetings - events organized by a group of economic operators, who draw-up a schedule of personal interviews with 25 companies. The operators propose these events to the Commission, who agrees to co-finance 50 events per year. The events last for two days and are usually held during specialist trade fairs. The participating companies receive a programme of face-to-face meetings ('agendas') specially arranged for them according to their profiles and products; d) TIPS System - information on-line service; e) the services of a Secretariat, based in Brussels.

---

165 COM (2999) 439, p.3 & 10.

The structure of the project consists of a unit in the Commission responsible for operating the project with input from an Advisory Committee as well as a Technical Secretariat for services providing. A Board under the Assistant Director General consisting of 3 representatives from DG RelExt and 3 from DG Enterprise make all the decisions. The Technical Secretariat consists of eight people, who devote 50% of their time promoting the programme and the rest providing support and organizing meetings.

From 1996 to 1999, the programme organized 156 Sectorial Meetings, in which more than 13.000 European and Latin American companies participated. Until April 2000, 210 commercial accords were registered (summing 89.3 million EURO), and 42 investment accords (summing 43.3 million EURO).

d) Business Cooperation Network (BC Net) & Business Cooperation Centre (BCC)

Although these initiatives were mainly designed to facilitate the cooperation among European firms by offering a matching service, firms from third countries could also participate in the database. The BCC was created as early as 1973 and the BC-Net in 1988, and both programmes were part of the European Commission Multi-Annual Programme to help and support enterprises, particularly small and medium (SMEs). They were managed by the DG Enterprise until 2000, when, following two negative evaluations and after a repositioning of the Commission's activities towards development policy and regulations, with less emphasis in direct actions management, they were closed down.

Both programmes were very similar, the main difference being that while BCC was designed as a scheme offering a "one-to-many" services, in which the local intermediary contacted by the SME would routinely look for a match, but also in parallel the profile would be disseminated among all other intermediaries who had access to the internet database, BC-Net was designed as a "one-to-one" scheme in which a fee was charged by the operation, which could be maintained confidential with only the contacted intermediary receiving the information and looking for matches. In practice, under BRE the intermediaries were more disseminators of information and under BC-Net they became actively engaged in assisting companies to move forward in their negotiations.[166]

The Southern Cone States intermediaries in the database were; from Argentina: Del Rio – Business Consultants, DEVNET Argentina, Fundación de Empresas – Eurocentro Córdoba, Eurocentro de Cooperación Empresarial Câmara Argentina de Comercio, Euroinvest, Eurocentro Mendoza, Internacional y Culto Argentina Cancilleria Argentina, Bolsa de Comercio de Mar del Plata; from Brazil: Indi, Governo do Rio Grande do Sul, América 2000 Consultoria e

[166] See Technopolis, 2000 & Homepage DG Enterprise

Representacao LTDA, Italian-Brazilian Chamber of Commerce of Minas, Federacao das Indústrias do Estado de Santa Catariana, Charneski & Associados S/C, Federacao das Indústrias do Estado do Rio de Janeiro, Federacao das Indústrias do Estado de Pernambuco; Paraguay: Bolsa de Subcontratacion del Paraguay – Eurocentro Paraguay; Uruguay: DEVNET Uruguay, Camara de Industrias del Uruguay. Information about the number of matches made by such intermediaries is not available, and therefore will be not considered. [167]

e) Synergy/ALURE

The EU has developed two cooperation programmes in the energy field of Latin America, both under the management of DG Energy and Transport. The first, Synergy, was created in 1980 to finance projects to help developing countries of Asia, Africa and Latin America to define, formulate and implement their energy policy, especially after the privatization of energy companies. It developed 14 projects in Latin America. Synergy was financed as a form of aid assistance, not involving FDI. ALURE, however, created in 1996, was designed within a framework of redirecting the focus from aid to economic cooperation, i.e., involving mutual gains, and exclusively in Latin America. The three declared objectives are to "improve the services of Latin American utilities, preferably in the growth of the electricity and natural gas sub-sectors, and to promote business relations with European companies familiar with the industry, such as utilities, financial operators and industrial firms, in particular small businesses; to contribute, where necessary, to the adaptation of legal and institutional frameworks; to promote sustainable economic and social development with relevant schemes". The initial phase of the programme (ALURE I), lasted for two years (1996-1997) and had a portfolio of 13 projects, with an EC contribution of 7 million euros, and the second phase of the programme (ALURE II) lasted a period of five years (1998- 2002) with a budget of 25 million euros. However, it was decided that ALURE will not be renewed, and Synergy closed down in 2000. The main reasons appointed for the suspension of both programmes are the political disagreements regarding future objectives of the programmes and the general reprioritization for cooperation with Latin America in the issue areas of information society, human rights, and poverty relief.[168]

---

[167] The database still exists and is managed by the Eurocenters (see Al-Invest); see http://europa.eu.int/comm/enterprise/networks/eic/eic.html

[168] The suspension of the programmes was criticized in a Report from the DG for Research of the European Parliament, which emphasized that the development of the energy sector is strategic, among others, to attain the "new" objectives of decreasing poverty and promoting the information society (by means of the ALIS programme, initiated in 2002. The report recommended that the Parliament try to create a new energy programme, EP, 2001, pp.22-24.

5.1.5) Level of cooperation of EU foreign policy

The indicators selected to analyze the level of cooperation of the EU foreign policy in the case of foreign direct investment are the number/budget and nature of the cooperation programmes under the EU development policy, and the characteristics of the commitments regarding FDI provisions in the bilateral agreements between the EU and the Southern Cone States, and Mercosur. Regarding FDI commitments, it was seen that they remain under the competence of member-states outside the EU system. Even if they have been negotiated by the Council and managed by the Commission, it would have been an example of "fourth pillar" development and not of EU initiatives. The only agreement that would be in this case was the one of 1995 with Mercosur, but this was not the case since it did not contain any FDI provisions, only references to cooperation (unlike the agreements with the CEEs and former Soviet States). The agreements with Argentina, Brazil, Paraguay, Uruguay and the 1992 agreement with Mercosur were signed by the EEC/EC, who did not have the power to negotiate such provisions. The informal political influence of the EU, independently of it formal competences, could be considered as favoring a cooperative approach with developing countries in general, when the position of the Commission in the discussions about the possible opening of negotiations for a multilateral FDI agreement within the WTO is analyzed. The Commission supported a scaled down version of a multilateral agreement at the WTO that would include neither pre-established national treatment nor investor-to-investor dispute settlement procedures, proposals usually advanced by developing countries.[169]

Table 30: FDI related issues in EU-SCS bilateral agreements

FDI related issues	1980-85	1995-2000
Commitments	-No	-No
Reference to cooperation in bilateral agreements	-Br-EEC 1980	-Arg-EEC 1991 -Urug-EEC 1991 -Br-EEC 1992 -Par-EEC 1992 -Mercosur-Ecs 1992 -Mercosur+MS-EC+MS 1995

Source: compiled by author

[169] Graham, 2000, p.186.

Regarding the programmes concerning FDI under the EU development policy, the main empirical findings are summarized in table 25. Although it was not possible to find information about specific operations and budget of Southern Cone States for all programmes, it can be seen that most programmes were created in late 80s and early 90s; only BCC existed prior to this, and it was not a program particularly designed for Latin America. It can be estimated, therefore, that the total budget allocation for FDI cooperation in the EU development policy for the Southern Cone States increased from 1980-85 to 1995-2000. The main characteristic of the nature of such programmes was that they focused on the creation of joint ventures among small and medium enterprises, and in attempts to improve the developmental impact of European FDI.

Table 31: EU programmes addressing FDI in the EU development policy for the SCSs

Program	1980-1985	1995-2000
EIB loans	Null (mandate to operate in LA was accorded in 1993)	% of the total loans to non-member states increased continuously from 1,96 in 1996 to 6,33 in 2000
ECIP	Null (created in 1988)	-
Al-Invest	Null (created in 1992)	From 1996 to 2000 42 investment accords with SCS
BCNet	Null (created in 1988)	-
BCC/BRE	Info about operations with SCS not found	-
Alure	Null (created in 1996)	-

With base on the empirical information described so far it can be argued that in the first period of observation, the level of cooperation was very low. The only indicator for cooperation was the reference to cooperation in the bilateral agreement between the EEC and Brazil in 1980. In the second period, although no commitments regarding FDI were included in bilateral agreements, all new agreements contained references to cooperation in articles related to economic cooperation. Moreover, the EU created programmes in its development policy addressing FDI that, among others, aimed at improving the developmental quality of European investments in the SCS, even if their actual impact can be considered relatively negligible in the context of the total amount of European FDI outflows to the Southern Cone States. The level of cooperation is evaluated as average. To conclude, it can be said that the level of cooperation did increase from 1980-85 to 1995-2000, even if it remained at a low level.

Table 32: The level of cooperation of the EU foreign policy behavior towards the SCS in foreign direct investment (very low, low, medium, high)

Indicators	1980-85	1995-2000
Agreements	No commitment, one ref to cooperation => coop very low	No commitment, 6 ref to coop=> coop low
Development policy programmes	(BCC-BRE)=> coop very low	EIB, ECIP, Al-Invest, BCNet, Alure, (BCC-BRE) => coop medium
Resulting level of cooperation	Very low	Medium

5.2) Independent variables and test of predictions

In order to explain why EU foreign policy behavior towards the Southern Cone States has become slightly more cooperative from the period of 1980-1985 to the period of 1995-2000 for the case study of foreign direct investments, the value of the independent variables in the approaches considered, the test of their predictions for each period of time and the covariance test are examined in sections 5.2.1, 5.2.2 and 5.2.3. Section 5.2.4 adds further observations and concludes with the evaluation of the explanations offered.

5.2.1) Neorealism

As seen in Chapter 4, the power position of the European Union can be said to have increased from the period of 1980-1985 to 1990-2000. Such increase was due to the polarity change in the international system, which allowed the EU to pursue a more independent foreign policy vis-à-vis the US, and increase EU's relative power position. The first step in analyzing the test of the Neorealist hypothesis, i.e., the covariance between independent and dependent variables, is therefore positive. Neorealism, however, does not offer explanations for the absolute level of cooperation in each period, i.e., it forecasts that the level of cooperation will be higher in a situation of lower differential of relative capabilities vis-à-vis stronger power and a multipolar system, than in a situation of a higher power differential in a bipolar system, but it does not specify if the level of cooperation in the first situation will be, for instance, medium or high, or in the second situation, low or very low.

Table 33: Test of Neorealist forecast for the case study of foreign direct investment

	1980-85	1990-95
Independent variable	High differential in relative capabilities between the US and the EU	Lower differential in relative capabilities between the US and the EU
Expected change of level of cooperation in the foreign policy behavior towards the SCSs	->	Higher
Observed level of cooperation in the EU foreign policy behavior towards the SCSs	Very low	Medium

5.2.2) Identity Constructivism

As analyzed in Chapter 4, from 1980 to 85 the level of homogeneity between the EU and SCS was very low: while the EU countries were liberal-democracies engaged in a process of regional integration, the SCS were protectionist dictatorships competing against each other. They shared a certain level of common fate in capitalism against communism in the context of the Cold War, but in the division of labor between the "allies", the Western hemisphere was seen as responsibility of the US, not the EU's, therefore inhibiting any initiatives from the latter. The role position of the SCSs was evaluated to be one of neglect; and the expected level of cooperation considered very low.

In the second period of observation, the level of homogeneity can be considered as high, after the SCS engaged in the process of democratization, economic liberalization and regional integration. The level of common fate decreased with the end of the Cold War. It was concluded that this change favored the beginning of the development of a collective identity between the EU and the SCSs; the EU came to see the SCSs as friends (benign clients). It was expected that the level of cooperation would increase to medium.

The test of covariance is therefore confirmed, since the level of cooperation increased from the first to the second period, and the explanation for the absolute level of cooperation in each period is also confirmed.

Table 34: Test of Identity Constructivism forecast for the FDI case study

	1980-85	1990-95
Independent variable	Neglected	Benign client
Expected level of cooperation in foreign policy behavior towards the SCSs	Very low/low	Medium/high
Observed level of cooperation in EU foreign policy behavior towards the SCSs	Very low	Medium

5.2.3) Utilitarian Liberalism

The independent variable "EU dominant interests" has not been analyzed yet given that it must be done separately for each case study. Organized actors in EU's FDI policy network, their interests and foreign policy preferences (section 5.2.3.1), as well as most assertive actors (section 5.2.3.2), are seen below.

5.2.3.1) Organized actors

Table 35: Organized actors in EU's FDI foreign policy network

Type	Main actors	Organized in 1980-85 /1995-2000	Foreign policy preferences
Political	a) European Parliament b) European Council and Council of Ministries	-yes/yes -yes/yes	-increase FDI and improve its developmental effect -advance national interests and increase their prestige within the EU
Administrative	c) European Commission d) European Investment Bank	-yes/yes -no/yes -yes/yes	-increase initiatives regarding FDI in general -increase number of FDI financed projects

	e) Economic and Social Committee		in general -improve developmental effect of FDI
Economic Pressure Groups	f) European Round Table of Industrialists g) Mercosur EU Business Forum	-yes/yes -no/yes	-increase profits and market share of EU firms - increase profit and market share of EU firms, and promote joint ventures
Political Advocacy Groups	h) Working Group EU-Me	-no/yes	- liberalization of FDI regime in the SCSs and bilateral agreements

a) European Parliament - an analysis of the most important resolutions regarding the Southern Cone States shows that the EP has continuously expressed its wish to foster cooperation between small and medium-sized enterprises (SMEs) from both regions as well as the expansion of BEI's activities to Latin America, although not as a priority in the agenda. It may be said that the EP was an organized actor in both periods and its general attitude was favorable to cooperation with Southern Cone States on the issue of FDI.

Table 36: FDI matters in EP resolutions regarding the SCSs

Resolution	Target	FDI related issues
12-10-83	LA	Demands the creation of a group of experts to study means to promote SMEs in LA (paragraph 14) and suggests the creation of a European-LA bank to finance mutual projects of investment (parag 15)
13-06-85	LA	Affirms the importance of EU capitals to LA to the latter's development and equilibrium of balance of payments (parag 6); demands LA countries to develop a more favorable environment to EU investments (parag 7); demands the creation of an EU-LA bank and the expansion of BEI activities in LA (parag 9)
13-06-85	LA	Recognizes the difficulties of countries and firms in LA to obtain capital and suggests the expansion of BEI activities to the region (parag 24)

14-04-89	Arg	Desires the intensification of the EU presence by means of investments and joint ventures in Argentina (parag 8); demands that Argentina subscribe the MIGA convention to favor EU FDI (parag 12); demands the expansion of BEI activities to LA (parag 15&16)
19-11-92	Br	Attributes importance to the increase of mutual beneficial investments and acknowledges the value of the ECIP programme (parag 13); acknowledges with satisfaction the approval of BEI activities in LA at ECOFIN in April (parag 15); demands that Brazil reviews its legislation about investment guarantees and protection of intellectual property (parag 16)
16-05-95	Me	Supports the inclusion in the Association agreement of the participation of the EU in investment projects in Me by means of the EC budget and BEI (parag 12); emphasizes the importance to promote SMEs (parag 13)
03-02-97	LA	Calls on the member states of the EU to continue to develop public or private investment policies in the LA region in order to continue to promote vital industrial cooperation and the transfer of technology via small and medium-sized undertakings or joint ventures (parag 7); calls on the Commission and the Council to use all possible instruments to promote investment by EU firms, in particular small and medium size enterprises, in LA, for example through the increase of funds for LA-Invest, ECIP and the EIB (parag 23)
15-01-99	DVP	Support for an European Code of Conduct of EU firms operating in developing countries

Source: Database in Annex I & IRELA, 1996.

b) European Council and Council of Ministries – the references to Latin America in the conclusions of the European Council Summits can be seen in the following table. FDI is only mentioned once, during the Spanish presidency in 1995, when the Council supported the extension of the EIB's activities to LA.

The relevant Council of Ministries for the case study of FDI would be the General Affairs, the Economic and Financial Affairs and the Development Councils, but it was not possible to obtain data on the meeting conclusions. It can be said, nonetheless, that it apparently member states preferred to deal with FDI issues on the national level; most of them have signed Bilateral Investment Treaties (BITs) with the SCSs. In the case of Spain, for instance, that became the major investor in Southern Cone States since the mid-90s, political initiatives in this direction were pursued at the national level.[170]

Table 37: Conclusions of the European Council Summits, emphasis on FDI matters

Year	Presidency	Summit	References to Latin America, FDI in bold
1980.1	Italy	-Luxemburg (April) -Venice (June)	- -
1980.2	Luxemburg	-Luxemburg (December)	-
1981.1	Netherlands	-Maastricht (March) -Luxemburg (June)	- -
1981.2	United Kingdom	-London (November)	-
1982.1	Belgium	-Brussels (March) -Brussels (June)	-Central America -
1982.2	Denmark	-Copenhagen (December)	-
1983.1	Germany	-Brussels (March) -Stuttgart (June)	 -Central America
1983.2	Greece	-	-
1984.1	France	-Brussels (March) -Fontainbleau (June)	- -
1984.2	Ireland	-Dublin (December)	-Central America
1985.1	Italy	-Brussels (March) -Milan (June)	- -

170 See EP, 2001, p.3

1985.2	Luxemburg	-Luxemburg (December)	-
1986.1	Netherlands	-Hague (June)	- discussed the situation regarding relations between the European Community and LA, in particular in the light of the enlargement of the Community to include Spain and Portugal; reaffirmed its desire to strengthen and develop these relations both on the political level and on the economic and technical level; asked the Commission to submit a document in accordance with the objectives set out in the Declaration annexed to the Accession Treaty; instructed the Ministers for Foreign Affairs to follow this matter closely and to submit reports to the European Council as and when necessary.
1986.2	United Kingdom	-London (December)	-
1987.1	Belgium	-Brussels (June)	-
1987.2	Denmark	-	-
1988.1	Germany	-Brussels (February) -Hanover (June)	- -discussed the situation in LA and underlined the fundamental importance of the rule of democracy and the normal functioning of democratic institutions as a key factor for stability in the sub-continent; Central America
1988.2	Greece	-Rhodes (December)	-
1989.1	Spain	-Madrid (June)	-supports the economic reforms in LA; calls for the continuous development of the political

			contacts and economic, technical, commercial and financial cooperation with LA; invites the Commission to develop cooperation policies differentiated to LA without prejudice against other regions; Central America
1989.2	France	-Strasbourg (December)	-Andean countries; Central America
1990.1	Ireland	-Dublin (June)	-states the interest to develop cooperation with LA
1990.2	Italy	-Rome (October) -Rome (December)	- -states the importance of the Rio Group Dialogue
1991.1	Luxemburg	-Luxemburg (June)	-
1991.2	Netherlands	-Maastricht (December)	-
1992.1	Portugal	-Lisbon (June)	- underlines the importance it attaches to the deepening of relations between the Community and LA as the means to support economic recovery and consolidation of democracy in that region; welcomes the signature of new framework agreements with Brazil and Paraguay; stresses the importance of supporting the efforts of economic integration which are developed at regional level, such as Mercosul; invites the Commission to present proposals with a view to intensifying and institutionalizing relations with Mercosul.
1992.2	United Kingdom	-Birmingham (October) -Edinburgh	- -

		(December)	
1993.1	Denmark	-Copenhagen (June)	-
1993.2	Belgium	-Brussels (October) -Brussels (December)	- -
1994.1	Greece	-Corfu (June)	-reaffirms the importance attributed to the relations with LA and its regional groups; welcomes the accession of Mexico to the OECD; confirms its desire to reinforce the political and economic relations with Mexico and Mercosur.
1994.2	Germany	-Essen (December)	-reaffirms the resolve expressed in the E's "basic paper" on its relations with the LA and Caribbean States to establish a new, comprehensive partnership between the two regions; urges the Council and the Commission, working on the basis of the Council report, to create as quickly as possible the conditions for an early opening of negotiations with the Mercosur States on an inter-regional framework agreement, including a Memorandum of Understanding, and to put ideas on the future form of treaty relations with Mexico and on the extension of relations with Chile into concrete form without delay.
1995.1	France	-Cannes (June)	-
1995.2	Spain	-Madrid (December)	- stresses the significant progress made in the process of

			strengthening relations with LA; requests the Council and the Commission to expedite implementation of the conclusions on enhancing cooperation between the European Union and Latin America in the period 1996-2000 (Annex 12); welcomes the signing in Madrid of the Inter-Regional Framework Agreement on Trade and Economic Cooperation between the European Union and Mercosur, the final objective of which is to achieve political and economic association; calls upon the EIB to step up its activity in Latin America in line with its financing procedures and criteria; Central America; Chile; Mexico; Cuba.
1996.1	Italy	-Florence (June)	-notes with satisfaction that relations with Latin America and the Caribbean have increased significantly, notably by: the progress in relations with Mercosur; renewal of the San Jose process between the European Union and Central America, and the Cochabamba declaration; the forthcoming opening of negotiations with Mexico; the perspectives for relations with the Andean Community
1996.2	Ireland	-Dublin (December)	-
1997.1	Netherlands	-Amsterdam (June)	- looks forward to a summit meeting of Heads of State and Government of the EU with Latin America and the Caribbean.

1998.1	Luxemburg	-Luxemburg (November) -Luxemburg (December)	- -
1998.2	United Kingdom	-Cardiff (June) - Vienna (December)	- -
1999.1	Germany	- Berlin (March) -Koln (June)	- - warmly welcomes the first Summit between the Heads of State and Government of the European Union, Latin America and the Caribbean, to be held in Rio de Janeiro on 28 and 29 June 1999. This historic event, in highlighting the excellent and close relations between the two regions, will launch a new strategic partnership, strengthening the political, economic and cultural understanding between our regions; Mexico; Central America
1999.2	Finland	-Tempere (October) -Helsinki (December)	- -
2000.1	Portugal	-Lisbon (March) -Sta Maria da Feira (October)	- -
2000.2	France	-Biarritz (October) -Nice (December)	- -

Source: Source: compiled by the author

c) Commission - The competence to negotiate and conclude FDI commitments in agreements with third countries remains with member-states and therefore outside the EU system. However, the Commission has tried – unsuccessfully - to expand its competences to this area in the late 1980s. One of the strategies adopted was support for the negotiation of a multilateral investment agreement at the WTO instead of at the OECD, since in the former it expected to have a larger role in the negotiations. The reasoning was that even if the negotiations succeeded, they would end up being an example of the 4th pillar, in which the EU institutions, and in particular the Commission, would be involved, triggering a process that could be favorable to the transfer of competences on its behalf. In order to gain support from developing countries to open the negotiations at the WTO, the EU even supported the exclusion of provisions about pre-establishment national treatment, and investor-to-investor dispute settlement. This was an interesting example of the Commission making a coalition with third countries against its member-states, with the aim of expanding its competences.

This informal political influence of the Commission, regardless of it formal competences, can be considered as favoring a cooperative approach with developing countries, even if motivated by its interest in increasing its competences.[171] Apart from that, the Commission supported the creation of a number of cooperation programmes to promote EU FDI in the SCSs, as can be seen in the table below.

Table 38: FDI in Commission communications regarding the SCSs

Document	Target	Reference to FDI
COM (1984) 105	LA	Proposes the access of Latin American countries to the European Investment Bank (EIB).
COM (1994) 428	Me	Proposes the establishment of several regional projects concerning, for instance, transport, energy, environment, telecommunications and the information society, to be financed by, among others, the EIB (p.17)
COM (1995) 495	LA	States that European FDI has played its part in the privatization process in LA (p.10) but that industrial promotion and investment should be strengthened using the ECIP, Al-Invest and EIB lending (p.17) and in the energy sector via the programme ALURE (p.18).
COM (1995) 504	Me	Promotion of exchange of information and the development of a legal environment conducive to investment, through the conclusion of BITs

[171] Graham, 2000, p.186; Torrent, 1998, 121.

		between the member states; promotion of joint ventures (Art.12); encouragement of technology transfer and investments in the energy sector (Art.13), transport (Art.14), information society and telecommunications (At.16)
COM (1995) 742	LA	Proposes a Community guarantee to the EIB against losses under loans for projects of mutual interest in Latin American and Asian countries with which the Community has concluded cooperation agreements
COM (1996) 429	LA	Technical issues about implementation of EIB loans to Asia and LA
COM (1999) 105	LA	Mentions that a enhanced cooperation will provide economic operators and investors prerequisites for productive and long term EU investment in LA
COM (1999) 600	Me	-
COM (2000) 670	LA	Prioritizes the information society, proposes the programme ALIS to improve investments in this area; implementation procedures are described in Annex 3

Source: compiled by the author

d) European Investment Bank- although the EIB possesses a quite independent decision-making structure, the approval of specific projects follows technical rather than political criteria. It is not its role to discriminate among regions or productive sectors. Concerning projects in the context of the development policy, it is responsible only for the implementation of projects. It can be said, however, that the EIB has an interest in increasing its operations in general, and in that sense, its position can be considered as favoring cooperation with Southern Cone States.

e) European Economic and Social Committee - The ESC established a dialogue with the Mercosur Economic and Social Consultative Forum (FCES), by means of a Memorandum of Understanding signed in December/1997, with a view to establishing regular exchanges of information and views. These inter-institutional contacts were consolidated during a second visit by an ESC delegation to Montevideo in May/1998. In February of 2000, the EU and Mercosur foreign ministers adopted the joint proposal advanced by the ESC and FCES of establishing a joint committee (JCC) in the framework of the Association agreement that had been in negotiation since 1999 to further their cooperation. Regarding FDI matters, it can be said that the ESC position has included a cooperative approach to the SCSs and a focus on the developmental effect of FDI.[172]

Table 39: FDI in the ESC opinions regarding the SCSs

Opinion nr.	Date	Target	Reference to FDI
102	26-01-1994	LA	States that in spite of the current efforts, full and effective use is still not being made of cooperation resources, principally because of the rigidity of procedures, and because economic and social operators are unaware of the possibilities available, particularly in the area of economic cooperation and access to EIB funds (parag 3.3); that the Latin American countries are trying to attract direct European investment because it can help to generate employment, to promote technology transfer and to modernize infrastructure, agriculture and industry. It can also contribute to the economic stability of the recipient country (parag 5.1), but that the world recession and investment requirements in the EU itself (arising from the internal market) and in other areas (such as Central and Eastern Europe) could lead to a diminishing flow of direct European investment to Latin America (5.2) and that against this backdrop, EU instruments for promoting cooperation investment, such as the Business Corporation Network and the EU-IIP have an important role to play. More could perhaps be done - e.g. through the EU representations in the various countries - to bring these instruments to the notice of potential investors. Member State financial incentives to encourage companies to invest in Latin America are likewise of primary importance (5.3); the Committee urges the Commission to prepare studies on European investment opportunities

[172] ESC, 2001.

			in Latin America and, in the light of its findings, to draw up proposals for expanding the range of EU instruments for promoting such investment. Similarly, it calls upon the Member States to take steps to back direct private and public investment in the region. (parag 5.5)
1176	25-10-1995	Me	supports an EU-Mercosur accord and states that it could also boost EU investment (parag 2.13); states that the presence of European firms in Mercosur has increased significantly in recent years (...) At the same time, the Committee notes recent research that suggests that there are still technical obstacles to the liberalization of capital flows between the EU and Mercosur, and is concerned that the inter-regional agreement should address that issue (parag 2.14); states that the Mercosur countries will require large-scale investment, particularly in infrastructure, that the EU can provide support in terms of know-how; and that resources could eventually be provided directly from European Commission budget lines, or through the European Investment Bank (parag 3.3)
1163	16-09-1998	Me, Chile	-
459	03-05-1999	LA	Advances that the EU economic objectives in LA should be focused on the stabilization of markets, international financial flows, and the promotion of direct investment as a stable source of financing for technological innovation and development of production (parag 2.8)
477	04-05-2000	Develo ping countri es	States that multinational companies, in their activities in developing and in transition countries, must respect the OECD Guidelines for Multinational Companies and the ILO's Tripartite Declaration on Multinational Companies and Social Policy (parag 4.2)
932	18-07-2001	Me,	States that investments by European firms in

		Chile	Mercosur (and Chile) not only offer these firms opportunities to benefit from the growth of the regional markets and to harness the region's human capital and resources for their productive processes, but also gives them an important role in promoting productive development, job creation, technological innovation and the training of human resources; European investment should be a positive factor in the consolidation of the basic characteristics of the social market economy; EU investors should follow the principles set out in the Resolution on EU standards for European enterprises operating in developing countries and the OECD's guidelines for multinational corporations (parag 3.7).
1326	25-10-2001	WTO	States that as regards investment-related objectives, codes of conduct for multinational companies ought to be encouraged, such as those being developed on the basis of the guidelines launched by the OECD. Special attention should be paid to freedom of transfer and protection against expropriation and other nationalization (parag 3.6.8)

Source: compiled by the author

f) European Round of Industrialists – the ERT was founded in 1983 by European industrial leaders with the objective of promoting European competitiveness and growth. Relevant issues are identified, analyzed, and then passed on to the political decision-makers at the national and European level by means of reports, position papers, and face-to-face discussions. At the European level, the ERT has contacts mainly with the Commission, the Council of Ministers and the Parliament, and also with the government holding the Presidency. In 1989, a Working Group on North-South relations was created, Chaired by Mr. Helmut O. Maucher, also Chairman and CEO of Nestle S/A, to address the issue of investments in the developing world. The group's main tasks were to increase the dialogue between European industry and the developing countries and to follow the changes in public policy on investment in those countries. In addition, the ERT wanted to learn from the host countries where they saw problems with investors, so that European industries could improve their cooperation with these countries. Since the first half of the 1990s, the working group on North-south relations has published a series of policy papers about FDI, including: "Survey on Improvements and Conditions for Investment in the Developing World", dated May 1993; "European Industry: a Partner of the Developing World – FDI as a tool for economic development", from August 1993; "Investment in the Development World – New Openings and Challenges for European Industry", from December 1996; "European Industry and the Developing World. For a Global Framework of Mutual Interest and Trust," dated May 1997; and "Improved Investment Conditions. Third Survey on improvements in conditions for investment in the developing world," dated June 2000. The reports from 1993, 1996 and 2000, particularly, offer a very detailed database on the improvements in investment conditions, remaining impediments and policy foci for the future in most developing countries.[173] Although there is evidence that EU institutions such as the Commission were aware of such documents, no evidence was found that they have been specifically used in any policy initiative.

g) Mercosur-European Union Business Forum – the MEBF, on the contrary, advanced to the Commission some very specific proposals regarding FDI, since the process of negotiations for the Association agreement started in 1999.[174] The MEBF Rio Declaration urged the EU and Mercosur governments to issue a comprehensive statement expressing their commitment to strong foreign direct investment protection and to open investment regimes, including: national treatment, common investment rules and procedures at all governmental levels, non-discriminatory access to government funds, civil research and development programs, free flow of investment-related capital, including free transfer of profits, elimination of tax legislation, policies and practices that discriminate against foreign investors, modification of tax laws regarding the treatment of foreign-earned income to encourage foreign investment and to prevent double taxation, limitation of national security exceptions in investment, narrowly circumscribed and applied in a transparent manner, and that foreign investment protection agreements should be speeded up. The MEBF also lobbies for support in the modernization and development of the infrastructure sector in Mercosur and joint efforts to provide financial resources for this purpose, such as from the European Investment Bank (EIB). Finally, the Rio Declaration also asks that the EU and the Mercosur governments provide easier access to investment financing for small and medium-sized enterprises (SMEs), and that they review their assistance programs, in particular to increase financial resources allocated to Al-Invest, and simplify the ECIP procedures and decision-making process. [175]

[173] For details about ERT in general, see Homepage: http://www.ert.be and Richardson, 2000. For the documents mentioned, see ERT, 1996, 1997 & 2000.

[174] For a brief historical background about the MEBF see Chapter 4, p.

[175] MEBF, 1999a, p.6-8.

In its official reaction to the MEBF Rio Declaration, the Commission announced that it agreed with MEBF's request for strong FDI protection and open investment regimes, calling for the EIB and EU member States to finance infrastructure projects in Mercosur. Such states, despite considering liberalization rather than privatization the most relevant factor for improving business conditions, had recently created an instrument to facilitate the participation of EU investors in the Mercosur privatization process through the new Facility 1B of the ECIP programme. The Commission also emphasized that great efforts had been made to improve the payment situation concerning the Al-Invest programme, and that both the Commission itself and Mercosur's governments were preparing a new SME cooperation project to be conducted under the 1995 Framework Cooperation Agreement.[176]

In the Mainz Statement, the MEBF also expresses support to developing WTO provisions for the treatment of FDI, and urges EU and Mercosur governments and the EU Commission to take action to fully implement the following commitments (in addition to the ones originated in the Rio Declaration): free movement of personnel; extinguishment of the obligation for non-executive directors to hold residence in the respective countries; clear stable and coherent support rules for all investors, in order not to distort competition; continuation of the privatization processes and availability of real-time information about such processes; and compliance by public authorities and state-owned companies with the obligations of foreign investment, particularly concerning financial payments deadlines, using the banking system if necessary. In terms of sectorial priorities, the areas of energy, tourism/transportation and information society/telecommunications were selected.[177]

The EU-Mercosur Action Plan on Business Facilitation, announced by the Commission during the 2nd EU-LAC Summit in Madrid was based to a large extent on the list of business facilitation measures prepared by the MEBF, originally presented to the negotiators of the Association Agreement in Sept/2001, and reformulated as a final proposal in the Buenos Aires Statement on Business Facilitation. The first list was much broader, including FDI proposals such as the easing up of work and residence permits, facilitation of remittances abroad, re-launching of financial assistance schemes to promote the creation of joint ventures between the EU and Mercosur SMEs such as AL-Invest and ECIP, which were suspended, assistance to build up the capacities of Mercosur countries' national export and investment promotion agencies (such as Fundacion Exportar of Argentina or Proparaguay) following the example of Commission initiatives in other developing countries and transitional economies, grants for feasibility and pre-feasibility studies in infrastructure projects in Mercosur, and EIB resources to

---

176 Marin, 1999, pp.10-11.

177 See MEBF, 1999b.

co-finance projects. The Buenos Aires Statement, used as a basis for the Commission's initiative, included only one recommendation on FDI, namely to encourage investments in the electronic commerce infrastructure of Mercosur countries, and focused on trade issues such as customs control, standards and technical regulations, and some aspects of electronic commerce.[178]

The MEBF Madrid Declaration contains recommendations on FDI that are far more detailed than previous declarations. Among the most important are: supporting negotiations for a multilateral FDI agreement at the WTO and TRIMs enhancement and update at the Doha Ministerial Conference; demanding that the EU and Mercosur governments include a chapter on FDI; demanding that these governments modify their tax regimes and sign new agreements on investment treatment, investment protection and avoidance of double taxation; requesting guarantees concerning political risks to infrastructure investments and an adequate regulatory framework, requesting liberalization of personnel movement; demanding improved cooperation regarding SMEs, in particular by enhancing effectiveness and providing proper funding to Al-Invest, in addition to relaunching ECIP (at the example of the new programmes EBAS and Pro-Invest for ACP countries); demanding the provision of technical assistance and funding to investment promotion agencies, especially in Mercosur, and finally; demanding improved transparency in government procurement markets, national treatment, and non-discrimination for foreign companies. The priority sectors selected were information society, electronic commerce, and telecommunications.[179] It is interesting to note that the energy sector, present in the Mainz Statement, was excluded. As seen in section 5.1.4.2.2e, the programme ALURE, designed to promote EU FDI in Mercosur in the emery sector was suspended in 2002. The new emphasis on electronic commerce was in line with the new focus on the information society by part of the Commission and with the creation of the programme ALIS to promote investments in this area. Although it was not possible to determine, in terms of time, whether the change in the priority sectors of the development policy was a reaction or a stimulus to the change in the priority areas advanced by the MEBF, it can be said that both the Commission and the business community had a desire for change, a position not shared by the European Parliament, who supported the continuation of ALURE and emphasized the importance of the energy sector to foster economic development in Southern Cone States.[180]

To conclude the observations on the MEBF, it can be said that it was not only an assertive actor in the EU FDI policy network, but also managed to exert a considerable influence on the PAS, especially via Commission. The Commission

[178] MEBF, 2001a, pp.4-5 & 2001b, p.15.
[179] MEBF, 2002, p.20-27.
180 See section 5.1.4.2.2e & EP, 2001.

was very receptive and supportive of the MEBF since its creation; the reasons pointed out are the need for expert information, and the need to improve the legitimacy of the proposals as a strategy for addressing the alleged lack of transparency and democratic deficit in the EU policymaking process.[181]

h) Working Group EU-Me – the working group took a position in favor of liberalizing the FDI regime in the SCSs, and increasing European FDI to the SCSs. The group recommended that the liberalization of investments should go hand in hand with that of trade. This is seen not only as a cross sectorial concession for access to the Mercosur market for European industrial products and services in exchange for access to the EU by Mercosur agricultural products, but also for the agricultural sector, for instance, with the opening of opportunities for European agro-businesses to invest in the SCSs and profit from the lower costs in agricultural production. In addition to liberalization, the SCSs should promote stable, non-discriminatory, and transparent regulatory FDI frameworks to benefit inflows. The Group recommended also the conclusion of a bi-regional investment agreement replacing the bilateral agreements between member-states, but it did not recommend specific commitments.[182]

5.2.3.2) Most assertive actors and strength of the dependent variable

After analyzing the initiatives and activities of mobilized actors in the EU foreign policy network for FDI, it is possible to conclude that the most assertive actors in the issue area of FDI for the period of 1980-85 were the Parliament, on the side of PAS, and the European Round Table of Industrialists (ERT) on the side of the private actors. Despite the low structural position of the former, given its lack of power, the Parliament enjoyed a high situational mobilization. It has consistently advanced the promotion of European FDI to the SCSs and supported EIB operation in the region. The Commission seems to have addressed this issue, but with less priority. There is no evidence that the Parliament depended on private actors such as the ERT in order to formulate and advance its preferences.

In the period of 1995-2000, the most assertive actors seem to have been the Commission, on the side of PAS, and the Mercosur-European Union Business Forum (MEBF) on the side of the private actors. The latter can be said to have a high situational and structural mobilization. The Commission, despite the lack of formal competences, also seems to have a high situational and structural position in the FDI policy network. There is strong evidence that the Commission has

---

[181] Other initiatives in that area were the organization of conferences with representatives from the civil society, business community, and academic community, to discuss and exchange views on the EU-Mercosur (and EU-Chile) association negotiations, such as I and II Conference with Civil Society on October 12, 2000 and February 12, 2002, respectively, in Brussels, and the Civil Society Consultation on Trade and Investment on the April 28, 1999, in Brussels.

[182] Chaire Mercosur, 2002, p.16.

counted on information and policy recommendation from the MEBF. This could have occurred due to a lack of resources and expertise of the Commission in the FDI area, given that it does not deal with FDI at the domestic (common market) level.

Table 40: Most assertive actors in the EU FDI policy network

Type of actor	1980-85	1995-2000
PAS	Parliament	Commission
Private	ERT	MEBF

Finally, proceeding with the measurement of the strength of the dependent variable represented by net gain-seeking foreign policy, for the period of 1980-85 societal interests in the EU foreign policy network regarding FDI seems to be weak. The only actor that manifested interest in promoting cooperation on this subject was the European Parliament. However, its decision-making powers both at the level of bilateral agreements and developmental policy were insufficient to establish a significant policy initiative. Among private actors, the ERT showed some interest in promoting FDI cooperation, but the efforts remained at a quite general level both in terms of policy suggestions and targeted areas.

In the period of 1995-2000, the value of the dependent variable seems to be medium. The Commission, the Parliament, the MEBF, the ESC, the EIB and the Working Group EU-Me have clear, highly pronounced and convergent preferences in the direction of promoting FDI cooperation with the Southern Cone States. Their influence was restricted, however, by their formal competences; the preferences of the dominant actors could not be translated into legal commitments on FDI in bilateral agreements, but they did have an impact on the design of programmes within developmental policy, favoring cooperation with Southern Cone States on FDI matters.

In both periods, the EU policy network for FDI seems to be better defined as pluralist than as monopolist or corporatist, and to fit in the EU regulatory model of the typology advanced by Helen Wallace (see section 4.2.3).

Table 41: Test of Utilitarian Liberalism forecasts for the FDI case study

	1980-85	1990-95
Independent variable	Weak societal common interests favoring cooperation	Medium societal common interests favoring cooperation
Expected level of cooperation in foreign policy behavior towards the SCSs	Very low	Medium

Observed level of cooperation in the EU foreign policy behavior towards the SCSs	Very low	Medium

5.3) Further observations and explanation of the level of cooperation of EU foreign policy behavior towards Southern Cone States

As seen above, the covariance test confirms forecasts derived from the three approaches, determining an increase in the level of cooperation in the EU foreign policy behavior towards the SCSs in the case of foreign direct investment. Neorealism, however, does not offer an explanation on the absolute level of cooperation for each period, and further observations actually weaken the covariance findings. The first relevant consideration is that there are no studies or economic simulations indicating that an increase of EU FDI would necessarily lead to a decrease or a barrier to the entrance of new US FDI, and vice-versa, unless this was implemented by means of discriminatory policies, which is unrealistic. Although countries have a limited capacity to absorb FDI, that was not the case in the Southern Cone States during the period under consideration. For developing countries that had not reached a level of saturation with new investments, the economic forecasts expect, on the contrary, that FDI would be attracted by the existence of other FDI, independently of where it comes from. That means that an increase of EU FDI would not necessarily improve the relative power position of the EU. The existence of EU FDI would not disfavor US FDI; on the contrary, it could have the effect of favoring it.[183]

Following this reasoning, EU policies that promote an increase in EU FDI by facilitating the formation of joint ventures and participation of small and medium-sized enterprises, or policies which aim at improving the quality of FDI in order to promote economic growth, such as is the case with EU policies regarding FDI within its development policy, do not necessarily contribute to the increase of the relative EU FDI vis-à-vis the US. Policies that could have this effect would be, for instance, the negotiation of FDI provisions granting better access to EU firms engaging in FDI than to firms from 3rd countries. Nevertheless, as seen, this was not the case in the analyzed period. Specific FDI commitments were not undertaken by the EU because it did not have the required competences, which remain with member-states. The EU has not pushed its member-states to negotiate such provisions either; on the contrary, it encouraged them to negotiate

[183] This forecast is confirmed by the patterns of FDI in Eastern Europe, where in parallel to the boom of European FDI in the 1990s, the US FDI also increased from 0,7 billion US$ in 1987 to 8,9 billion US$ in 1997. The case of Mexico is also illustrative; although NAFTA created trade diversion from the EU to the US, the same did not happen in FDI. See Nunnenkamp, 2001, p.141.

BITs on FDI protection and promotion and to avoid double taxation, such as stated in Art.12 of the 1995 Agreement with Mercosur. In addition, most BITs signed by member-states have followed the trend to include the non-discriminatory and most-favored-nation treatment.

A second observation that also weakens the Neorealist explanation is that, although the EU has used conditionality in its foreign policy towards the SCSs, its content, i.e., the preservation of democracy and the respect for human rights, was actually shared by the latter. The use of conditionality cannot be seen therefore as a "price" which the target country has to pay in order to obtain cooperation, as advanced by Neorealism, but rather a "gift" to help them attain their own purpose of preserving democracy and human rights.

Both Identity Constructivism and Utilitarian Liberalism were successful in their forecasts about the absolute level of cooperation in both periods and in the covariance test.

Table 42: Observed and forecasted level of cooperation for the FDI case study

	1980-85	1995-2000
Observed level of cooperation in the EU foreign policy behavior	Very low	Medium
Neorealist forecast	->	Higher
Identity Constructivist forecast	Very low	Medium
Utilitarian Liberalist forecast	Very low	Medium

Chapter 6 - Case Study 2: Agricultural Trade

6.1) Case description and dependent variable

Agricultural trade is an extremely complex topic, not only on account of its political sensitivity, but also due to its technical aspects. Although the EU also exports agricultural goods to the SCS, and the general background information of this chapter covers both EU imports and exports, the case study focuses on EU imports, or SCS exports, since the latter are the object of dispute in bilateral/bi-regional relations. Different theoretical approaches attribute differently the role of agricultural exports in economic development (section 6.1.1). For developing countries in general, and the Southern Cone States in particular, agriculture is the major component of their exports, particularly to developed countries, such as the EU and its member-states (section 6.1.2). Despite the liberal international trade regime established by GATT and its successor WTO, agriculture remains one of the most protected areas (section 6.1.3). The EU has a common commercial policy, which, in the case of agriculture, is under the exclusive competence of the Community. It also has a number of trade instruments to be used against unfair trade practices or to achieve specific goals such as cooperation with third countries. The Southern Cone States, however, have not been addressed by these instruments. On the contrary, they have suffered from protective instruments such as high tariffs, subsidies and price controls in the context of the common agricultural policy (section 6.1.4). The level of cooperation of EU foreign policy behavior to Southern Cone States from 1980-85 to 1995-2000 does not seem to have changed much. Despite efforts made at the GATT/WTO level, and of CAP reform, the substantive effect, in terms of opening up the Common Market to agricultural exports from the SCS, was negligible (section 6.1.5).

6.1.1) Role of agricultural trade in economic development

According to the prevailing generally sanctioned theory of international trade, the Factor Proportion Hypothesis, or Heckscher-Ohlin Theorem (a reformulation of Ricardo's theory of comparative advantages which takes into consideration opportunity costs), countries should specialize in producing and exporting goods in which their comparative advantage is the greatest, and should import goods in which it is lowest.[184] Given their less advanced stage of development, the competitiveness of Southern Cone States tends to decrease as

---

[184] See Trebilcock & Howse, 1999, Ch.1; Sirc, 1975; Guillochon, 1979.

the level of technological sophistication in production increases. With a few exceptions (such as the Brazilian aircraft industry, or Argentine and Brazilian footwear industry), most of the products in which the Southern Cone States are competitive in the world market are agricultural (Brazil: coffee, cocoa, sugar, soybean, beef meat, poultry and orange juice; Argentina: beef meat, soy, wheat; Paraguay: soybean and cotton; Uruguay: beef meat, rice and wool). Therefore, according to the prevailing economic theory Southern Cone States would be able to maximize their trade revenues and, therefore, their capital to promote economic growth, by maximizing their exports of the specific (agricultural) products in which they have the greater competitiveness.

This premise has been contested by structural development theories in the 50s and 60s, which claimed that the decreasing terms of trade between manufactured goods and commodities due to inelasticity of commodity demand, among others, posed an obstacle to the development of peripheral countries. Unlike the developed countries, in which the inadequate use of savings could be corrected by governmental intervention as advanced by Keynesian approaches, the crucial problem in developing countries was held be the insufficient level of savings, which required different remedies. The main developmental strategy advanced was the promotion of domestic industrialization and the substitution of imports. Exports were important to equilibrate the balance of payments, but not seen as a key variable to promote domestic economic growth. Moreover, instead of focusing on the (most competitive) agricultural products, diversification should be promoted.[185] The alleged lack of ties between agriculture and the domestic economic system was also seen as discrediting agricultural export-led strategies for economic growth.[186]

Southern Cone States adopted the imports substitution model as their main strategy for promoting economic growth until the late 1980s, and the limited success obtained is well documented. This acknowledgement, complemented by new studies showing positive results concerning agricultural linkages, the phenomenon of economic globalization, and also World Bank and IMF's conditions to solve the debt crisis, among others, led to a revival of export-led development strategies in the Southern Cone States. Considering that, apart from

[185] The structural economic theory and the model of import substitutions were developed within the ECLAC (UN Economic Commission for Latin America), right after its creation in 1948, mostly in the works of its first General Secretary, the Argentinean Raul Prebish, and other Latin American economists such as Celso Furtado and Osvaldo Sunkel. Its central ideas inspired both the creation of the UNCTAD and the movement for the creation of a New International Economic Order (see section 6.1.3), as well as the dependency theory; a political thread which linked the development process to the power structure and social class behavior both at the international and domestic levels, developed among others by Fernando Henrique Cardoso, Enzo Faletto and Jose Medina Echavarria. For a detailed analysis of the structural and dependency theories, see Bielschowsky, 2000, and Bielschowsky, 1988, Ch.2.

[186] Hirshman 1958 in Valdes, 1991, p.87.

exceptional cases, agricultural products continue to be the only area in which such countries have a chance to compete in the world markets with developed countries, agricultural exports assumed again a pivotal position.[187] In order for the new developmental strategy to be successful (according to orthodox theory), two basic requirements must be fulfilled. The first is that, on the domestic side, they promote economic liberalization and privatization of state-led industries, which have largely occurred, particularly in Argentina.[188] The second requirement is that a free trade system prevails at the international level, allowing countries to realize the benefits of their comparative advantages. While the international trade regime represented in the GATT/WTO promotes the liberalization of trade, it has been less effective in promoting the liberalization of trade in agricultural products, as will be seen next.

6.1.2) Flows and trends in agricultural trade

World trade in agricultural products increased significantly since 1980, especially during the early 1990s, in response, among other factors, to the strong economic growth worldwide. Food demand grows faster in relatively rapidly growing developing economies that show a substantial growth in the income *per capita*. At a certain level of income, diets change from largely cereal-based to include animal products, which further increase the demand for animal foodstuffs. However, when countries become relatively wealthy, the increase in food demand slows down. Agricultural trade is therefore highly sensitive to economic performance in developing countries; in fact, after reaching a peak in 1996, flows declined as a consequence of the decrease in demand caused by the economic crisis in Russia and in Asian and Latin American countries.[189]

Southern Cone States are all net exporters of agricultural products; their coverage ratios (ratio between exports and imports) in the periods 1980-1989 and 1990-1997 were 3,8 and 4,4 for Argentina; 2,8 and 2,3 for Brazil; 4,7 and 3,0 for Paraguay; and 3,5 and 3,1 for Uruguay. Among the largest net importers, we find Japan and Southern East Asian countries, with a ratio of 0,2 for both periods and some EU countries such as Germany (0,4 and 0,5 for each period), Italy (0,4 for both periods) and the UK (0,5 and 0,7 for each period).[190]

---

[187] See , Richards, 1997; Blake, 1998;Cruz Junier et al, 1993; Hojman, 1994; Valdes, 1991; Trebilcock & Howse, 1999, Ch.14; Orden et all, 2003.

[188] See the evaluation of the liberalization of agricultural markets in the WTO Trade Policy Reviews Argentina 1999, Brazil 1996 & 2000; Paraguay 1997 and Uruguay 1998. All four countries are praised for the unilateral liberalizing measures adopted, despite some remaining protection, specially in Brazil, such as to sugar and alcohol.

[189] Vaillant & Nin, 2002, pp.306-307.

[190] Vaillant & Nin, 2002, p.310.

As regards bilateral flows with the EU, agricultural products are the main component of exports (see Table 43; even if the data refers to 2001, the patterns did not change much since 1980). In this respect, the composition of the balance of trade between the EU and the SCS can be said to follow the traditional North-South patterns, in which the main products imported by the EU are agricultural, and the main products exported are manufactured goods such as machinery, transports materials, and chemical products. Among the agricultural exports to the EU most are bulk commodities (non-processed foodstuffs); the main products from Brazil are coffee, sugar, orange, soy and bovine meat; from Argentina, sunflower, soy, wheat and maize; from Paraguay, soy, coffee and sugar; and from Uruguay bovine meat, fish and citrus fruits.[191] Most tropical products exported from the SCS to the EU face low tariffs, with some exceptions such as sugar and bananas, which are subject to special regimes within the EU. Temperate products, such as cereals, and bovine meat and dairy products face higher tariffs or difficulties in market access due to EU subsidies and other measures in the context of common agricultural policy (see below).

Table 43: Main products of EU-LA (in 2000) and EU-Southern Cone States (in 2001) trade in goods (millions of euros/ % of total)

Products	Imp. from LA	Exp. to LA	Imp. from SCS	Exp. to SCS
Agricultural	18.680 (55,3%)	3.086	13.169 (74,2%)	847
Energy	4.292	558	281	181
Machinery	4.401	18.010	1.005	8.241
Transp.Material	3.986	10.418	2.246	4.996
Chemical	1.916	8.724	848	4.360
Textiles & Cloth.	508	1.222	198	351
Total	33.783		17.747	

Source: EU-DG Trade Homepage

A look at the total flows of trade in goods (agricultural and non agricultural) between the EU and the SCS shows that the percentage participation of the region in both EU imports and exports decreased from 1980 to 2000; and that the trade balance of the EU decreased from 1.751 million euros to 173 million euros (Table 2). This same trend can be seen in the EU-Latin America patterns (Table 3), although in this case the total balance is positive to the EU for an amount of 5.704 million euros.

191 Vaillant, 2000, p.18.

Table 44: EU trade in goods with the Southern Cone States (Millions of euros and %)

	1980	1990	2000
Imports (share of EU total)	7.705 (2.8)	14.208 (3.3)	24.374 (2.4)
Exports (share of EU total)	5.954 (2.9)	5.657 (1.4)	24.200 (2.5)
Trade Balance	-1.751	-8.551	-173

Source: EU-DG Trade Homepage

Table 45: EU trade in goods with Latin America (Millions of euros and %)

	1980	1990	2000
Imports (share EU total)	17.809 (6.3)	27.051 (6.1)	48.982 (4.8)
Exports (share of EU total)	14.270 (6.7)	16.939 (4.3)	54.686 (5.8)
Trade Balance	-3.539	-10.112	5.704

Source: EU-DG Trade Homepage

When only agricultural goods are considered, the EU has a long-standing trade deficit with the SCS. Still, from 1990 to 1996, SCS agricultural exports to the EU increased by 11,9%, while SCS agricultural imports increased by 237%. As mentioned above, SCS exports are concentrated on a few products, notably soy and its by-products (such as animal feed), coffee, tobacco, bovine meat and fruits. EU exports are also concentrated in three groups of products - alcoholic beverages, dairy products, and cocoa derivatives.[192]

6.1.3) International cooperation regarding agricultural trade

The first initiatives of international agricultural trade cooperation were not taken by governments, but by national agricultural associations, in the form of periodic congresses held during international exhibitions and fairs, such as the ones of 1848 in Brussels, 1878 in Paris, 1885 in Budapest, 1889 in Paris again and 1891 in the Hague. In the latter, it was decided to create a permanent institution, the International Commission on Agriculture in order to examine the rural economy, provide technical information and to promote the coordination of the production and sale of agricultural commodities. The first governmental initiative was the creation of the International Institute of Agriculture (IIA), in 1905. Although the original proposal by the American David Lublin was to give it the power to manage international commodity markets, the Institute ended up being a

[192] EC, DG-Trade, 1998, pp.6-7.

research body responsible for compiling statistical data and organizing conferences and congresses. In 1945, it was dissolved and its library and staff were transferred to the Food and Agriculture Organization (FAO). The creation of FAO is due to the successful demand of the "four Geneva colleagues" Frank McDougall, Andre Mayer, Frank Boudreau and John Boyd Orr, made to the US President Roosevelt requesting support for the preparation of a United Nations Conference to discuss food and agriculture. The conference took place in Hot Springs, Virginia from May 10 to June 3, 1943, and in its final act the participating states agreed, among other things, on the need for international action to increase world agricultural production, individual governmental responsibility to ensure sufficient food, and on the establishment of an interim commission to draw up a Constitution for the organization. FAO, however, came to have a predominately technical and advisory function, a predictable result given the incompatibility between the management of agricultural markets at the multilateral level, and the responsibility attributed to national governments to "ensure sufficient food" in their domestic societies, as agreed in Hot Springs, an incompatibility that contributed to the failure of negotiations that would create the International Trade Organization (ITO). [193]

The ITO was supposed to be the third pillar of the Breton Woods system, together with the World Bank and the International Monetary Fund (IMF). In 1946, the UN Economic and Social Council established a Preparatory Committee constituted by 50 representatives from different countries to draft a charter, which had been negotiated during the UN Conference on Trade and Employment held from 11-21-1947 to 03-24-1948 in Havana, Cuba. The resulting draft, the Havana Charter (UN doc. E/Conf.2/78) was quite ambitious, including rules on employment, restrictive business practices, and on commodities. Concerning the latter, it included a mechanism to stabilize world prices and to manage surpluses and temporary crisis situations, very much in line with the failed proposal on the creation of a World Food Board by FAO (Chapter VI). Before the charter was approved, 23 of the 50 participants decided to negotiate tariff concessions among themselves, which was done in negotiations that took place from April to October

[193] It is interesting to note that The League of Nations Pact and the Constitution of the International Labor Organization, created after World War I did not make any references to agriculture. It was only with the overproduction in the context of the crisis of 1929 and consequent collapse of agricultural prices that attempts to strengthen international cooperation and upgrade the IIA took place. The New Deal subsidies for agricultural commodities and the UK Agricultural Marketing Act of 1931 marked the beginning of governmental intervention in the production and trade of agriculture commodities, and the necessity to regulate it at the international level. The First International Wheat Agreement was signed in 1933. In 1930, the until then small health section of the League of Nations was extended to include nutrition problems, with the creation of a Technical Commission on Nutrition and a Mixed Committee for food problems, when the "four Geneva colleagues" worked together. Marchisio & Di Blasé, 1991, Ch1.

1947.[194] The combined package of trade rules and tariff concessions became known as the General Agreement on Tariffs and Trade (GATT), which became effective in January 1948, while the Havana Charter was still being negotiated. Although the latter was finally agreed in March 1948, the legislative bodies of some countries refused to ratify it, including the US Congress. With the faltering of the Charter, GATT remained the only multilateral instrument ruling international trade from 1948 to 1995, when the World Trade Organization (WTO) was established. Rather than substituting the GATT, WTO incorporated it alongside new agreements on trade in services (GATS), Trade-Related Aspects of Intellectual Properties (TRIPs), and related measures (such as the Trade Related Investment Measures, TRIMs or the Agriculture Agreement, both under the GATT), annexes, decisions and understandings, in one formal international organization.[195]

The GATT Agreement of 1947 did apply to agricultural trade, but it allowed countries to use import quotas and export subsidies, in contrast to the regime governing industrial goods. As a result, trade in agriculture became highly distorted, as tariff reductions were practically transferred to non-tariff protective measures. Trade rules and further tariff reductions were negotiated again in subsequent "rounds" (see Table 4). In the Kennedy Round (1964-67), agricultural issues were considered for the first time as part of the total package of negotiations, but achievements were very limited; some tariff cuts and trade limitations were removed for non-basic items, and an arrangement about cereals was concluded. In the Tokyo Round (1973-79), negotiations on bovine meat and dairy products took place, but because they were not accepted by full GATT signatories, they were informally called "codes." Particularly the dairy code was never very effective since major exporting countries did not sign it. Both codes were terminated in 1997 and their issue areas included in the Agricultural Agreement of the Uruguay Round. Most important, an agreement on tropical products was reached, including reduction of import duties and other trade barriers.[196]

The Uruguay Round (1986-94) included for the first time substantial negotiations concerning agricultural products, including border and behind-the-border trade instruments. Together with the Agreement on Agriculture itself, the Agreement on Sanitary and Phytosanitary Standards and the Ministerial Decision concerning Least-Developed and Net Food-Importing Developing Countries provide a framework for a long-term reform of agricultural trade and domestic

[194] The 23 founding members were Australia, Belgium, Brazil, Burma, Canada, Ceylon, Chile, China, Cuba, Czechoslovakia, France, India, Lebanon, Luxemburg, Netherlands, New Zealand, Norway, Pakistan, Southern Rhodesia, Syria, South Africa, United Kingdom and the United States.

[195] See WTO, 2001.

[196] For details about the Kennedy Round, see Andrews, 1973, Ch.8.

policies. The Agreement on Textiles and Clothing also provided for the eventual elimination of the Multifibre Arrangement after a ten-year transition period. This change is attributed mainly to pressure on the part of the US, which was facing a growing deficit in its balance of agricultural goods, mainly vis-à-vis the EU. The prevailing idea was that despite lower competitiveness, domestic support for agriculture in the EU, as advanced by the Common Agricultural Policy (CAP) was distorting the market. US dissatisfaction gained support from other major agricultural exporting countries, in particular the members of the Cairns Group.[197] However, negotiations were extremely difficult, and at times risked the successful conclusion of the whole round. Many studies describe these negotiations in great detail, yet, for the purpose if this study it is enough to state that the main breakthrough was the Blair House Agreement, concluded on a bilateral basis between the US and the EU in November 1992. [198]

The specific commitments adopted in the Agreement on Agriculture were largely based on the Blair House agreement, with some modifications demanded by the French government, to the dissatisfaction of other countries, which saw the multilateral agreement being negotiated on a bilateral basis between the US and the EU. The most important final commitments are: a) regarding domestic support (production subsidies to agriculture) – minimum reduction of 20%, calculated with basis on the Aggregate Measure of Support (AMS), specified in Art.1 (a), 6 and Annex 3.; exceptions were provided to subsidies with no distorting effects, such as early retirement schemes (green box), and some specific cases, such as direct payment to farmers (blue box); b) export subsidies - reduction of 21% in terms of volume, and 36% in terms of total cash (modifying the operation of Art.XVI of the General Agreement which allows export subsidies on primary products); c)non-tariff border measures (such as import quotas, VERs and the EU variable import levy) – existing measures must be converted into tariffs (the so-called "tariffication"), according to calculation methods attached to Annex 5, and new measures were prohibited (modifying Art. XI:2 (c) of the General Agreement, which permitted quantitative restrictions on agricultural and fisheries products where necessary to the enforcement of the domestic marketing scheme). In addition, existing measures were to be reduced to the extent required to allow

---

[197] The Cairns Group was formed in 1986 at the initiative of the government of Australia to coordinate the members position's during the Uruguay Round. After the conclusion of the latter, the Group continued to work in the promotion and early implementation of the commitments, having submitted joint proposals to the new round of negotiations. The original members were Argentina, Australia, Brazil, Canada, Chile, Colombia, Fiji, Hungary, Indonesia, Malaysia, New Zeeland, Philippines, Thailand, and Uruguay. They were joined later by Paraguay (in 1997), Bolivia, South Africa, Costa Rica and Guatemala, although Fiji and Hungary left. For a discussion about the past and future prospects for the success of the Cairns Group as a coalition, see Vaillant & Nin, 2002. For details about its activities, see http://www.cairnsgroup.org.

[198] For details about negotiations, see Paarlberg, 1997; Patterson, 1997; Coleman & Tangermann, 1998; Gardner, 1996; Ackrill, 2000.

foreign producers a minimum of 3% market access for each product category, rising to 5% in the end of the 6th year; d) tariffs – all tariffs were to be bound (commitment not to increase (later) tariffs above the agreed level); all tariffs (including existing non-tariff border measures that have been converted to tariffs) were to be reduced by a simple average of 36% to developed countries and 24% to developing countries, with a minimum reduction of 15% and 10% respectively on each product category (tariff line), with the exception of those products for which special treatment had been negotiated.

All commitments of the Agriculture Agreement were to be achieved over a 6-year period for developed countries, with 1986-8 as the base period, and 10 years for developing countries; the least developed countries were exempted entirely. Apart from these commitments, one important provision of the Agreement on Agriculture was the special safeguard measure permitting imposition of an additional level of duty (but not re-imposition of non-tariff measures) when imports of a particular product exceeded a trigger level in a given year, or when the price of imports fell below a trigger price (trigger level and trigger price definition and calculations set in Art.5.5 (a)-(c). The agreement created a new instrument, the tariff rate quotas (TRQs), to guarantee minimum levels of market access in the face of higher MFN tariffs resulting from tariffication. TRQs work similarly as quotas, but instead of limiting the total amount of imports, they stipulate higher tariffs for imports above the stipulated amount (for details see section 6.1.4.1.2 below).[199]

Despite its achievements, the Agreement on Agriculture recognized its shortcomings implicitly in that it included in Art.20 a mandate for the initiation of further negotiations one year before the end of the implementation period, i.e., in 1999. Studies show that, as of 2002, the effect of the agreement upon the improvement of market access for agricultural commodities in OECD member countries has been actually insignificant.[200] Following the abortive attempt to launch a comprehensive round of global trade negotiations in Seattle in November 1999, the agricultural negotiations were formally initiated in January 2000.[201] When the new global round of negotiations was finally launched at the 2001 Ministerial Conference in Doha, Qatar, the negotiations on agriculture were incorporated in its agenda as part of the single final undertaking, seen as beneficial on account of it offering the use of cross-issue linkages to overcome

[199] Trebilcock & Howser, 1995, pp.57-63; Matthews & Laroche-Dupraz, 2002; EC DG Trade, 2003.

[200] For critical evaluation of the effects of the Agricultural Agreement, see Matthews, 2000b; Priyadaeshi, 2002; Orden et al, 2003; Bouzas & Svarzman, 2000.

[201] External NGO pressure, unresolved differences on the scope of the negotiations among member-states, mainly the US (which advanced a narrowly focused agenda) and the EU (who supported a more comprehensive agenda) as well as internal procedural WTO problems have been advanced as causes for the Seattle failure. Matthews, 2000a, p.3.

deadlocks. Since the agricultural negotiations within the Doha Round are not yet concluded (according to the mandate they must be finished before 1st January 2005), and as, in any case, they exceed the period of time under consideration in this study, they are not included in the analysis.

Regarding the other two agriculture-related agreements of the Uruguay Round, the Agreement on Sanitary and Phytosanitary Standards supplemented the Agreement on Technical Barriers to Trade (signed in the Tokyo Round and extended in the Uruguay Round), covering topics specific to agriculture. The agreement encourages members to base their measures on international standards, but allows them to maintain or introduce measures that result in higher standards when there is scientific justification, or as a consequence of consistent risk decisions based on appropriate risk assessment. Art.5.7 allows temporary measures when scientific evidence is insufficient and requires that additional information be sought. The WTO dispute-settlement panel rulings made an important contribution to the interpretation of this agreement. The panel on hormone treated beef, a case filed by the EU against imports from the US (WT/DS26), held with the US that the EU had failed to base its ban of imports on a scientific risk assessment, and ordered the EU to bring its domestic regulations to compliance with WTO law. The ruling, therefore, stipulated that the complainant must prove that a given technique is safe, instead of putting the burden of proof on the user of the new technique, which would be a much more exigent requirement. [202]

The Ministerial Decision Concerning Least-Developed and Net Food-Importing Developing Countries recognizes that despite increasing opportunities for trade expansion and economic growth to the benefit of all participants, generated by the progressive implementation of the results of the Uruguay Round, and the elimination of subsidies in developed countries and consequent decrease in their domestic production, might have negative effects in terms of availability of adequate supplies of basic foodstuffs from external sources on reasonable terms and conditions, including short-term difficulties in financing normal levels of commercial imports of basic foodstuffs (paragraphs 1, 2). As remedies, the Decision provides the increase of food aid commitments; technical and financial assistance to improve these countries' agricultural productivity and infrastructure, favorable treatment for agricultural export credits, access to the resources of the IMF and World Bank to assist during short-term difficulties in financing normal levels of commercial imports (Paragraphs 3,4,5). However, the Decision is not

---

[202] The international standards recognized by the Agreement are the ones advanced by the FAO/WHO Codex Alimentarius Commission (for food), the International Office of Epizootics (for animal health), and FAOs Secretariat of the International Plant Protection (for plant health). Governments can add other international organizations or agreements whose membership is open to all WTO members. For details about the beef case, and also the dispute about genetically modified foods (GMOs), see Matthews, 2000b, pp.13-15 and Pollack, 2002, pp.19-21.

legally binding, and has largely not been adhered to the Food Aid Convention in 1999 actually lowered the minimum guaranteed quantities that donors intend to provide. On export credits, no agreement has been reached on how assistance might be provided. As regards financial access, most countries were already benefiting from the IMF/World Bank special facilities, but no further increase was decided.[203] Here the diverging immediate interests of developing countries that are competitive exporters of agricultural products that expect to benefit from liberalization, such as the members of the Cairns Group (among them the Southern Cone States), and the countries primarily addressed in the Ministerial decision should be noted.

Table 46: GATT/WTO Instruments concerning agricultural trade

Place, Year	Instruments concerning agriculture
Geneva 1947	-tariffs
Annecy 1949	-tariffs
Torquay 1950-1951	-tariffs
Geneva 1956	-tariffs
Dillon Round 1960-62	-tariffs
Kennedy Round 1964-67	-tariffs -Arrangement on grains -Anti-Dumping Agreement -Arrangement covering cotton textiles in 1962 as an exception to GATT rules
Tokyo Round 1973-79	-tariffs -Arrangement on bovine meat -Arrangement on dairy products -Arrangement on tropical products exported by developing countries -Arrangement on textiles (Multifibre Arrangement – MFA)
Uruguay Round 1986-1994	-Agreement on Agriculture (market access, subsidies, domestic support) -Agreement on Sanitary and Phytosanitary Standards -Ministerial Decision Concerning Least-Developed and Net Food-Importing Developing Countries -Agreement on Textiles and Clothing
Doha Round 2002-(2005?)	-in process of negotiation

203 Matthews, 2000b, pp.12-13.

Source: compiled by the author

Apart from FAO and GATT/WTO, the United Nations Conference of Trade and Development (UNCTAD) has also addressed international cooperation in agricultural trade. Since its creation, in 1964, it has been the key developing-country forum for the formulation of principles and policies for development and trade, particularly in relation to agricultural goods. UNCTAD has often taken a critical position towards the activities and results achieved by both FAO and GATT, in particular their sectorial and technical approach, and towards the lack of priority in addressing the growing trade imbalances that disfavor developing countries. Some of its initiatives were the inclusion of Chapter IV in the GATT Agreement, entitled "Trade and Development," in 1965, the inclusion of a waiver to the MFN clause of the GATT favoring developing countries (enabling clause), in 1971, and the creation of the Integrated Programme for Commodities, in 1976.

The latter was proposed by UNCTAD in the context of the New International Economic Order (NIEO), with the main goal of promoting price stabilization. The two pillars of the programme were the conclusion of International Commodity Agreements (such as banana, bauxite, tropical woods, cocoa, coffee, rubber, cotton, copper, tin, hard fibers and jute, manganese, iron ore, phosphates, sugar, tea and meat), by which producer countries were assigned export quotas, with the global total of such quotas determined in such a way as to sustain world prices at an acceptable level, some of them including stabilization funds to purchase surplus productions at times of oversupply; and a System of Export Earnings Compensation that would provide loans or grants to countries facing a decline below a certain level due to supply and price fluctuations of commodity prices. Both initiatives were not very successful, due to internal coordination problems as well as lack of support from developed countries to create a Common Fund to finance the stabilization funds and the exports compensations loans. [204]

Chapter IV of the GATT essentially confers a "special and differential status" to developing countries, which are allowed to pursue certain protective measures and face longer periods of implementation of liberalizing measures. Despite the fact that most provisions of Chapter IV do not have a clearly binding or mandatory character, developing countries are encouraged to request consultations with individual developed countries or with the GATT Council when provisions are not complied with.[205]

---

[204] The NIEO was initially proposed in Resolution 3202 (S-VI) of the 6th Special Session of the UN General Assembly in May 1974, entitled Programme of Action for the Establishment of a New International Economic Order. About UNCTAD initiatives see FAO, 1979, p.193; Trebilcock & Howser, 1999, Ch.14; Calvert, 114-116.

[205] Trebilcock & Howser, 1999,p. 371.

The enabling clause was adopted by GATT members on 25 June 1971 (BISD 18S/24), originally for a period of 10 years, and subsequently renewed on 28 November 1979 for an indefinite period of time by the Decision on Differential and More Favorable Treatment Reciprocity and Fuller Participation of Developing Countries (L/4903). The clause created a legal framework for the Generalized System of Tariff Preferences, under which developed countries were authorized to establish individual Generalized Schemes of Tariff Preferences advancing non-reciprocal preferences towards developing countries. It is important to note that the enabling clause allowed for discrimination in favor of developing countries but no discrimination between them. This rule has created problems for the EU regarding the preferences accorded to ACP countries in the context of the Lome Conventions (see section 6.1.4.1.2). In 1994, WTO members agreed on an Understanding in Respect of Waivers, which explicitly states that requests for new waivers or extensions of existing waivers must describe the measures which the member proposes to take, the specific policy objectives and the reasons which prevent the member from achieving its politic objectives by measures consistent with its obligations under GATT 1994 (Art.1); it further stipulates that any waiver in effect on the date of effectiveness of the WTO Agreement shall terminate unless extended according to the procedures of Art.1 and Art.9 of the WTO Agreement (Art.2). The Understanding also explicitly encourages members to bring cases to the WTO dispute settlement (Art3.). The Understanding was complemented by the Decision on Waiver adopted on 06-15-1999, in which the MFN waivers are extended until 05-30-2009 to allow preferential treatment for products of the least-developed countries (as designated by the UN) on a generalized, non-reciprocal and non-discriminatory basis (Art.1,2). The Decision stipulated that the exceptional circumstances justifying the Waiver must be reviewed annually. In short, the new waiver regulations put Waiver use under closer scrutiny, restricted to the LDCs, which are classified according to technical criteria and not based on historical relationships, and in principle for a limited time.[206]

6.1.4) Agricultural trade in the EU foreign policy

6.1.4.1) Common commercial policy (CCP)

6.1.4.1.1) General features

[206] The enabling clause is also the legal basis for regional arrangements and the Global System of Trade Preferences (GSTP), by which developing countries exchange trade concessions among themselves. See EC DG Trade, 2003; WTO Homepage for original documents, and Trebilcock & Howse, 1999, Ch.14.

The common commercial policy is based on three main principles: a common external tariff, common trade agreements with third countries, and the uniform application of trade instruments across member-states. These principles are set out in Articles 131-134/TEU (ex 110-116/TEC). Art. 131 takes a liberal approach in that it states that the CCP should contribute to the common interest of the member states in promoting the harmonious development of international trade and the progressive suppression of restrictions to international exchanges as well as tariff reduction.

The scope and competences of the CCP are addressed in Art.133. However, since the article originally contained only an indicative list of component policies, it was actually left open to interpretation. In a series of cases and opinions, such as Commission v. Council (ERTA), Opinion 1/75 (OECD Local Cost Standard), Kramer and others (Fisheries), Opinion 1/76 (Rhine Navigation), Opinion 1/78 (International Rubber Agreement), Opinion 2/91 (ILO), Opinion 2/92 (OECD National Treatment Instrument), and Opinion 1/94 (Uruguay Round), the European Court of Justice (ECJ) clarified the scope and competences of the CCP. The two main effects of ECJ jurisprudence upon the scope and competences of the CCP consisted first of all, in the establishment of a parallelism between the internal development of the EU and its exclusive external competence, i.e., the doctrine of implied powers, as established in the 1971 ERTA case; and second, in the specification of component policies. While in most cases the ECJ is said to have taken a pro-integration position, i.e., increasing the exclusive competences of the Commission, in the Kramer case of 1976 and in Opinion 1/94 it favored the position of member-states vis-à-vis the Commission. The former excluded fisheries from the scope of CCP. The latter stipulated that the areas of intellectual property and trade in services (except for cross border services) remained under mixed competence. [207]

The trend towards limiting the exclusive competences of the Community was codified in the amendments to Art.133 made by the Treaties of Amsterdam and Nice (see Table 5). Although the general rule for trade in services and the commercial aspects of intellectual property remained under exclusive competence, Council unanimity came to be required. This unanimity requirement was also extended to fields in which the Community had not yet exercised its powers, and a list of exceptions was included, such as cultural and audiovisual services. [208]

Although Opinion 1/94 is seen as disfavoring the Commission, given the growing importance of trade in services vis-à-vis trade in goods, the fact remains that with respect to agricultural trade and the application of technical barriers to

[207] See Young, 2000, pp.102-105; Peterson & Bomberg, pp.90-91.

[208] Cremona, 2000, p.7 Meunier & Nicoladis, 2001, pp.7-8.

trade the Opinion confirmed the Community's exclusive competence. On agricultural trade agreements, the Opinion states "the fact that the commitments that became effective under that Agreement (on Agriculture) require internal measures to be adopted on the basis of Article 43 (new Art. 37) of the Treaty does not prevent the international commitments themselves from being entered pursuant to Article 113 alone." On the application of technical barriers to trade, the Opinion states that it was not concerned with the harmonization of standards (in which case it would fall into mixed competence given that complete harmonization in the area has not yet been achieved) but about avoiding unnecessary obstacles to international trade (in which case it falls within the scope of the CCP).[209]

Table 47: Art.133 (ex-113) and its amendments

1. ~~After the transitional period has ended, t~~The common commercial policy shall be based on uniform principles, particularly in regard to changes in tariff rates, the conclusion of tariff and trade agreements, the achievement of uniformity in measures of liberalization, export policy and measures to protect trade such as those to be taken in case of dumping or subsidies.
2. The Commission shall submit proposals to the Council for implementing the common commercial policy
3. Where agreements with ~~third countries~~ one or more States or international organizations need to be negotiated, the Commission shall make recommendations to the Council, which shall authorize the Commission to open the necessary negotiations. *The Council and the Commission shall be responsible for ensuring that the agreements negotiated are compatible with internal Community policies and rules.* The Commission shall conduct these negotiations in consultation with a special committee appointed by the Council to assist the Commission in this task and within the framework of such directives as the Council may issue to it. *The Commission shall report regularly to the special committee on the progress of negotiations.* The relevant provisions of Article 228 shall apply.
4. In exercising the powers conferred upon it by this Article, the Council shall act by a qualified majority.
*5.*The Council, acting unanimously on a proposal from the Commission and after consulting the European Parliament, may extend the application of paragraphs 1 to 4 to international negotiations and agreements on services and intellectual property insofar as they are not covered by these paragraphs. Paragraphs 1 to 4 shall also apply to the negotiation and conclusion of agreements in the field of trade in services and the commercial aspects of

209 Cremona, 2000, pp.9-10. Meunier & Nicoladis, 1999, pp.488-493.

intellectual property, insofar as those agreements are not covered by the said paragraphs and without prejudice to paragraph 6.

By way of derogation from paragraph 4, the Council shall act unanimously when negotiating and concluding and agreement in one of the fields referred to in the first subparagraph, where that agreement included provisions for which unanimity is required for the adoption of internal rules or where it relates to a field in which the Community has not yet exercised the powers conferred upon it by this Treaty by adopting internal rules.

The Council shall act unanimously with respect to the negotiation and conclusion of a horizontal agreement insofar as it also concerns the preceding subparagraph or the second subparagraph of paragraph 6.

This paragraph shall not affect the right of the Member States to maintain and conclude agreements with third countries or international organizations insofar as such agreements comply with Community law and other relevant international agreements.

6. An agreement may not be concluded by the Council if it includes provisions that could go beyond the Community's internal powers, in particular by leading to harmonization of the laws or regulations of the Member States in an area for which this Treaty rules out such harmonization.

In this regard, by way of derogation from the first subparagraph of paragraph 5, agreements relating to trade in cultural and audiovisual services, educational services, and social and human health services, shall fall within the shared competence of the Community and its Member States. Consequently, in addition to a Community decision taken in accordance with the relevant provisions of Article 300, the negotiation of such agreements shall require the common accord of the Member States. Agreements thus negotiated shall be concluded jointly by the Community and the Member States.

The negotiation and conclusion of international agreements in the field of transport shall continue to be governed by the provisions of Title V and Article 300.

7. Without prejudice to the first subparagraph of paragraph 6, the Council, acting unanimously on a proposal from the Commission and after consulting the European Parliament, may extend the application of paragraphs 1 to 4 to international negotiations and agreements on intellectual property insofar as they are not covered by paragraph 5.

Note: ~~strikethrough~~ and bold are alterations made by TEU
Paragraph 5 *(in italic)* was added by the Treaty of Amsterdam
~~Double-strikethrough~~ and *Italic* (except parag 5) are alterations of the Treaty of Nice

The process of decision-making in the trade area is also set out in Art. 133. The Commission has the power of initiative, as in other areas, elaborating proposals for the initiation and content of international trade negotiations. In the process of elaboration of proposals, the Commission is free to consult interest groups and other EU institutions such as the Parliament or the Economic and Social Committee. Once the proposal is concluded, it will be discussed in Committee 133, which is composed by senior civil servants and trade experts from the member-states and Commission representatives. The Committee examines and amends the proposal on a consensual basis and then transmits it to the Coreper. Coreper examines and amends the proposal as well and sends it on to the Council of General Affairs, which then hands out a negotiating mandate to the Commission. The mandate is agreed by qualified majority for most cases, and unanimity for services and intellectual property, as set out in the amendments to the Treaties of Amsterdam and Nice. Commission officials representing the Union under the authority of the designated Commissioner(s) conduct the international trade negotiations, within the limits set by the Council's mandate (note that even in negotiations involving issues of mixed competence the Commission represents the member-states during the negotiations). At the conclusion of the negotiations, the Council approves or rejects the trade agreement, by qualified majority or unanimity. The Parliament has no formal decision-making powers in the agreements concluded under Art.133, although it is normally consulted under the Luns-Westerterp procedure.[210]

Next to trade-only agreements, cooperation and association agreements concluded based on Art.300/TEU (ex-228) and Art.310/TEU (ex-238), respectively, often include trade (i.e. tariff) issues, such as the second and third generation agreements signed with the SCS. In such cases, the trade components of the agreements are negotiated according to the procedures of Art.133, but the total resulting agreement must follow the procedures set by Art.300 or Art.310. The main difference is that Council decisions regarding the mandate and final approval must be adopted by QMV or by unanimity, as stipulated in the Articles, and the Parliament has formal powers in that its assent is required.

Table 42: Art.300 (ex-228) and its amendments

1. Where this Treaty provides for the conclusion of agreements between the Community and one or more states or international organizations, ~~such agreement shall be negotiated by the Commission. Subject to the powers vested in the Commission in this field, such agreements shall be concluded by the Council, after consulting the Assembly where required by this Treaty.~~ ~~The Council, the Commission or a member state may obtain beforehand the opinion of the Court of Justice as to whether an agreement envisaged is compatible with the provisions of this Treaty. Where the opinion of the Court of~~

[210] Meunier & Nicoladis, 1999, p.480; Cremona, 2000, p.19; Woolcock, 2001, pp.378-387. About the Luns-Westerterp procedure see Chapter 4, p.

~~Justice is adverse, the agreement may enter into force only in accordance with Article 236.~~
the Commission shall make recommendations to the Council, which shall authorize the Commission to open the necessary recommendations. The Commission shall conduct these negotiations in consultation with special committees appointed by the Council to assist it in this task and within the framework of such directives as the Council may issue to it.

In exercising the powers conferred upon it by this paragraph, the Council shall act by a qualified majority, except in the cases *where the first subparagraph 2 provides that the Council shall act unanimously.* ~~provided for in the second sentence of paragraph 2, for which it shall act unanimously.~~

2. ~~Agreements concluded under these conditions shall be binding on the institutions of the Community and on Member States.~~ Subject to the powers vested in the Commission in this field, *the signing, which may be accompanied by a decision on provisional application before entry into force, and the conclusion of the agreements, shall be* decided ~~the agreements shall be~~ concluded by the Council, acting by a qualified majority on a proposal from the Commission. The Council shall act unanimously when the agreement covers a field for which unanimity is required for the adoption of internal rules, and for the agreements referred to in Article ~~238~~ *310.*

By way of derogation from the rules laid down in paragraph 3, the same procedures shall apply for a decision to suspend the application of an agreement, and for the purpose of establishing the positions to be adopted on behalf of the Community in a body set up by an agreement based on Article 310, when that body is called upon to adopt decisions having legal effects, with the exception of decisions supplementing or amending the institutional framework of the agreement.

The European Parliament shall be immediately and fully informed on any decision under this paragraph concerning the provisional application or the suspension of agreements, or the establishment of the Community position in a body set up by an agreement based on Article 310.

3. The Council shall conclude agreements after consulting the European Parliament, except for the agreements referred to in Article ~~113(3~~), *133(3)* including cases where the agreement covers a field for which the procedure referred to in Article ~~189b~~ *251* or that referred to in Article ~~189c~~ *252* is required for the adoption of internal rules. The European Parliament shall deliver its opinion within a time-limit that the Council may lay down according to the urgency of the matter. In the absence of an opinion within that time-limit, the Council may act.

By way of derogation from the previous subparagraph, agreements referred to in Article ~~238~~ *310*, other agreements establishing a specific institutional framework by organizing cooperation procedures, agreements having important budgetary

implications for the Community and agreements entailing amendment of an act adopted under the procedure referred to in Article ~~189b~~ *251* shall be concluded after the assent of the European Parliament has been obtained The Council and the European Parliament may, in an urgent situation, agree upon a time-limit for the assent
4. When concluding an agreement, the Council may, by way of derogation from paragraph 2, authorize the Commission to approve modifications on behalf of the Community where the agreement provides for them to be adopted by a simplified procedure or by a body set up by the agreement; it may attach specific conditions to such authorization.
5. When the Council envisages concluding an agreement which calls for amendments to this Treaty, the amendments must first be adopted in accordance with the procedure laid down in Article ~~N~~ *48* of the Treaty ~~of the~~ *on* European Union.
6. The European Parliament, the Council, the Commission or a Member State may obtain the opinion of the Court of Justice as to whether an agreement envisaged is compatible with the provisions of this Treaty. Where the opinion of the Court of Justice is adverse, the agreement may enter into force only in accordance with Article ~~N~~ *48* of the Treaty on European Union.
7. Agreements concluded under the conditions set out in this Article shall be binding on the institutions of the Community and on Member States.

Note: ~~strikethrough~~ and bold are alterations made by TEU
~~Double strikethrough~~ and *Italic* are alterations of the Treaty of Amsterdam
superscript was removed and underline added by the Treaty of Nice

Table 48: Art.310 (ex-238) and its amendments

1.The Community may conclude with a ~~Third State, a union of States~~ one or more States or ~~an~~ international organizations agreements establishing an association involving reciprocal rights and obligations, common actions and special procedure. ~~These agreements shall be concluded by the Council, acting unanimously after consulting the Assembly.~~ ~~Where such agreements call for amendments to this Treaty, these amendments shall first be adopted in accordance with the procedure laid down in Article 236.~~

Note: ~~strikethrough~~ and bold are alterations made by TEU

The secondary legislation regarding the CCP is the common rules for exports, and the common rules for imports. The common export regime was established by Regulation (EEC) No 2603/1969 (amended by Regulations 2603/69; 2604/69; 234/71; 1078/71; 2182/71; 1275/75; 1170/76; 1934/82; 3918/91) and is based on the principle of freedom of export, i.e., exports are not subject to quantitative restrictions (Art.1), with the objective of defining procedures enabling the Community to implement, where necessary, the surveillance and protective measures required. The regulation applies to all industrial and agricultural products covered by the EC Treaty, but regarding the latter it is complementary to the regulation establishing the common organization of agricultural markets and the special regulations for processed agricultural products (Preamble) - for the CAP, see section 6.1.4.2. Protective measures may be adopted by the Council (by QMV) upon proposal by the Commission in order to prevent or remedy a critical situation brought about by a shortage of essential products, or to allow international commitments entered into by the Community or all the member states to be fulfilled, in particular those relating to trade in primary products (Art6 & 7). Since its establishment, and in particular for the period from 1980 to 2000, legislation for the common export regime did not change much, and in the case of agricultural products, the Community has had exclusive competences to negotiate and implement agreements with 3rd parties.[211]

The common import regime, on the contrary, has been substantially modified since its establishment by Regulation (EEC) No 1439/74. It was amended by regulations 3279/75; 516/77; revoked by 926/79; which in turn was revoked by 288/82; revoked by 517/94 (covering textiles), 518/94 and 519/94 (covering Albania, CIS, North Korea, China, Mongolia and Vietnam). Regulation 3285/94, which so far has remained effective, revoked, in turn, regulation 518/94. It applies to all imports originating in 3rd countries, except cases covered by Regulations 517/94 and 519/94, and on a complementary basis the regulations on agricultural products covered by market organizations (see section 6.1.4.2 about the CAP below), being amended by regulations 139/96; 2315/96; 2474/2000. It is beyond the scope of this research to analyze all modifications to the common import regime of the EU. The relevant point is to note that major modifications reflect to a large extent the re-regulation of aspects of the import regime for which competences were transferred from member-states to the Community with the implementation of the Common Market, as stated in the Single European Act of 1986 (into force in 1992), and adaptation to new agreements signed under the GATT/WTO agreements.

A common feature of the regime for the period of 1980-2000 is that the general rule is free importation, though with three basic exceptions: safeguarding measures, which may be applied to imports that increase in such quantities and are made under such conditions as to cause or threaten to cause serious injury to Community industries, provided there is a Community interest to do so; surveillance measures for the system of automatic import licensing; and the imposition of quotas. In addition, imports can be affected by the application of

[211] EU Homepage, summaries of legislation, common rules for exports; and Regulation (EEC) No 2603/69.

measures against "unfair practices" from third countries, as stated in the Anti-dumping, Anti-subsidy, and Trade Barriers Regulations. These instruments are seen in detail below.[212]

6.1.4.1.2) Trade instruments

Countries, and for that purpose, common unions, have a number of instruments at their disposal to use in order to achieve economic or political goals. Trade instruments can be classified as traditional border (tariffs, quotas), traditional behind-the-border (on the active side, export and production subsidies, imports licensing, etc; and on the passive side, countervailing duties, anti-dumping, etc), and "new" behind-the-border (technical regulations and standards, rules of origin, competition policy).[213] Under the (liberal) international trade regime of the GATT/WTO, the use of trade instruments is regulated and restricted to particular cases. When a third country is found to promote unfair trade measures, i.e., contravenes against GATT/WTO norms, the affected country is allowed to apply measures to compensate this violation. The measures vary, but usually consist in the suspension of imports from the third country, imposition of import quotas or higher tariffs/duties. The GATT/WTO has rules defining what constitutes unfair trade and defines procedures on how to deal with it. These are reflected in the EU regulations, as seen above.

This section will analyze the instruments from the perspective of their cooperative effects upon the SCS agricultural exports. From this perspective, two categories of instruments may be distinguished; the first category is the CCP border instruments, basically tariffs and quotas. The higher the tariffs applied to the agricultural products exported by the SCS, the lower the level of cooperation; the lower the designated quota for SCS in a specific agricultural product, the lower the level of cooperation.

The second category of instruments are the CCP instruments against unfair practices in SCS exports (on account of, for example, benefits through production or export subsidies, or because their prices are dumped). In principle, these instruments should not have a political (cooperative) meaning, i.e., they should be

---

[212] EU Homepage, summaries of legislation, common rules for imports; and above mentioned regulations.

[213] Tariffs are defined here as a trade instrument, despite the fact that the CCP differentiates between the "common external tariff" and (other) "trade instruments". This differentiation was done because while the EU came to have a common external tariff when it became a custom union, uniform application of the (other) trade instruments remained under the competence of member-states until the completion of the Common Market, in 1992. The "new behind-the-border" instruments are in fact not new at all, the novelty being the acknowledgement that they can be used intentionally as protectionist barriers to trade, and for this reason were included in the Uruguay Round.

applied technically to the pertinent cases, and their use should be seen as an indicator of SCS uncooperative behavior, not of the EU's. However, it has been pointed out that in many cases these instruments have been used in a biased manner in order to find a perpetrator even when there is none. This has been done either by distortions in the procedures of the EU's internal regulations, or by simply not following them very closely.

a) Tariffs and the Pyramid of Preferences - the most traditional instrument of trade policy consists in tariffs applied to imported products. As a customs union, the EU has unified the tariffs of its member-states vis-à-vis 3rd countries, creating a common external tariff for each product. The importance of tariffs in EU trade policy has been declining; the average MFN tariff from non-agricultural products was as low as 4.4% in 1999. For "sensitive" products, such as electronics, chemicals, pharmaceuticals and agricultural goods, tariffs are higher, but the average MFN tariff for agricultural products also decreased from 26,7% in 1995 to 17,9% in 2000. Average MFN tariffs are not, however, a good indication of market access for specific products. Some of the most important products for SCS exports have to face tariff peaks, such as bovine meat (above 80%), grains (above 50%), sugar (above 65%) and fruits. Moreover, when summed up with equivalent tariffs, the final tariffs applied to some of these products have reached, reach for instance, 108% for bovine meat, 92,3% for rice, 60% for wheat flour, 48,7% for maize, 68% for refined cane sugar, 29% for oranges and 127% for bananas in 2000. [214]

A second feature of the EU tariff system is tariff escalation, where tariffs increase with the degree of processing of imported goods. Indicative calculations show that equivalent tariffs on SCSs exports in 2000 are 19% for raw materials, 14% for goods corresponding to first-level processing, 20% for second level, and 29% for third-level processing.[215] No data is available for previous periods, but the Uruguay Round, for instance, did not address it, so it probably did not change much proportionally over the period 1980 to 2000. This system stands accused of hampering the development of the food processing industry in agricultural export countries, a fact recognized by the Commission.[216]

A third feature of the EU tariff system is that tariffs are not applied equally for all third countries, despite the centrality of the MFN principle in the GATT/WTO agreements. The EU has concluded a number of preferential trade agreements with different countries and regions, in which lower tariffs are accorded, constituting what is referred to as the EU "pyramid of preferences," a reflection of its political priorities. In the period from 1980 to 2000 the most

---

214 Bureau, 2002, p.330.

215 Bureau, 2002, p.334.

216 EC/DG Trade, 2003b, p.4; Bouzas & Svarzman, 2000, pp.18-19; Howell et al, 1992, pp. 419-420; Vaillant, 2000, pp. 18-19.

beneficial treatment was accorded to ACP countries that are signatories of the Lome/Cotonou agreements (more than 80% of exports enter the EU with duty free on a non-reciprocal basis).[217] In second place were the countries that concluded free-trade agreements (a FTA must include a minimum of 80% of total exports with reciprocal duty free exports). In third place were the countries that benefited from specific non-reciprocal tariffs under the SGP (with an average of 54% of non-reciprocal duty free exports). Last, come the countries that were only subject to MFN, with an average of 20% of duty free access.[218]

Apart from beneficial treatment for some products under the SGP (see below), the SCS have mostly benefited from MFN tariffs, ranking, therefore, at the end of the pyramid of preferences. If the FTA negotiations with Mercosur in the context of the Association agreement succeed, it will represent an improvement in duty-free access to the EU market. In March 2003, the tariff offers of the EU reached 91% and of Mercosur 83, 5% of traded products (see chapter 2, p.24), including tariffs for agricultural products, but this agreement is not yet concluded.

b) Quotas and Tariff Rate Quotas (TRQs) - quotas are the second most traditional trade instrument; until 1993, they were used only at the national level in the EU, not by the Community, but the Uruguay Round prohibited its use shortly after; as a result, quotas were not used much as a trade instrument by the Community.

Despite the prohibition of quotas, the Uruguay Round continued to allow the use of the system of tariff rate quotas (TRQs), by which higher tariffs are to be

---

217 The preferences accorded to the ACP countries were originally allowed by the GATT 1947, as long as they remained equal or below the tariffs existing when it became effective (Art.1(2)). These tariffs were modified at the first Lome Convention in 1975, with basis on the waiver introduced in the GATT in 1971 (Art 25), which allowed the granting of new preferential treatment to developing countries. This clause however, requires that preferential access be extended to all developing countries. While this "non-conformity" was ignored for years, it was put under strain by the Understanding in Respect of Waivers signed in 1994 , and the panels brought to the WTO dispute settlement against the EU import regime for bananas (WT/DS16; 27; 105; 158). In the Decision on Waiver (WT/L/304), signed in 1999, and Decision on the ACP-EC Partnership Agreement (WT/MIN(01)/15), in 2001, an extension of the exclusive waiver to the ACP, was agreed effective until 2007. These negotiations were reflected in the reformulation of the EU policy towards the ACP, as stated in the Green Paper on the EU-ACP relations of 1996 and the Cotonou Agreement. The latter, concluded in 2000, replaced the Lome Conventions and instead of according trade preferences, provided for the conclusion of free-trade agreements with ACP subgroups. For further descriptive details and analysis of the effects of the Cotonou agreement and this shift of approach (often critical) see: Trebilcock & Howse, 1999, p.373-375; Holland, 2002, Ch.7&8; Döpcke, 2002; Dickson, 2000; Martenczuk, 2000.

218 In 2001, only nine WTO members were subject to exclusively MFN treatment by the EU in all product categories, although they accounted for 45.2% of EU's total imports in goods: Australia, Canada, Chinese Taipei, Hong Kong, China, Japan, Republic of Korea, New Zeeland, Singapore, and the United States. All other countries benefit from some sort of preferential treatment in at least one product. WTO, 2002, p.2.

paid on imports exceeding the "arranged volumes." TRQs were indirectly introduced in Art.4, which specifies that "market access concessions contained in the Schedules relate to bindings and reductions or tariffs *and to other market access commitments as specified therein*" (italics added). These other market access commitments were set out in the Agreement on Modalities for establishment under the Reform Programme, and were never formally adopted, remaining as suggestions or guidelines for the determination and management of TRQs. They explicitly state that TRQs should be introduced on an MFN basis, but this has not been general practice. Art.XIII of the GATT Agreement also sets out rules to govern the administration of TRQs. [219]

The EU established 85 TRQs for agricultural products in its Schedule as a result from the Uruguay Round, and more were added later. It distinguished in its notifications to the WTO between current access (44), intended to safeguard historical quantities imported under special arrangements, minimum access quotas (36), opened to meet minimum access obligations required by the Agriculture Agreement, and non-tarified product quotas (6), opened for products that did not have to undergo tariffication. Four products stand out with respect to the importance of their TRQs in terms of the volume of imports covered: manioc, arrowroot and sweet potatoes (benefiting Thailand and Indonesia); maize (benefiting the US); bananas (benefiting ACP); and sugar (benefiting ACP countries and India). Other products where sizeable TRQs have been opened include meats, a few dairy products, eggs, fruits and vegetables, and cereals. In 2001, 14% of the EU's agricultural imports from developing countries were subject to TRQs, although the fill rate (weighted by value) was 76%, sugar, dairy products and fruits and vegetables being above the average.[220]

TRQs have been held to perpetuate the quota system given the prohibitive out-quota tariffs, and, thus, inhibiting market access to newcomers, even if they are by definition temporary, as their value will be eroded by successive rounds of MFN tariff reductions. Moreover, in the case of the EU, the current access quotas are used to maintain previously existing preferential access arrangements, reproducing the pyramid of preferences and disfavoring countries at the pyramid bottom, such as the SCS.[221]

c) Anti-Dumping - dumping occurs when the price of a product exported from one country is less than the comparable price in the ordinary course of trade for the same product when destined for domestic consumption, or less than the cost of production plus reasonable addition for selling costs and profits. The GATT 1947 Agreement (Art.6), clarified and expanded by the Code on Anti-

---

[219] Matthews & Laroche-Dupraz, 2002, pp.15-16.
[220] Matthews & Laroche-Dupraz, 2002, p.19.
[221] See Trebilcock & Howser, 1995, pp.57-63; Matthews & Laroche-Dupraz, 2002; EU DG Trade Homepage, trade policy instruments (September 2002).

Dumping Measures of the Tokyo Round, and the WTO Anti-Dumping Agreement, allows the use of anti-dumping corrective measures, such as charging duties corresponding to the differential between the fair and unfair price, when it is evidenced that the dumping negatively affects producers of the importer country.

The EU introduced a unified anti-dumping regulation in 1968 (EC 459/68) to replace the previously disparate national regimes, which was subsequently reviewed a number of times at EU's initiative, or to conform to new GATT/WTO rules. It was amended by Regulation 1681/79, which was revoked by 3017/79, amended by 1580/82, revoked by 2176/84, amended by 1761/87, and revoked by 2423/88, 3283/94, and 384/96. The current EU provisions, as stated in the Basic Regulation on Anti-Dumping (EC 384/96), require three main tests to apply anti-dumping measures: evidence of dumping, injury, or threat of injury to an EU industry, and demonstration that the imposition of anti-dumping duties would be in the interest of the EU. The Commission decides whether the EU initiates an investigation in response to complaints by or on behalf of an EU industry (which must represent 50% of the sector concerned), although member-states are consulted via an Advisory Committee, chaired by the Commission. It is also the Commission who evaluates whether the case requires anti-dumping measures (in most countries the decision to open a process and the evaluation are done by separate agencies), although it conducts hearings and sends out questionnaires to survey the preferences of the industry. Finally, it is also the Commission which determines which remedies will be used, mostly duties or price initiatives. The Commission has the power to impose provisional anti-dumping measures, which stand for 6 months, with a possible extension to 9 months (unless the Council decides by QMV to reverse the Commission's decision). However, in order to impose definitive action (which can last 5 years) the case must be discussed in Coreper, and approved by the Council of Ministers by simple majority vote (until the Uruguay round its was QMV).[222]

As noted before, anti-dumping is considered a legitimate instrument to be used against unfair trade practices on the part of the exporter. However, it has been pointed out that the EU has often used it as a means to protect the domestic market from external competition, by the use of legal interpretations that bias the calculations in favor of finding dumping. From 1980 to 1990, out of 430 proceedings initiated, 129 (30%) were terminated without protective measures, an unusually high proportion of cases accepted. From 1990 to 1997, this proportion decreased to about 20% (about 55 cases out of 271). Considering the whole period from 1980 to 1997, most cases were against industries from Eastern Europe (28%), Asian Tigers (11%), China (11%), Japan (8%) and the US (5%). Other developing countries accounted for 21%. In terms of the issue area, most cases

[222] Woolcock, 2001, pp. 389-391; Bourgeois & Messerlin, 1998, pp.127-133.

were in chemicals, iron, steel and machinery; and only two cases concerned agricultural products. Criticism of this practice has come from member-states such as the UK, Germany and the Netherlands, who feared the negative effects that the distorted use of anti-dumping could have on inward FDI, and from the 3rd countries themselves, particularly Japan and East Asia during the 1980s. Some of these cases were submitted to dispute settlement in the GATT/WTO, but often a diplomatic solution was attempted.[223]

d) Anti-subsidy - not all types of subsidies are prohibited by the GATT agreements. A country is allowed to apply countervailing duties to offset subsidies from third parties only if the subsidies fall into the categories stipulated in the Tokyo Round Subsidy Code, and after the Uruguay Round, the WTO Subsidy Agreement. The latter defined three categories of subsidies, which apply to both industrial and agricultural goods (except when complying with the Agriculture Agreement), and cover both export and domestic subsidies: a) subsidies that require recipients to meet certain export targets, or to use domestic goods instead of imported goods, are prohibited; b) actionable subsidies for which the complaining country has to show that the subsidy has an adverse effect on its interests; c) non-actionable subsidies, such as those for industrial research, pre-competitive development activity, assistance to disadvantaged regions, adaptation to new environmental regulations, etc.

The first EU common rules for anti-subsidies were established together with the rules against dumping by Regulation 2176/84. After the Uruguay Round, it came to be addressed specifically by the Regulation concerning protection against subsidized imports, which became effective on January 1st, 1995. The Regulation only concerns imports from outside the EU, providing for the imposition of countervailing duties on goods that have been subsidized by the governments of non-EU countries. Three conditions must be met before countervailing duties can be imposed: the subsidy must be specific (it must be an export subsidy, or a subsidy limited to a company, an industry or a group of companies or industries); it must cause material injury to a Community industry (the import sales must have caused or threatened to cause damage to a substantial part of the industry within the EC, such as loss of market share, reduced prices for producers and resulting pressure on production, sales, profits, productivity, etc), and it must be in the interest of the Community (the costs for the Community of taking measures must not be disproportionate to the benefits). As with anti-dumping action, the Commission conducts the investigation, and imposes provisional and definitive measures in the coal and steel sectors, while in other areas such measures must be approved by the Council of Ministers. Complaint

[223] Hindley, 1992, pp. 89-96; Howell et al, 1992, pp. 414-416; Bourgeois & Messerlin, 1998, pp.134-137.

and investigation procedures are similar to those governing Anti-dumping actions.[224]

e) Technical regulations and standards - the EU addresses these issues in the Trade Barrier Regulation (EC 3286/94) and its predecessor the New Commercial Policy Instrument (EC 2641/84). These regulations cover a range of trade barriers, such as standards, rules of origin, and competition policy and apply to goods, services not involving the relocation of persons, and intellectual property rights where the violation of an international right has an impact on trade between the EU and a 3rd country. The TBR substituted the NCPI by request of some member-states, particularly France, who complained about the lack of efficiency of the latter resulting from the requirement of QMV in the Council for final approval. The TBR, instead, requires only simple majority, and contains two new additional elements, covering the so-called non-violation cases of GATT/WTO (cases that are not illegal but nevertheless harmful) and allowing for individual firms to request the initiation of investigations by the Commission, next to entire industries and member-states.

Some aspects covered by the TBR, such as technical standards, were already addressed in the Tokyo Round with the signature of a Code on Technical Barriers to Trade. The code was expanded in the WTO Technical Barriers to Trade Agreement, and the Sanitary and Phytosanitary Agreement to specific issues regarding agricultural products. With regard to rules of origin the first ever agreement on the subject at the multilateral level was the WTO Agreement on Rules of Origin. It requires members to ensure that their rules are transparent, do not distort or disrupt trade, and set the long-term goal of common "harmonized" rules of origin among WTO members, with a few specific exceptions. The importance of the rules of origin is that they set the criteria used to define where a product was made. While in the case of manufactured goods assembled with parts that may have been produced in many countries it may be used as a protective measure, in the case of agricultural products it is less relevant.

The Commission is mainly responsible for deciding and implementing TBRs. Within 45 days after the filing of a complaint, the Commission rules on its admissibility, after consulting member-states. If it is held admissible, an investigation is formally initiated and announced in the Official Journal. The Commission has then up to 7 months to consider the case, after which it can either terminate the procedure (if the 3rd country voluntarily takes steps to eliminate the adverse effects of injury in question), suspend it (if the 3rd country agrees to seek an amicable solution, such as to conclude a new agreement), or to initiate an international (WTO or other) dispute settlement against the 3rd country (after consultation with the Article 133 Committee). If the case goes to the WTO and the third party fails to comply with the panel decision, the TBR provides a basis

---

[224] EU Homepage, DG Trade, Trade policy instruments, Anti-Subsidy (April 2000).

for imposing retaliatory measures, such as sanctions, against the third country, subject to approval by QMV in the Council. The Commission may also propose retaliatory action in cases where there is no dispute-settlement machinery. As in the case of anti-dumping, the EU has been accused of using technical regulations and standards with protectionist purposes, to compensate tariff reduction in the GATT/WTO rounds.[225]

f) Safeguard measures - the GATT Agreement allows countries to restrict imports of a product temporarily by means of, for example, import quotas (Art.19), if its domestic industry is seriously injured or threatened due to a surge in imports. Such measures have rarely been used, in most cases governments have preferred to persuade the accused country to "voluntarily" restrain its exports. The WTO agreement on Safeguard Measures prohibited these "gray measures" arrangements and set time limits (a sunset clause) for all safeguard actions. Bilateral measures not modified to conform to the agreement were phased out at the end of 1998. Countries were allowed to keep one of these measures an extra year (until the end of 1999), with the EU being the only one exercise this option with respect to its restrictions on imports of cars from Japan. If, after investigation, a case of improper safeguard measures is found, the country who is restricting the imports must theoretically give something in return to the exporter, i.e., compensation. If both parts do not reach an agreement, the exporter can retaliate by taking equivalent action. Developing countries are to some extent shielded from safeguard measures, since their exports can be restricted only if they correspond to more than 3% of the imports of the specific product, or 9% together with other developing countries.

Safeguard measures are included in the Regulations on the common regime of imports (since 1980): 288/82 (Title V, Arts.15-18), 518/94 (Title V, Arts.14-17) and 3285/94 (Title V, Arts.16-22). They may be applied to imports that increase in such quantities and are made under such conditions as to cause or threaten to cause serious injury to the Community industry, provided that there is a Community interest to do so. At the request of a member-state or at the Commission's initiative, an investigation may be initiated based on which measures should be applied on a case-by-case basis.

g) Surveillance of import licensing - the WTO negotiated an Agreement on Import Licensing, expanding from the Tokyo Round code on the issue, which requires that governments improve information, transparency and efficiency in the concession of import licenses, not taking more that 30 days to deal with an application. As for the case of safeguards, procedures to adopt surveillance of import licensing are included in the regulation on the common import regime (since 1980): 288/82 (Title IV, Arts.10-14), 518/94 (Title IV, Arts.9-13) and 3285/94 (Title IV, Arts.11-15). Where the trend in imports of a product

[225] EC Regulation 3286/94; Woolcock, 2001, pp.391-393.

originating in a 3rd country threatens to cause injury to Community producers, and where the interests of the Community so require, imports of that product may be subject to retrospective or prior Community surveillance, for a maximum period of six months. Products under prior surveillance may be put into free circulation only upon presenting an import document, which must be endorsed by the competent authority designated by member states, free of charge, for any quantity requested and within a maximum of five working days of receipt by the competent national authority of a declaration from any Community importer.

6.1.4.2) Common agricultural policy (CAP)

The common agricultural policy is not, strictly speaking, part of EU foreign policy. It has, however, a direct impact upon EU agricultural trade, insofar as it complements regulations concerning common import and common export regimes of the EU. Its instruments, such as export and production subsidies, affect world prices and the demand for agricultural products, especially dairy products, cereals, sugar, and bovine meat, with the last three being of particular importance for SCS exports. The higher the protective CAP measures, the lower internal prices drop, and lower the demand for SCS exports. Before analyzing CAP effects upon the SCSs exports, this section provides a brief historical background of the CAP and its reforms.

The common agriculture policy (CAP) was established by Articles 38-47 of the Treaty of Rome. Art. 39 (1) set out the objectives of CAP, notably to increase agricultural productivity though the promotion of technical progress and the optimum utilization of factors of production, especially labor, to ensure a fair standard of living for the agricultural community, in particular by increasing individual earnings for those engaged in agriculture, to stabilize markets, to assure the availability of supplies, and to ensure that supplies reach consumers at reasonable prices. Art.43 (1) requested the Commission to hold a member-state conference to compare member states' agricultural policies, as well as their resources and needs, which took place in Stresa, Italy in July 1958.

After Stresa, a special committee chaired by the first commissioner for agriculture, the Dutchman Sicco Mansholt, was established to study how to create a common domestic market and, as a necessary consequence, a common trade policy vis-à-vis 3rd countries in this area. In 1962, the committee established a special agency to control and supervise the flows of trade in agriculture in order to set rules and regulations. The original idea was to use three instruments: variable import levies for products such as wheat, coarse grains, sugar and dairy products; import quotas for live cattle; and quality control for fruits, vegetables, and wine. In emergencies, special purchases, intervention levies, and destruction of surplus would be used to maintain desired prices in the internal market. The prices for each product were to be decided every year by the Council of Agriculture.

The first price policy was announced in 1964, establishing common prices for grains, pigs, poultry, and dairy products. Yet, the Agriculture Council approved the agreements only in 1967, after controversial discussions among member-states, mainly between Germany and France. Once implemented, the system effectively isolated the internal market from international competition. This fact, combined with the general economic growth of member-states, and the increase of productivity due to technical improvements, led to a rapid transformation of the EU from net importer of agricultural products to exporter. Moreover, the overproduction led to the accumulation of surpluses. Shortly after the system began to work, it became clear that reforms had to be implemented in order to equilibrate the market and contain the increasing costs for the EU. In 1968, Mansholt proposed a plan (Agriculture 1980) in which the emphasis lay on moving away from price support towards structural reforms. However, the plan was rejected, especially by Germany, and supported by the Community Farming Pressure Group (COPA). The modified version, proposed in 1969, known as the Mini Mansholt Plan, was approved by the Council in March of 1971, parallel to a demonstration that gathered more than 80.000 farmers in Brussels, but was never implemented, on account of poor harvests and an increase in world prices in 1973-4, which took off some of the pressure for reform.[226]

This situation remained the same until the 1980s, when the distorting effects of CAP were felt by EU's main trading partner in agricultural products, the United States. The US did also have protective domestic agricultural policies, but in face of its increasing deficit, and in combination with the perception that American agriculture was actually more competitive than EU's, it reverted its position and decided to pursue a unilateral and multilateral liberalization strategy. At the unilateral level, measures such as the 1985 Farm Bill, reducing subsidies by 20%, and the 1990 Budget Reconciliation Act were implemented. At the multilateral level, as seen above, the US applied pressure to include broad liberalization in agricultural products in the agenda of the Uruguay Round.

On the part of the EU, the first sign of change towards reforms was the establishment of dairy quotas approved by the Agriculture Council in March 1984, and the establishment of budget stabilizers approved by the European Council in February 1988 as part of a group of measures to contain the increasing misbalance of the EU budget.[227] In July 1991, agriculture commissioner Ray Mac Sherry issued a package of reform proposals based on Commission communications' COM (91) 100 & COM (91) 258/3. This proposal was quite radical, and in light of both the internal (costs) and external pressures (US,

[226] For more details about the historical developments of CAP see George, 1996, pp.172-193; Howarth, 1992; Marsh, 1997; Andrews, 1973, pp.12-24; Ackrill, 2000; Grant, 1997, Ch3.

[227] For details about both measures and the political dynamics of their adoption see Moyer & Josling, 1990, pp.66-99 & Ackrill, 2000, pp.85-92.

Uruguay Round) was approved by the Council in May 1992. The reform covered about 75% of the EU agricultural production, including cereals, oilseeds, protein crops, tobacco, milk, beef and sheep meet, and its main feature was the partial switch from support based on high prices to support based on direct payments to farmers (partial because prices, although lower, remained above world levels for most cases). This shift implied a move away from prices and market guidance towards an income policy, and a transfer of the financial support from consumers to taxpayers. [228]

In 1997, the agriculture commissioner Franz Fischler proposed a new major reform to the CAP, as part of the Commission's Agenda 2000 budget package to prepare for EU enlargement. Although the major concern was to accommodate CEE countries, the reform must be seen in the context of the necessity of addressing the shortcomings of the reform of 1992 (budgetary pressure even in the absence of enlargement), and the expected pressures from future negotiations within the WTO. The reforms were adopted by the Berlin Council in 1999, including an extension of the price cuts advanced by the 1992 reform to the sectors of cereals and bovine meat, new price cuts in the sectors of dairy products, olive oil and wine, and progressive replacement of price support by income support. The reforms can potentially result in greater market access for the SCS, but since their implementation exceeds the period of time relevant to the present study, it will not be analyzed in detail.[229]

Many studies attempt to explain the causality between the EU's liberalization of agricultural policies (CAP reforms) and the GATT/WTO rounds, with different findings.[230] For the purposes of this study, the important point is to note that since the end of 1980s the EU trade policy for agricultural products has changed significantly as a result of both the GATT/WTO agricultural negotiations and the CAP reforms. From 1992 to 2001, EU exports subsidies decreased from 25% to 5,2% concerning farm exports; which had a positive effect on the SCS, since about 19% of export subsides in 1994 were for bovine meat and 17% for wheat, two products where SCS are competitive. As regards domestic subsidies, the achievements were not as significant. The EU justifies the maintenance of domestic farm support as a political choice based on the "multifunctionality" of agriculture.[231] It recognizes that the elimination of domestic support would favor

---

[228] For content and political dynamics underlying the MacSherry Reform, see Ackril, 2000, pp.92-107.

[229] See Akcrill, 2000, Ch4; EP 1999.

[230] For the case of the 1992 reforms and the Uruguay Round, see Paarlberg, 1997; Patterson, 1997; Coleman & Tangermann, 1998; Gardner, 1996; Ackrill, 2000.

[231] The "multifunctionality" of agriculture is a concept that attributes to agriculture a number of functions apart from the production of food and fibers, such as the protection of environment, preservation of landscapes and rural employment. In other words, agriculture is seen as producing both commodity, and non-commodity outputs, and some of the non-commodity ones are

some developing countries such as Argentina and Brazil, but that their gains would come at the cost of greater food insecurity and rural deprivation in many other developing and developed countries.[232]

6.1.4.3) Developmental policy

Since the general features of EU developmental policy were already examined in section 5.1.4.4, in this section only the specific programmes concerning agriculture are described. Two programmes are of particular interest, the System of Generalized Preferences (SGP), and the programmes relating to cooperation in the area of technical norms and standards, and animal and vegetable health.

The EU's Scheme of Generalized Preferences (SGP) was created in 1971 based on the GATT enabling clause of the same year.[233] It has been renewed a number of times to accommodate changes at the development level of benefiting countries and the level of competitiveness of their specific sectors (countries which "graduate" to higher stages of development, or to higher levels of competitiveness of the specific product are excluded from the GSP), as well as changes in relevant GATT/WTO provisions. The original scheme was renewed in 1980. In 1994 a new regulation was issued (No.3281/94) for 1995-1998, which was replaced by regulation No.2820/98 for 1999-2001, and No.2501/2001 for 2002-2004. Agricultural products were included since 1996 as stated in the EC regulation 1256/96 for 1996-1999. The products and countries benefiting from GSP are listed in the annexes of the regulations. While the SGP originally addressed only developing countries in general, it later included other specific arrangements, such as special incentives for protection of labor rights; protection of the environment; and anti drug production and trafficking measures. In 2002, the Initiative Everything but Arms was created to favor least developed countries (LDCs). Each arrangement of the scheme must benefit all developing countries covered by the specifications. Different products are covered by each category, and different categories may grant different tariff preferences for the same product. Until 1995, the preferences were implemented in the form of quotas and ceilings for the beneficiary countries and products. Since then, given the prohibition of the use of quotas as a result of the Uruguay Round, preferences are

---

considered positive externalities, or public goods. Such broad definition of agriculture implies restrictions in the liberalization of agriculture, as advanced by the GATT/WTO, and is often accused of masking protectionist intentions. It has been addressed as the "Lampedusa effect", in reference to the famous statement in the novel "The Leopard", from Tomasi di Lampedusa, "if we want that everything continues to be the same, it is necessary that everything changes". Laurent, 2000, p.50.

232 EC/DG Trade, 2003b, pp.7-8, WTO, 1994, p.25; Laurent, 2000.

233 See section 6.1.3 p.162.

implemented via reduction of the MFN tariffs. Where the MFN is zero, it becomes impossible to grant preferences for the product.[234]

The SCS have been addressed in the general scheme since 1971, but agricultural products (with the exception of a few processed products) were not covered until 1996. The SCSs initially benefited from this scheme, but Argentina, Brazil, and Uruguay were excluded in 1999, as they had "graduated" in a number of product categories such as meat and dairy products in the case of Argentina; meat, coffee, and tobacco in the case of Brazil, and meat in the case of Uruguay. Regulation 2501/2001 removed further tariff preferences of Argentina and Brazil.[235]

The projects on technical standards, and animal and vegetable health, were advanced in the 1992 Agreement with Mercosur, and they were also supported in the MEBF Business Facilitation Measures. The latter was initiated in 1993 and focused on the eradication of foot-and-mouth disease, which has affected the export of meat from the SCS to the EU. The former was initiated in 1994 and aimed at improving the level of harmonization between the EU and SCS technical standards. Both types of programmes contribute directly to the increase of trade by lifting barriers to trade as a result of increased compatibility between regulatory systems, and indirectly by decreasing the probability that such instruments were used distortedly. Since the establishment of the Common Market, the EU promotes the transfer of knowledge and best practices in the area of technical standards to third countries. Once such countries achieve compatible regulatory systems, they can sign mutual recognition agreements (which apply to one or more categories of products), but this was not the case with the SCS, at least until the end of 2000.[236]

6.1.5) The level of cooperation of EU foreign policy

Following, the level of cooperation of each policy instrument regarding agricultural trade will be analyzed: the EU common commercial policy, the common agricultural policy, and the developmental policy. However, it is important to note that, until the completion of the Single European Market in 1992 (initiated in 1985), a number of trade instruments, such as quotas and technical barriers to trade were under the competence of member states. In terms of trade relations, until 1992, the EU was a customs union, with a common external tariff system under exclusive competence of the Community, but without a full common import and export regime, in terms of internal regulations. Only

---

[234] See EC/DG Trade 2003a and original regulations. For the definition of developing countries, see section 5.1.4.2.1, p.105).

[235] Regulation EC No.2820/98 Annex II Part I; Regulation 2501/2001 Annex I.

[236] See EU DG External Relations homepage: description des projects de cooperation UE-Mercosur and EC-DG Enterprise, 2000, pp.62-65.

with the harmonization of its "domestic" trade regulations, trade instruments other than tariffs were progressively transferred to the EU level. Therefore, only the instruments that have remained under the competence of the Community throughout the whole period of observation will be considered as indicators, i.e. tariff instruments (common external tariff and preferential tariffs), anti-dumping, and subsidies in the context of the Common Agricultural Policy, so as to avoid distortions.[237]

As regards tariffs, despite the general decrease of MFN average tariffs for agricultural products resulting from the Uruguay Round, the most important products for the SCS are subject to tariff peaks. The general behavior of the EU during the Uruguay Round cannot be defined as cooperative vis-à-vis the SCS (represented in the Cairns Group). The EU was reluctant to liberalize agricultural trade during the negotiations, and the resulting texts reflected the bilateral negotiations with the US. The SCS considered the Uruguay Round a success only to the extent that it represented an opportunity to rewrite the rules governing agricultural trade, rather than achieving a substantial reduction in protection. As regards the SGP, preferential tariffs to agricultural products were included only in 1996, but some were excluded again in 1999. The launching of negotiations with Mercosur for the conclusion of an FTA that included agricultural products, in 1999, can be said to represent a clear step towards more cooperation. A definitive evaluation of this initiative can only take place after the end of the negotiations, when the specific commitments are known. So far, it has been pointed out that, despite the fact that EU's liberalization offer has reached 91,5% of the products exported by Mercosur, it does not include some of the products in which the SCS are most competitive, such as meat, sugar, soy oil, tobacco and processed products, which remain the most protected sectors within the EU.[238]

As seen above, a decrease of the use of anti-dumping measures against the SCSs is considered as an indicator of improvement of cooperation. In terms of the complaints of the EU, only "abusive" complaints should be taken into consideration as an indicator of (un)cooperative behavior, since in the case of legitimate complaints against unfair trade practices on part of the SCS the EU would be merely exercising its rights. Determining which complaints are abusive requires a deep knowledge of all cases and their technicalities. Since this data was not available, a second best option would be to look at the number of successful cases brought by the SCS against the use of anti-dumping measures on the part of

---

[237] Interestingly enough, despite its enormous effect on extra-EU trade, the Single European Act contained only one mention of the rest of the world; "the Community's trading partners will not be offered the benefits from the enlarged Community market without themselves being forced to make concessions" (Art.??) , and treated the entire initiative as a purely European concern. See Page, 2002, p.130-131; Torrent, 2002, p.216.
[238] See Folha de Sao Paulo, Editorial, 22/03/2003.

the EU. A decrease in the number of successful cases by the SCSs indicates an increase in cooperation on the part of the EU. As is seen in the following table, there was only one case brought against the use of anti-dumping measures by the EU in 1994 for agricultural products, but such use was found to be legitimate. This indicator can be interpreted as a sign that the EU did not use the imposition of anti-dumping measures in a distorted way in the case of agricultural products. The analysis of non-agricultural products also supports this argument.

Table 49: Trade disputes between the EU and the SCS brought to GATT (adopted panels) /WTO (adopted panels and disputes going on) dispute-settlement mechanisms

Complainant	Respondent	Date *1	Code and dispute
Uruguay #	*2	02-1962 (16-11-1962)	BISD 11S/95; BISD13S/35 & BISD13S/45 Restrictive measures concerning temperate primary products such as wheat, rice, and bovine meat
Brazil	ECs #	10-11-1978 (10-11-1980)	BISD27S/69 ECs export refunds for sugar
EEC #	Brazil	23-12-1992 (28-04-1994)	SCM/179 Countervailing duties on milk powder and certain types of milk
Brazil	EC #	05-04-1994 (12-06-1995)	BISD Anti-dumping duties on imports of cotton yarn
Uruguay	EC	17-01-1996 (request for consultation)	WT/DS25 Implementation of Uruguay Round commitments concerning rice
Brazil #	EC	12-06-1997 (13-07-1998)	WT/DS69 Measures affecting importation of certain poultry products
EC	Argentina	15-09-1997 (suspended in 29-07-1998)	WT/DS77 Measures affecting textiles, clothing and footwear
EC	Brazil	20-05-1997 (request for consultation)	WT/DS81 Measures affecting trade and investment in the automotive sector
EC	Brazil	13-01-1998 (request for consultation)	WT/DS116 Measures affecting payment terms of imports
EC #	Argentina	11-06-1998	WT/DS121 Safeguard measures on

		(14-12-1999)	imports of footwear
EC	Argentina	In consultation since 29-09-1998	WT/DS145 Countervailing duties on imports of wheat gluten
Brazil	EC	11-12-1998 (request for consultations)	WT/DS154 Measures affecting differential and favorable treatment of coffee
EC #	Argentina	04-06-1999 (16-02-2001)	WT/DS155 Measures on the export of bovine hides and the import of finished leather
EC	Argentina	In consultation since 14-01-1999	WT/DS157 Anti-dumping measures on imports of drill bits from Italy
EC	Brazil	In consultation since 14-10-1999	WT/DS183 Measures on import licensing and minimum import prices for textiles, sorbitol and carboxymethylcallulose, etc.
EC #	Argentina	06-11-2000 (28-09-2001)	WT/DS189 Anti-dumping measures on ceramic floor tiles from Italy
Brazil	EC	12-10-2000 (request for consultation)	WT/DS209 Measures applied under the EC's GSP scheme affecting soluble coffee
Brazil	EC #	07-06-2001 (07-03-2003)	WT/DS219 Anti-dumping duties on malleable cast iron tube or pipe fittings
Argentina	EC	In consultation since 04-09-2002	WT/DS263 Measures affecting imports of wine
Brazil	EC	In consultation since 27-09-2002	WT/DS266 Export subsidies in sugar
Brazil	EC	In consultation since 11-10-2002	WT/DS269 Customs classification of frozen boneless chicken

Source: compiled by author with data from WTO & EC/DG Trade Homepages.

# indicates who won the panel. When not indicated, the panel is not yet finished

*1 If not indicated otherwise, date of establishment of panel and (data of panel /appellate body report)

*2 Austria, *Belgium*, Canada, Czechoslovakia, Denmark, Finland, *France, Germany*, *Italy,* Japan, *Netherlands,* Norway, Sweden. (Italic: EU members at the time). In the two additional reports adopted in 03-03-1965, Uruguay complained about the noncompliance with the recommendation of the report dated 11-16-1962.

As regards the measures in the context of the CAP, it was seen that the EU has been engaged in a process of reforming the CAP since the late 1980s. This is expected to benefit the SCS, since they are competitive in a number of products that are supposed to be liberalized (a reform of the CAP will not necessarily benefit all developing countries; the non-competitive and net food importers will actually be damaged, since it is expected that world prices for the affected products will rise). Even if the effect of the already implemented commitments from the reforms of 1992 and 1999 do not seem to have benefited the SCSs significantly, it is still the case that the reforms must be seen as an improvement in the level of cooperation with the SCSs.

As far as the EU's development policy is concerned, the two programmes mentioned above - technical norms and animal and vegetable health - indicate an improvement in the level of cooperation of EU foreign policy from the first to the second period, since they were initiated in 1994 and 1993, respectively. Although their impact is diffuse, it should not be underestimated, especially in the case of EU meat imports.

To conclude, an analysis of the indicators shows that the level of cooperation in the EU foreign policy behavior was very low for the period of 1980-85, and increased slightly in the period of 1995-2000, supporting the statement that EU foreign policy behavior towards the SCS has become more cooperative although at a very low level. The conclusion of the FTA Agreement, the developments of the CAP reforms, as well the agricultural commitments from the Doha Round, which should take place in the next 5 years, will be decisive to make a more definitive argument.

Table 50: The level of cooperation of the EU foreign policy behavior towards the SCS in agricultural trade (very low, low, medium, high)

Indicators	1980-85	1995-2000
Tariffs	High tariffs , bottom of the pyramid of preferences =>coop. very low	Lower tariffs, SGP (although decreasing after 1999), possibility

		of FTA =>coop. low
Anti-Dumping cases lost by the EU at GATT/WTO	0 =>no effect to coop	0 =>no effect to coop
CAP	Subsidies =>coop. null	Reforms =>coop. very low
Developmental policy programmes	No => coop. null	After 1993 animal and vegetable health and 1994 technical norms =>coop. low
Resulting level of cooperation	Very low	Low

6.2) Independent variables and test of forecasts

In order to explain why the level of EU foreign policy behavior towards the Southern Cone States has become more cooperative from the period of 1980-1985 to the period of 1995-2000 in the case of agricultural trade, the value for the independent variables in the approaches being taken into consideration, and the test of their forecasts for each period of time, as well as the covariance test, are examined in sections 6.2.1, 6.2.2 and 6.2.3. Section 6.2.4 makes further observations and concludes with an evaluation of the different explanatory approaches.

6.2.1) Neorealism

As seen in Chapter 4, and 5.2.1, the power position of the European Union can be said to have increased from the period from 1980-1985 to 1990-2000, given the change of polarity of the international system and the increase of the EU's relative power position. Since the observed level of cooperation increased from the first to the second period, the covariance test is confirmed. Neorealism, however, does not explain the absolute level of cooperation in each period; it could have been, for instance, low or very low in the first period, and medium or high in the second.

Table 51: Test of Neorealist forecast for the agricultural trade case study

	1980-85	1990-95
Independent variable	High differential in relative capabilities between the US and the EU	Lower differential in relative capabilities between the US and the EU
Expected level of cooperation in the EU foreign policy behavior towards the SCSs	->	higher
Observed level of cooperation in the EU foreign policy behavior towards the SCSs	Very Low	Low

6.2.2) Identity Constructivism

As analyzed in Chapter 4, and item 5.2.2, the role position of the SCSs was considered to be one of neglect in the first period, and benign client in the second. The expected level of cooperation would be therefore low for the first period and medium for the second. The test of covariance of Identity Constructivism is confirmed, since the level of cooperation increased from the first to the second period. It overestimates, however, the absolute level of cooperation for the second period.

Table 52: Test of the Identity Constructivism forecast for the agricultural trade case study

	1980-85	1990-95
Independent variable	Neglect	Benign client
Expected level of cooperation in the foreign policy behavior towards the SCSs	Very low/low	Medium/high
Observed level of cooperation in the EU foreign policy behavior towards the SCSs	Very low	Low

6.2.3) Utilitarian Liberalism

The values of the independent variable "EU dominant interests" has not been yet determined given that it must be done separately for each case study. The organized actors in the EU agricultural trade policy network, their interests, and foreign policy preferences, can be seen in section 6.2.3.1, and the most assertive in section 6.2.3.2.

6.2.3.1) Organized actors

Table 53: Organized actors in the EU agricultural trade foreign policy network

Type	Main actors	Organized in 1980-85 /1995-2000	Foreign policy preferences
Political	a) European Parliament b) European Council and Council of Ministries	-yes/yes -yes/yes	-improve market access to SCSs exports -advance their national interests and increase their prestige within the EU
Administrative	c) European Commission d) Economic and Social Committee	-yes/yes -yes/yes	-trade liberalization, subject to multifunctionality of agriculture -trade liberalization, subject to multifunctionality of agriculture
Political-Administrative	e)Special Committee on Agriculture (SCA), Committee 133	-yes/yes	-extend policymaking power; increase financial means conditioned to not increase of national contribution

Economic Pressure Groups	f)MEBF g)COPA/COGECA	-no/yes -yes/yes	-trade liberalization -preserve market protection
Political Advocacy Groups	h)CIDSE i)Working Group EU-Me	-no/yes -no/yes	-improve market access to SCSs exports -trade liberalization

a) European Parliament - an analysis of the most important EP resolutions regarding the Southern Cone States indicates that the EP has shown a few concerns in respect of the use of the SGP but, as seen, this instrument did not actually include agricultural products until 1986. The first clear concern regarding agricultural trade appeared only in the two resolutions of 13-6-1985, in which the CAP and the liberalization of tropical products at the multilateral level are addressed. EP can hardly be considered as a mobilized actor in the issue area for the period of 1980-85. In the second period, it addressed the issue a couple of times, but despite the support of Paraguayan exports of bovine meat (resolution of 16-2-89), it can not be said that the EP took a strong position in favor of an increase of cooperation with the SCSs regarding agricultural trade; the resolution of 16-5-95, for instance, shows general satisfaction with the results of the Uruguay Round.

Table 54: Agricultural trade matters in the EP resolutions regarding the SCSs

Resolution	Target	Agricultural trade-related issues
22-04-82	Argentina	Approves the sanction applied to imports from Argentina in the context of the Falklands War (parag 4)
14-10-82	LA	Insists in the possibility of increasing the efficacy of the SPG of the EC, insufficiently used by the Central American countries, and favors the extension of resources and means of the EC to promote the exports of these countries (paragraph 12).
12-10-83	LA	Calls the attention to the decreasing participation of LA in the imports from the EC and asks for improvement in the SPG to Latin-American countries with the aim of abolishing commercial barriers (paragraph 8)

13-06-85	LA	Claims that the EC could perform an essential contribution to LA countries by opening more its markets to their exports (parag 3); notes that this objective is conditioned to the efforts to restructure the sensitive sectors from the EC (such as metallurgy and textiles) and restructure the CAP (parag 4); regrets that no practical implementation has followed the recommendations of the Final Act of the VI Interparliamentary Conference between CE-LA such as in respect to (d) the improvement of the SPG to LA (parag 9).
13-06-85	LA	Insists that the EC assists LA countries to improve their use of the SPG (parag 7); calls the communitarian institutions and member states to work in forums such as the UNCTAD an GATT in favor of the improvement of commercial conditions for tropical products and the conclusion of agreements for commodities (parag 31).
16-02-89	Par	Emphasizes that more than half of the Uruguayan exports to the EC are agricultural and derivatives, and that only 20% of such exports benefit from the SPG, indicating a mismatch between Uruguayan exports and EC demand for imports (parag 6); shows concerns for the losses of Uruguay in its exports of bovine meat to the CEE and 3rd parties in consequence of the CAP and asks the Commission and the Council to establish quotas to these countries for the exports of high quality bovine meat (parag 7);
16-05-95	Me	Urges the Framework Agreement to include the political commitment to negotiate the establishment of a FTA for trade in industrial goods and services, and the progressive reciprocal liberalization in agricultural goods (parag 2); is convinced that the final agreement of the Uruguay Round concerning the liberalization of agricultural exchanges will have a positive effect in improving the access of Mercosur to international markets (…) and that in this context considers the margin to offer additional concessions is very limited (parag 7)
03-02-97	LA	Considers it vital for the EU to support integration between the emerging countries of LA through the

		flexible application of advantages conferred by the SGP on a regional basis and, in this sense, supports the notion that where an emerging country no longer benefits from the GSP, the system of regional accumulation might continue to be applied to components from that country used by the remaining countries belonging to the same regional grouping (parag 15); insists that trade protectionist measures which discriminate against LA products, i.e. agricultural subsidies, need to be addressed within the EU to support and encourage growing trade links between these two regions (parag 22)

b) European Council and Council of Ministries - no references regarding agricultural trade with the SCSs were found in the European Council Summit conclusions, as can be seen in Table contained in section 5.2.3(b). The relevant Ministerial Councils for the case study of agricultural trade would be the General Affairs, the Agricultural, and the Development Councils. It was not possible to obtain data about the conclusions of the meeting, but it can be said that, at least in the context of the CAP, it does not seem to be the case that member states were concerned with the SCSs. Even the studies which attribute the main cause of the CAP reforms to the Uruguay Round (and not to domestic factors), emphasize the pressure exerted by the United States, rather than that of the Cairns Group, in the negotiations. This claim is confirmed by the fact that the resulting agreement was to a large extend based on the Blair House Agreement, concluded between the EU and the US only.[239]

It should be emphasized that despite the general effort on the part of Portugal and Spain to develop closer relations with LA, this does not seem to have had a direct positive effect upon EU trade policy (including agricultural trade) with LA. On the contrary, these countries had to renounce all trade agreements previously concluded with third nations upon their EU entry, including those with LA. As latecomers to the EU, they were in no position to lay down conditions that would benefit LA in the realm of the CCP, as France and the UK did with regard to their former colonies. In fact, the reverse happened; membership in the EU required fundamental changes in their commercial policies, several of which have had detrimental repercussions upon LA. Spain, for instance, is a net importer of agricultural products, in particular cereals and meet, and with the adoption of the CAP it has increasingly shifted its supply from LA to the EU. Secondly, by joining the Lome Convention, its imports from tropical products such as sugar, coffee, and cocoa, were shifted towards the ACP. Thirdly, as a full member of the

[239] See section 6.1.4.2.

EU, Spain has been able to expand its exports of traditional manufactured products to the EU at the expense of LA. As a result, Spain's exports to LA dropped from 5.8% of its total in 1985 to 5,6% in 1993; and most importantly, its imports dropped from 11,4% in 1985 to 4,4% in 1993. One specific trade measure favoring LA countries, attributed to the pressure of Portugal and Spain, was the granting of special tariffs under the SGP to the Andean countries (Bolivia, Colombia, Ecuador, and Peru) and Central American countries, under the programme to combat drugs, but this initiative did not affect the Southern Cone States.[240]

c) Commission – In general, the position of the Commission seems to have changed from the first to the second period to a more liberal approach regarding the EU agricultural policy, both in the context of the CAP and CCP. However, it did not address agricultural trade issues in its communications on the SCSs before the mid-90s. It was only in 1999 that it demanded a mandate to open negotiations on agricultural matters with the SCSs. As far as development programmes are concerned, it can be seen that the main interests of the Commission have been the promotion of standards harmonization and customs matters. The role it played in the CAP is not analyzed here, but as in the case of the member-states, it is clear that the Commission did not have the SCS in mind when deciding about the CAP reforms. In general, the attitude of the Commission may be considered as nearly not mobilized in the first period, and as mobilized and slightly favoring cooperation in the second.

Table 55: Agricultural trade subjects in Commission communications regarding the SCSs

Document	Target	Reference to agricultural trade
COM (1994) 428	Me	Proposes the gradual liberalization of agricultural trade and cooperation in trade issues; states that the Commission will attempt to reconcile the dictates of the CAP with the Community's international commitments, including those relating to the WTO; proposes cooperation in the fields of harmonization of standards and trade policy instruments such as antidumping rules etc (p.16)
COM (1995) 495	LA	States that the EU has done much to counter the trade imbalances with LA via the SGP and exemptions from certain custom duties in the CAP; the reforms of the CAP and the farm-trade provisions of the GATT, the phasing out of the Multifiber Arrangement in 10 years (p. 9) but that

[240] Banklanoff, 1996, pp.112-113; Page, 2002, pp.132-134.

		the Union must foster freer trade in both direction and offer LA products greater access to its market in order to promote a smooth integration of those countries to the world economy (p.17)
COM (1995) 504	Me	Supports the establishment of FTA, cooperation in agrifood standards and customs matters (Chapter II)
COM (1999) 105	LA	Supports the establishment of a FTA in general
COM (2000) 670	LA	Only mentions the promotion of trade as a general priority

d) European Economic and Social Committee - The ESC established a dialogue with the Mercosur Economic and Social Consultative Forum (FCES), by means of a Memorandum of Understanding signed in December/1997, with a view to establishing regular exchanges of information and views. These inter-institutional contacts were consolidated during a second visit by an ESC delegation to Montevideo in May/1998. In February of 2000 the EU and Mercosur foreign ministers adopted the joint proposal advanced by the ESC and the FCES for the establishment of a joint committee (JCC) in the framework of the Association agreement, in negotiation since 1999, to further their cooperation. In terms of agricultural trade, it can be said that the ESC has not taken a very cooperative position towards the SCSs, in that it evaluates the current situation as satisfactory (except from opinion 195) and prioritizes the multifunctionality of agriculture and the necessity to maintain a level of self-sufficiency in certain sectors for security reasons.[241]

Table 56: Agricultural trade subjects in ESC opinions regarding the SCSs

Opinion nr.	Date	Target	References to agricultural trade
102	26-01-1994	LA	States that LA demands center around improved access to European markets and that the recent GATT Agreement, which commits the EU to reduce external agricultural protection and export refunds by the year 2000, will certainly make it easier for agricultural produce from the countries of the South to enter the Community and international markets, but in order to boost their agricultural exports the Latin American

[241] ESC, 2001.

			countries will also have to improve quality and market their products more competitively and effectively (presentation, packaging, etc.), and comply more strictly with the relevant plant and animal health standards (parag 4.1); accepts that harmonization of technical, environmental and health standards does complicate the entry of products not meeting the established requirements (parag 4.2) and that in view of this new situation, the Commission needs to launch a major information initiative among Latin American operators to ensure that they can meet the new requirements and adequately exploit the new market opportunities (parag 4.3). This could include an advisory project for LA exporters, not only in relation to the new conditions and standards, but also offering technical advice on how to improve the quality of their products and to meet technical requirements for packaging, labeling, health aspects, etc.; the Committee further recommends that the GSP arrangements for the three Andean Pact and six Central American countries be extended and that an evaluation be made of any (negative) repercussions about the exports of countries not covered by these arrangements (parag 4.6)
1176	25-10-1995	Me	States that a trade agreement should be advantageous in terms of longer-term EU trade strategy. Recent initiatives, such as NAFTA and the Miami Summit of 9-11 December 1994, suggest a strengthened US presence in Latin America. The possibility of hemisphere-wide free trade (as envisaged at the Miami Summit) and of continued Mercosur expansion in South America, make an agreement with Mercosur crucial to consolidate the EU's continued presence in Latin America, and sustain its privileged

			access to one of the world's largest markets (parag 2.12); that difficulties might arise in the agricultural sector because all Mercosur countries, in particular Argentina and Uruguay, are exporters of high quality agricultural goods, such as wheat, beef and wine which would compete with the EU produce from Member States. The complete elimination of EU trade barriers to agricultural imports from Mercosur would affect the CAP, and might provoke complaints from third countries exporting the same products to the European Market (parag 4.2.4); that the Committee wishes to express its concern that any EU-Mercosur free-trade agreement should be compatible with the Union's international obligations as regards the WTO, while conforming to the norms of the CAP (4.2.5).
459	03-05-1999	LA	States that although the development of trade between the EU and Latin America has generally been satisfactory, there are some structural problems. Despite the growth in EU exports to Latin America, there has been a drop in the EU's relative share of Latin American foreign trade (...) From the Latin America perspective, the persistence of a growing trade deficit with the EU since 1993 is a cause for concern, and this has prompted demands for better access to European markets, mainly for agricultural products (parag 2.7)
932	18-07-2001	Me, Chile	States that a important feature for Mercosur countries of the liberalization of their trade with the EU would be the opportunity to eliminate or reduce import tariffs on certain products, particularly in the agricultural and fishing sectors, which make up the greater part of their sales to the EU and where they enjoy comparative advantages (parag 3.6); but that the compliance with the commitments entered into in the Uruguay

			Round and that both the completed and expected reforms of the CAP should prevent problems in the agricultural sector to become an insuperable obstacle to the new association agreement (parag 4.7).
1326	25-10-2001	WTO	As for agriculture-related objectives, the Committee underlines the need to strike a balance between several essential requirements: increasing world food supply; extending market access for developing countries in particular; quality, food safety and consumer protection requirements; the multi-functional and social aspects of agriculture and not just its economic aspects, as legitimately championed by the EU; the well-being of farm animals; the protection of bio-diversity and traditional know-how; rural environment protection and support for restructuring; and an overall balance in the concessions granted by all the partners in their attempts to secure increased market access. The structured opening up of trade in agricultural products, reductions in import measures and in both internal and external subsidies must be carried out gradually (parag 3.6.6)
195	27-02-2002	LA	States that the decision taken at the beginning of 2001 under the Everything But Arms agreement also confirms that the EU is serious about continuing to open its borders to the least developed countries, but this by no means goes far enough and that a greater impact could have been achieved by allowing access for processed agricultural products. It also states that less than 80% of trade concessions for developing countries in the form of tariff-free import quotas for unprocessed agricultural products have been used in the past few years, because of the increasingly rigorous EU food safety requirements (parag 1.10)
26	23-01-2002	CAP	Notes that since the last two CAP reforms

			and the WTO agreements the EU's degree of self-sufficiency in plant proteins has again fallen, last year sinking below 25%. This constantly deteriorating situation does raise the question of Europe's dependence on imports, entailing risks in the supply of plant proteins to European livestock farmers (parag 1.5.1); Supply of this commodity is concentrated - geographically speaking - in three countries, namely the United States, Brazil and Argentina, which between them make up 80% of world production (parag 3.3.2); the major cut-backs in aid are discouraging farmers from cultivating oilseed and protein crops. This is leading to a situation where the EU is becoming increasingly vulnerable. The Committee therefore remains skeptical about the idea that there would be only benefits and no risks for economic operators in obtaining nearly all their supplies of protein-rich plant substances in the international market; the concentration of supply in certain countries necessarily entails a climatic risk; if this risk should materialize, it could be long-lasting and cause farmers in these countries to alter their output (by reducing the acreage used for such crops). This climatic risk, although a very real one (this was the basis for the 1973 embargo decision), has never been taken into account by the Commission either in its policies or in its decisions. In addition, it should be noted that in value terms, purchases of plant protein from third countries constitute a major item of the Community's trade deficit (parag 3.8, 3.9)

e) Special Committee on Agriculture (SCA), Committee 133 – the position of these committees is assumed to be in line with the position of the Ministerial Councils, given the difficulties in obtaining specific empirical data.

f) Mercosur EU Business Forum – the MEBF has taken a position in favor of trade liberalization, including agriculture. The interest in liberalization is advanced by import-export firms and also European agribusiness companies. The latter, who have been increasingly investing in the SCSs, see opportunity gains from selling their (SCSs produced) products back to Europe at cheaper prices once market access is secured.[242] The most important MEBF recommendations advanced in the area of agricultural trade are examined next.

The MEBF Rio Declaration of 1999 contains recommendations on customs procedures, trade facilitation, rules of origin, standards and regulatory cooperation, and trade-defense instruments, which were prepared by the Working Group on Market Access. The declaration calls on EU and Mercosur officials to study the document with great care and to incorporate its recommendations into the EU-Mercosur meeting to take place in the margins of the 1st EU-LAC Summit in Rio later that year. The most relevant recommendations are: the elimination of tariff and non-tariff barriers to trade; the improvement of a regulatory framework with a high level of protection with respect to health and safety, but without unnecessarily duplicating procedures; the improvement of the convergence and modernization of customs practices and the conclusion of an agreement on a Protocol on Mutual Administrative Assistance on customs matters; support for the work of the World Customs Organization to harmonize non-preferential rules of origin; the establishment of a permanent channel of dialogue between the authorities of the sanitary/phytosanitary and environment protection areas, in order to increase the transparency of the standard-setting process; the promotion of standards harmonization and technical regulations, based on international standards as laid down, for example, by the International Standards Organization (ISO); FAO (Codex Alimentarius) etc; and finally, the abstention of using trade defense instruments not compatible with WTO rules, ads well as applying appropriate instruments such as antidumping in a fair and transparent way.

The response from the Commission to the Rio Declaration welcomes MEBF recommendations, in particular for the development of a transparent and efficient regulatory framework with high levels of protection with respect to health and safety. In that respect the Commission states that it will post a veterinary member of the Food and Veterinary office (FVO) of the DG XXIV with the Commission's delegation in Montevideo as from 16-8-1999 to carry out regular inspection missions in order to ensure that trade can take place in as safe a manner as possible. As to the Protocol on Mutual Administrative Assistance on customs matters, the Commission remarked that it would need to be part of an institutional framework in the bilateral agreement and would require the development of an institutional framework within Mercosur as well. Concerning standards, the Commission emphasized that is had a long experience in the area and was willing to share it with Mercosur countries as it was doing already in cooperation projects. The Commission thought, however, that the establishment

[242] Se Chaire Mercosur, 2000, p.9

of a permanent channel of dialogue in the sanitary/phytosanitary area would duplicate the work of the WTO Sanitary and Phytosanitary Committee. As to the trade-defense instruments, the Commission welcomed the recommendations but stated that Mercosur member states must improve their compliance with WTO rules such as in the cases of the Argentine safeguards measures on imports of footwear and anti-dumping measures, and the Brazilian failure to undertake mid-term reviews in relation to its application of safeguard measures in relation to the import of toys.

The MEBF Mainz Statement of 1999 basically reaffirms the recommendations of the Rio Declaration, emphasizing the importance of a strong commitment from all parties to the liberalization negotiations of the Association agreement to cover all sectors, including agribusiness. Among the new recommendations was the establishment of a bilateral dispute settlement mechanism; the implementation of business facilitation measures independently of the negotiation process; the necessity to remove production and export subsidies and incentive programmes, especially in the agricultural sector; and the orientation to avoid using environmental standards as non-tariff barriers to trade.

The EU-Mercosur Action Plan on Business Facilitation, announced by the Commission at the 2nd EU-LAC Summit in Madrid was based to a large extent on the list of business facilitation measures prepared by the MEBF, originally presented to the Association Agreement negotiators in Sep. 2001, and reformulated in a final proposal by means of the Buenos Aires Statement on Business Facilitation. As regards agricultural trade, the first list recommended the simplification of customs procedures and labeling systems; the granting of better GSP status or the increase in the rates of tariff quotas granted to products originating in Mercosur countries. The final list is focused on detailed recommendations concerning the harmonization of customs procedures, standards, and technical regulations, not making any references to GSP or tariff quotas. The Madrid Declaration of 2002 provides detailed recommendations for the removal of tariff and non-tariff barriers to trade between the EU and the SCSs (Ch.2). It states that the serious economic crisis that some Mercosur countries faced should encourage the two regions to pursue a trade agreement that would remove obstacles to trade, allowing both sides to benefit from their competitive advantages, since EU foreign investors and exports could be negatively affected if Mercosur did not reach a current accounts position sustainable in the long term (p.9). As regards subsidies to the agricultural sector, there is a divergence between EU and SCS members of the MEBF; while the former supports the view that they should be negotiated at the WTO level, the latter emphasize that the liberalization proposals exchanged between the EU and Mercosur were subject to conditionality, such as the phasing out of agricultural subsidies, given that the removal of tariffs without the elimination of non-tariff barriers and subsidies would have very limited actual impact on trade. Despite the different opinions, both EU and Mercosur members of the MEBF emphasize the great importance of a solution to the agriculture issue and encourage the negotiators to make every effort to achieve rapid progress on this matter (p.9-19). As regards non-tariff barriers and measures that distort trade, the MEBF urged negotiators to make this a priority and establish means to achieve this goal, such as compiling a comprehensive list in which all trade barriers would be identified and a standstill clause agreed for NTBs. (p.10). Other recommendations are that the negotiations between the two blocks should provide mechanisms for special and differential treatment, including the possibility of asymmetrical trade liberalization in order to reduce the gap in terms of economic development. (p.11), that tariff peaks should be reduced rapidly in order to eliminate distortions, that import licenses should be granted automatically, customs procedures and documentation should be harmonized (in that respect the MEBF recalled its Buenos Aires Statement), that international standards would be used as prescribed in the WTO Agreement on Technical Barriers to Trade, that bilateral negotiations on mutual recognition agreements for sanitary and phytosanitary measures would be accelerated, that the antidumping instrument should not be used for protectionist purposes, and that labeling requirements and compulsory warehousing should be avoided (pp.11-14).

g) COPA/COGECA – The Committee of Agriculture Organizations (COPA) was founded in 1958 as an umbrella group for national farming organizations; the General Committee of Agricultural Cooperation (COGECA) was founded in 1959 as a confederation of agricultural cooperatives. Both organizations merged their Brussels secretariats in 1962, and have a reputation for having a very close relation with the Commission, especially with DG Agriculture. There is a consensus among authors that their influence has been decreasing, especially since the end of the 1980s, which is confirmed by their recent recurrent criticism of the Commission's positions, such as the press release entitled "The Commission goes too far in its first WTO negotiation proposals" from 17-12-2002. The activities of COPA/COGECA are described in detail in the study of the CAP and CAP reform, and will not again be reproduced here. No evidence was found of a direct reference by the COPA/COGECA to the SCSs, but in a press release of November 2000 (PR(00)60F1) they state that the EU should not conclude bilateral trade agreements (such as the one under negotiation with Mercosur) before the end of the WTO round and that these should not result in further concessions by European agriculture (parag 8), as well as that the EU has already given a large range of trade preferences to developing countries and should not extend duty-free access to EU imports, despite its recognition of the need to ensure that developing countries fully benefit from expanding world trade (parag 9). To conclude, it can be said that the COPA/COGECA interest in maintaining the protection of the EU agricultural markets must be seen as disfavoring a cooperative approach to the SCSs. [243]

h) International Cooperation for Development and Solidarity – the CIDSE (originally the acronym stood for *Cooperation Internationale pour Developpement Socio-Economique*) is a coordination body for Catholic aid agencies formally established in 1967. Its main aim is to provide effective aid to the South, based on the social teachings of the church, in particular the two Encyclicals on development: *Populorum Progressio* from 1967, and *Sollicitudo Rei Socialis* from 1987. In 2002, it consisted of 15 member organizations from Europe and North America, which develop and implement field projects, but also work with the preparation of studies and policy recommendations, which are made available to the public in printed and on-line publications. It has a Secretariat in Brussels, where the Board of Directors and the Executive Committee meet, but most activities are decided and implemented in a decentralized manner.[244]

CIDSE has a Task Group on EU, the Trade, and Food Security (TG1), which is charged with the question of life forms patenting and the agricultural trade. The group developed an advocacy work specifically targeted at European institutions, as part of the lobby coordination among the Brussels-based development and humanitarian aid networks. In a paper called Food Security and the WTO, from 2001. CIDSE criticizes the EU position in both the Uruguay and Doha negotiations on agriculture. It accuses the Uruguay Round Agriculture Agreement to have legitimized the use of subsidies in developed countries, while narrowing the options available to developing countries, which have unilaterally liberalized their trade regimes (often as part of structural adjustment programmes) in reforms that they are prevented from reversing by the WTO. It accuses the EU (and the US) of having introduced exemptions into the agreement, enabling them to increase their support to farmers, leading to the dumping of subsidized food to the world market with damaging effects on southern producers, while at the same time net food-importing developing countries have failed to reap the benefits from lower costs, partly because of corporate control of the global food business. The paper maintains that CIDSE's members do not support the EU's proposal for a broad round of negotiations at Doha, and that, instead, WTO's priorities should include: giving serious attention to the many difficulties in implementing the Uruguay Round of trade agreements, bringing the agriculture negotiations to a successful and pro-poor conclusion, introducing impact assessment as a central activity, both in reviewing past agreements and policies, and in designing new ones; and, in general, it advocates broader institutional reform of the WTO to

[243] About COPA/COGECA see Greenwood, 1997, Grant, 1995 Howel et al, 1992 and their homepage http://www.copa-cogeca.be/ .
[244] For details, see homepage: http://www.cidse.org.

ensure greater transparency, and equal participation by developing country members, as well as a greatly enhanced role for special and differential treatment for developing countries, focusing on measures to end poverty and food insecurity.

In a statement submitted together with Caritas Internationalis in the preparatory committee for the International Conference Financing for Development of the General Assembly, in January 2002, CIDSE advanced the following specific demands with regard to trade liberalization by developed countries (such as the EU): prevent the abuses of anti-dumping measures; eliminate export subsidies and reduce production subsidies; reduce tariff peaks and eliminate tariff escalation; accelerate the reduction of trade barriers in textiles and clothing. It also proposes that the Conference should explicitly mention the negative impact of trade liberalization on developing countries and the need for flexibility to allow these countries to protect themselves, particularly with regard to agriculture and food security, and that the requirement of further liberalization on the part of developing countries should be explicitly linked to progress by developed countries in providing greater market access and reducing support to agriculture.[245] Although not specifically addressed to EU policies towards the SCSs, the CIDSE positions can be said to favor a more cooperative approach on the part of the EU towards developing countries in what regards its agricultural and trade policies.

i) Working Group EU-Me – the working group has adopted a position in favor of agricultural trade liberalization. The central argument is that the establishment of a free-trade area would enable effective international specialization, which on its turn would generate considerable welfare improvements in the Mercosur and certain specific improvements in the EU. Apart from certain European farmers, who would suffer the negative effects from competition with Mercosur imports, producers in both regions would benefit from a better allocation of productive resources and the reciprocal opening of markets. Partial liberalization excluding sensitive sectors and particularly agriculture would have the advantage of minimizing the impact of structural adjustment on the sectors with exposure to competition, but would reduce collective welfare gains. In order to dissolve the "agricultural deadlock" in the bi-regional negotiations, the Working Group proposes new solutions. One of such solutions concerns the bovine meat and poultry market, consisting of a segmentation of the European market into an upmarket, supplied by fresh domestic products, and a less demanding market supplied by imported frozen foods.

In addition, the Group advances two specific recommendations: the replacement of European production subsidies and guaranteed prices by direct

[245] See CIDSE, 2001 and CIDSE 2002.

transfers to European farmers (such as are already in place through CAP reforms), and the linking of trade liberalization to investment liberalization for the European agribusiness investors in the SCSs. The first policy would pave the way for a compromise, in which Mercosur could accept the idea of intervention in agricultural markets, justified by agricultural multifunctionality as a legitimate requirement of any modern society, but which does not transfer the costs of such a policy to competitive producers in other areas of the world. The second policy, i.e., the linking of trade and investment liberalization, would help to disassociate agribusiness interests from small farmers' interests; large European agribusinesses could benefit from trade liberalization as mentioned above, and small farmers would be supported by other means.[246]

6.2.3.2) Most assertive actors and strength of the dependent variable

The most assertive actors in the period of 1980-85 seem to have been the Council of Ministries, which has been, on the whole, in favor of protection for the European agricultural market. They enjoyed a high situational and structural mobilization. The most powerful interest groups were the farmers' lobbies such as the COPA/COGECA, which also enjoyed high situational and structural mobilization. The resulting CCP and CAP have in general not been favorable to the SCSs. The Commission apparently also took a more protective approach to agricultural policy, and did not address this question in its documents that refer to the SCSs. The Parliament did not address the matter in its resolutions concerning the SCSs either.

In the period of 1995-2000, the interests advanced by the Council of Ministries were not as convergent. While some member-states such as France still prioritized protection of the agricultural market, others, such as Germany, adopted a more liberal approach. The Commission also seems to have taken a more liberal stance towards agricultural trade as well; despite its commitment to the concept of agricultural multifunctionality, most initiatives from the Commission in the context of CAP reforms and CCP can be seen as favoring liberalization and therefore the SCSs. On the side of private actors, the farmers' lobbies seem to have decreased its structural mobilization and influence over the Commission, whereas MEBF's seems to have increased. Advocacy groups, such as CIDSE and the Working Group EU-Me, adopted a cooperative approach to the SCSs but do not seem to have had a strong influence on the Commission.

Table 57: Most assertive actors in the EU agricultural trade policy network

Type of actor	1980-85	1995-2000
PAS	Council of Ministries	Commission

[246] See Chaire Mercosur, 2000, pp.10, 16-19.

Private	COPA/COGECA	MEBF

Finally, in measuring the strength of the dependent variable "gain-seeking foreign policy," it can be said that for the period of 1980-85 there were no societal interests favoring cooperation with the SCSs. On the contrary, societal interests in the EU foreign policy network regarding agricultural trade seem to disfavor cooperation, resulting in a very low level of cooperation, as predicted. In the period of 1995-2000, the value of the dependent variable seems to be "weak," but still favoring cooperation, with the result of a low level of cooperation, again as predicted.

To conclude, Utilitarian Liberalism successfully explains both the absolute level of cooperation in the periods of 1908-85 and 1995-2000 and the increase in the level of cooperation from one period to the other. The agricultural policy network seems to be better described as pluralist, rather than monopolist or corporatist. It seems to fit most adequately the community method in the classification proposed by Helen Wallace (see section 4.2.3).

Table 58: Test of Utilitarian Liberalism forecasts in the case of agricultural trade

	1980-85	1990-95
Independent variable	No societal common interests favoring cooperation; strong societal common interests disfavoring cooperation	Weak societal common interests favoring cooperation
Expected level of cooperation in the foreign policy behavior towards the SCSs	Very Low	Low
Observed level of cooperation in the EU foreign policy behavior towards the SCSs	Very low	Low

6.3) Further observations and explanation of the level of cooperation of the EU foreign policy behavior towards the Southern Cone States

As seen above, the covariance test confirms the three approaches forecast concerning an increase in the level of cooperation of the EU foreign policy behavior towards the SCSs in the case of agricultural trade. Neorealism does not offer an explanation for the absolute level of cooperation in each period, but further observations support its main prediction. Unlike the case for FDI, a number of economic studies show the trade diversion effects against the EU in the case of conclusion of a FTAA without counterpart.[247] Utilitarian liberalism successfully offers an explanation for the absolute level of cooperation in both periods and covariance. Identity Constructivism does offer an explanation for covariance, but overestimates the absolute level of cooperation in the second period.

Table 59: Observed and forecasted level of cooperation in the case of agricultural trade

	1980-85	1995-2000
Observed level of cooperation in the EU foreign policy behavior	Very low	Low
Neorealist forecast	->	Higher
Identity Constructivist forecast	Very low/low	Medium/high
Utilitarian Liberalist forecast	Very Low	Low

[247] See Giordano & Watanuki, 2000.

The main objective of the present study has been to find answers for two questions: whether or not EU foreign policy behavior towards Southern Cone States has become more cooperative since the mid-to-end 1980s, and why a change, if any, occurred. Another objective has been to address these questions in a methodologically systematic fashion in order to fill the gap existing in present literature on this subject.

Two case studies were selected for their representativeness of most conflictive aspects in the bi-regional relationship, as well as for methodological considerations, namely, foreign direct investment and agricultural trade.

The analysis developed for the first question was based on a descriptive inference of the level of the EU foreign policy behavior towards Southern Cone States. This level was analyzed based on a number of indicators in the relevant EU policies, and classified as very low, low, medium, or high for the periods 1980-85 and 1995-2000.

A comparison of the results of the analysis, as set out in Chapters 5.1 and 6.1, leads to the conclusion that for the case of foreign direct investment, the observed level of cooperation was very low in the first period, and medium in the second period, therefore indicating that the level of cooperation has increased. For the agricultural trade case study, the observed level of cooperation was found to be very low in the period of 1980-1985 and low in the period of 1995-2000, even if at low levels, the level of cooperation may be said to have increased as well.

The analysis developed to answer the second question, i.e., why this change has occurred, took into consideration the hypotheses advanced by three IR theoretical approaches: Neorealism, Identity Constructivism, and Utilitarian Liberalism. In addition to allowing empirical testing, these hypotheses address the three most recurrent theses in the literature concerning the relations between the EU and the SCSs, namely, the EU attempt to counterbalance US hegemony in the region, the processes of democratization, economic liberalization, and regional integration that took place in the Southern Cone States, and the accession of Portugal and Spain to the EU.

The analysis developed in Chapter 5.2 leads to the conclusion that the increase of cooperation in the foreign direct investment case may be explained by two groups of factors: the first relates to the processes of democratization, economic liberalization, and regional integration, resulting in the initiation of a process of collective identity formation, as advanced by Identity Constructivism. The second concerns the particular interests of the European Commission, and economic pressure groups such as the Mercosur-European Union Business Forum. The influence of Portugal and Spain does not seem to have played a strong direct role; although these countries supported the increase of cooperative programmes in the context of the development policy, they have ultimately preferred to approach FDI matters at the national level, outside the EU system. The counterbalancing of US hegemony does not seem to have played a role in the increase of cooperation of EU foreign policy in the FDI case. Cooperative policies advanced by the EU focused on the promotion of joint ventures among small and medium-sized enterprises and the improvement of developmental effects of FDI, and not on discriminatory policies that could disfavor the FDI coming from third parties, such as the US.

For the case of agricultural trade, analyzed in Chapter 6.2, the counterbalancing effect does seem to have played a major role in the increase of cooperation of EU foreign policy behavior towards the SCSs. The fact that the EU proposed to open negotiations for a free trade agreement in 1999, including the liberalization of agricultural products, is clearly a reaction to the expected effects of trade diversion that would result from the conclusion of the Free Trade Areas of the Americas (FTAA). Specific EU domestic interests also seem to have contributed to an increased level of cooperation in agricultural trade, especially the shift in member-states positions observed in the Council of Ministries and in the Commission, moving towards a less protective approach to the domestic market. The decreasing influence of farmers' lobbies and the increase of that of business lobbies, which include agribusiness sectors, also seem to have played a major role. As for the FDI case study, Portugal and Spain do not seem to have had a particular strong cooperative influence on the resulting EU foreign policy behavior.

Concluding, it can be said that the level of cooperation of the EU foreign policy behavior towards the SCSs did increase from 1980-1985 to 1995-2000 in the cases of FDI and agricultural trade. It should be stressed, however, that this increase of cooperation, although existent, remained at relatively low levels. Even for the case of FDI, where the increase was more significant, cooperation seems to be more symbolic than substantial, given its low impact in the total European outflows to the SCSs.

A final comment that should be made is that the conclusions found for the two case studies should not be transferred to other issue-areas. As mentioned, these cases were chosen mainly because of their representativeness in the most problematic areas of the bi-regional relationship, what might cause a bias towards less cooperation. In fact, greater cooperation seems to have happened between both regions in other areas, such as international security and international governance. A broader study covering other issue-areas would have to be developed in order to show a complete picture of the EU foreign policy towards Latin American Southern Cone States.

Bibliography

- Ackrill, Robert, *The Common Agricultural Policy*, Sheffield Academic Press, 2000.
- Adler, Emanuel, *Seizing the Middle Ground: Constructivism in World Politics*, in: European Journal of International Relations, Vol.3, No.3, 1997.
- Alexopoulos, A. & McCarthy P.A., *Theory Synthesis in IR - Problems & Possibilities*, in: EUI Working Papers RSC, No.95/14, 1995.
- Alinson, G., *Essence of Decision: Explaining the Cuban Missile Crisis*, Boston, Little Brown, 1971.
- Allen, David & M.Smith, Western *Europe's Presence in the Contemporary International Arena*, in: Review of International Studies 16(3), 1990.
- Allen, David, *Who speaks for Europe?: the search for an effective and coherent external policy*, in : Peterson J & Helene Sjursen, A Common Foreign Policy for Europe ? Competing visions of the CFSP, 1998.
- Almeida, Paulo Roberto, *Cronologia da Integração Latino-Americana no contexto do Sistema Econômico Internacional*, in: Boletim de Integração Latino-Americana, No.16, 1995.
- Anderson & Eliansen, *Policy Making in the European Community*, 1993.
- Andrews, Stanley, *Agriculture and the Common Market*, The Iowa State University Press, 1973.
- Annino Antonio & Aymard Maurice (a cura di), *Il Mercato Posible. Sindicati Globalizzazione Merocusr e CEE*, Robertino Editore, 1995.
- Ayuso, Anna, *La relación euro-latinoamericana a través del proceso de integración regional europea*, in: Afers Internacionals, No.32, 1996.
- Azambuja, Marcos Castrioto, *O relacionamento Brail-Argentina: de rivais a socios*, Soares, in Fonseca Junior, Gelson & Sergio Henrique Nabuco de Castro (orgs), Temas de Politica Externa Brasileira II, Vol.2, Editora Paz e Terra, 1994.
- Babarinde, Olufemi, *The European Union's Relations with the South: A Commitment to Development?,* in : Rhodes, Carolyn (ed.), The European Union in the world community, Lynne Rienner Publishers, Inc., 1998.
- Baer, Monica, *O Financiamento Externo da Economia Brasileira diante das mudancas no contexto internacional: uma avaliacao do periodo recente*, Cadernos do IPRI, Edicao Especial, 1993.
- Baker, James Calvin, Foreign *direct investment in les developed countries: the role of ICSID and MIGA*, Greenwood Publishing Group Inc, 1999.
- Baklanoff, Eric, *Spain's Economic Strategy toward the "Nations of its historical community": the reconquest of Latin America?*, in Journal of Interamerican Studies and World Affairs, Vol.38, Bo.1, 1996.

- Barbé, Esther, *The External Dissenter : Spain*, in: Stavridis, Stelios & Christopher Hill (eds.), Domestic Sources of Foreign Policy, Oxford, Washington DC, 1996.
- Barbosa, Rubens A., *Perspectivas das Relações Brasil-CE*, in: Boletim de Diplomacia Econômica, No.14, 1993.
- Barbosa, Rubens Amb., *Regional Common Markets: The Case of Mercosur*, in: Foreign Direct Investment. OECD countries and Dynamic economies of Asia and Latin America, OECD, 1995.
- Barreto Filho, Fernando Paulo de Mello, *O Tratamento Nacional de Investimentos Estrangeiros,* Colecao de Altos Estudos do Instituto Rio Branco, 1999.
- Barrios, Harald, *Uber den Neoliberalismus hinaus. Vier Thesen zur aktuellen Debatte um Entwicklungstheorie und – praxis in Lateinamerika*, in: Manfred Mols & Rainer Ohlschläager (Hrsg.), In Vorbereitung auf das 21.Jarhundert: Lateinamerikas Entwisclungsrfahrungen und-perspektiven, Verlag Vervuert, 2000.
- Barry, Lisandro, *Competition in the Attraction of Foreign Investments: The Argentinean Case,* in: Foreign Direct Investment Policy and Promotion in Latin America, OECD, 1999.
- Batista Jr., Paulo Nogueira, *O eterno retorno do mesmo*, in: Dividas externas na América Latina e a crise financeira internacional, Konrad Adenauer Stiftung, Pesquisas nr.15, 1999.
- Bauman, Renato, *O modo de insercao da America Latina na economia mundial dos anos 90*, in: Dividas externas na América Latina e a crise financeira internacional, Konrad Adenauer Stiftung, Pesquisas nr.15, 1999.
- Beinhardt, Gerd, *The Relations between European Community and Latin America. The Community's Point of View*, in: Institut d'Etudes Europeennes Université Libre de Bruxelles, Colloques Europeens, *La Communaute Europeenne et L'Amerique Latine*, Bruxelles, 9 et 10 mai 1980, Editions de l'Universite de Bruxelles, 1981.
- Bennett, Andrew & George, Alexander, *Process Tracing in Case Study Research.* Paper presented at the Mac Arthur Foundation Workshop on Case Study Methods, Belfer Center for Science and International Affairs, Harvard University, Oct.17-18, 1997.
- Bergsten, C.Fred, *Open Regionalism*, in: The World Economy, Vol.20, No.5, 1997.
- Berrocal, Luciano, *La politique latino-américaine de l'Espagne: quelques éléments d'analyze*, in: Institut d'Etudes Europeennes Université Libre de Bruxelles, Colloques Europeens, *La Communaute Europeenne et L'Amerique Latine*, Bruxelles, 9 et 10 mai 1980, Editions de l'Universite de Bruxelles, 1981.

- Bhagwati, J, in Irwin, Douglas (ed), *Political Economy and International Economics – Jagdish Bhagwati*, MIT Press, 1991.
- Bhagwati, J, *The Theory of Political Economy, Economic Policy and Foreign Investment*, in Irwin, Douglas (ed). *Jagdish Bhagwati. Political Economy and International Economics,* MIT Press, 1991.
- Biersteker, Thomas & Cynthia Weber, *The Social Construction of State Sovereignty*, in: Biersteker, Thomas & Cynthia Weber(eds), State Sovereignty as Social Construct, Cambridge University Press, 1996.
- Bitsch Marie-Therese, *Histoire de la construction europeene*, Editions Complexe, 1996.
- Blake, Charles, *Economic Reforms and Democratisation in Argentina and Uruguay: the tortoise and the hare revisited?* in Journal of Interamerican Studies and World Affairs, Vol.40, No.3, 1998.
- Bodemer, Klaus, *Auf dem Weg zu einer strategischen Partnerschaft ? – Die europäisch – leteinamerikanischen Beziehungen an der Wende zum 21. Jahrhundert*, in : Wulfdiether Zippel(Hrsg.), Die Beziehungen zwischen der EU und den Mercosur-Staaten, Nomos, Baden-Baden, 2001.
- Boeckh, Andreas, *Lateinamerikanische Entwicklungsvorstellen zwischn Nachahmung und Eigenstäandigkeit: Historische Erfahrungen und künftige Perspekiven*, in Manfred Mols & Rainer Ohlschläager (Hrsg.), In Vorbereitung auf das 21.Jarhundert: Lateinamerikas Entwisclungsrfahrungen und-perspektiven, Verlag Vervuert, 2000.
- Bonalumi, Gilberto, *La política exterior de la Unión Europea: El caso Mercosur*, in: Pozo, Carlos Francisco Molina del, *Integracion Eurolatinoamericana*, Ediciones Ciudad Argentina, Buenos Aires, 1996.
- Borzel, Tanja, *Policy Networks A New Paradigm for European Governance?* EUI Working Paper RSC No.97/19, 1997.
- Bourgeois, Jacques & Patrick Messerlin, *The European Community's Experience*, in: Brooking Trade Forum, 1998.
- Bouwen, Pieter, *Corporate lobbying in the European Union: the logic of access*, in: Journal of European Public Policy, 2002.
- Bouzas, Roberto, *Is Mercosur withering as a customs Union?* in Giodano, Paolo (ed), An integrated approach to the EU-Mercosur Association, Chaire Mercosur Sciences Po, 2002.
- Bouzas, Roberto, *Mercosur's External Trade Negotiations*, in: Roett, Riordan (ed), *Mercosur: regional integration, world markets*, Lynne Rienner Publishers Inc, London & Boulder, 1999.
- Bouzas, Roberto, *Trade flows and protection structure: the magnitude of the problem*, Chaire Mercosur, *Annual Report 2000*, Sciences Po, Paris, 2000.
- Bradford, Colin, *Mobilising international investment for Latin America*, OECD, 1992.

- Brady, Linda, *A proposal*, in Callahan, Patrick, Brady, Linda & Argaret G (eds), Describing Foreign Policy Behaviour, Sage, 1982.
- Breslin, Shaun, Christophre Hughes, Nicola Phillips & Ben Rosamond (eds), *New regionalisms in the global political economy*, Routlede, 2002.
- Bretherton, Charlotte & John Vogler, *The European Union as a Global Actor*, Routledge, London & New York, 1999.
- Brugnoli, Alberto, *Italia-Argentina: un'alleanza di successo?,* in: Relazioni Internazionali, 1999.
- Brugnoli, Alberto, *Trade and foreign direct investment in the manufacturing sector*, Chaire Mercosur, *Annual Report 2000*, Sciences Po, Paris, 2000.
- Brum, Argemiro, *Integração do Cone Sul*, Editora Unijuí, Rio Grande do Sul, 1995.
- Bull, Hedley, *Civilian Power Europe: A contradiction in terms*?, in: Journal of Common Market Studies, 21, 2, 1982.
- Bulmer, S., *Analysing EPC: the case for two-tier analysis* in: Holland, M. (ed), The future of EPC, Macmillan, 1991.
- Bureau, Jean-Christophe, *The Agricultural Issue in EU-Mercosur Integration: Beyond the Gridlock*, in Giodano, Paolo (ed), An integrated approach to the EU-Mercosur Association, Chaire Mercosur Sciences Po, 2002.
- Cafruny, Alan & Glenda G Rosenthal (eds), *The State of the European Community. The Maastricht Debates and Beyond*, Lynne Rienner Publishers Inc., 1993.
- Calderón, Alvaro, *Relaciones Unión Europea-América Latina. Mecanismos de Cooperación financiera*, in: Pozo, Carlos Francisco Molina del, *Integracion Eurolatinoamericana*, Ediciones Ciudad Argentina, Buenos Aires, 1996.
- Camerana, Ludovico Incisa di, *Italia e America Latina: dallo strabismo all'attenzione*, in: Relazioni Internazionali, Ottobre 1995.
- Camerana, Ludovico Incisa di, *L'America Latina tra gli Stati Uniti e l'Europa*, in: Relazioni Internazionali, 1999.
- Cameron, Fraser, *Building a common foreign policy: do institutions matter?*, in : Peterson J & Helene Sjursen, A Common Foreign Policy for Europe ? Competing visions of the CFSP, 1998.
- Cameron, Fraser, *The European Union as a Global Actor: Far from Pushing its Political Weight Around*, in : Rhodes, Carolyn (ed.), The European Union in the world community, Lynne Rienner Publishers, Inc., 1998.
- Cameron, Fraser, *The Foreign Policy and Security Policy of the European Union*, Sheffield Academic Press Ltd, 1999.
- Campbell, David, *Writing Security. United States Foreign Policy and the Politics of Identity*, University of Minnesota Press, 1992.
- Caporaso, J.A., *Across the Great Divide: Integrating Comparative and International Politics*, in: EUI Working Papers RSC, No.97/58, 1997.

- Cardoso, Eliana, *Fluxos de capitais para a América Latina na década de 90: crise, contágio e políticas de ajuste* , in: Dividas externas na América Latina e a crise financeira internacional, Konrad Adenauer Stiftung, Pesquisas nr.15, 1999.
- Cardoso, F.H. e Enzo Faletto, *Dependencia e subsedenvolvimento na America Latina*, 1969, reprinted in Bielschowsky, *Cinquenta anos de pensamento na CEPAL*, Editora Record, 2000.
- Cardoso, Fernando Henrique, Conferência pronunciada por Sua Excelência o Senhor Ministro de Estado das Relações Exteriores, Senador Fernando Henrique Cardoso, no Royal Institute for International Affairs (Chatham House) sobre o tema: *"O Brasil e a Integração Européia"*, Londres, em 28 de janeiro de 1993, in: Boletim de Diplomacia Econômica, No.14, 1993.
- Carlsnaes, W. & S.Smith (eds), *EC and changing perspectives in Europe*, London, Sage, 1994.
- Carlsnaes, Walter, *Foreign Policy*, in Carlsnaes... (eds), Handbook of International Relations, Sage, 2002.
- Carlsnaes, Walter, *Ideology and Foreign Policy: problems of comparative conceptualisation*, Oxford, Blackwell, 1986.
- Carlsnaes, Walter, *In Lieu of a Conclusion: Compatibility and the Agency-Structure Issue in Foreign Policy Analysis*, in: Carlsnaes, Walter & Steve Smith, *EC and Changing Perspectives in Europe*, Sage Publications Ltd., London, 1994.
- Carlsnaes, Walter, *The Agency-Structure Problem in Foreign Policy Analysis*, in: International Studies Quarterly, No.36, 1992.
- Carneiro, Dionisio Dias, *Capital Flows and Brazilian Economic Performance*, in: Capital Flows and Investment performance. Lessons from Latin America, OECD, 1998.
- Carrasquilla, Ricardo Schembri, *La integración latinoamericana: entre el modelo comunitario europeo y el libre comercio,* in: Pozo, Carlos Francisco Molina del, *Integracion Eurolatinoamericana*, Ediciones Ciudad Argentina, Buenos Aires, 1996.
- CEPAL, *América Latina en la Agenda de Transformaciones Estructurales de la Unión Europea: una contribuición de la Cepal a la Cumbre de Jefes de Estado y de Gobierno de américa Latina y el Caribe y de la Unión Europea*, Santiago, 1999.
- CEPAL, *La inversion extranjera en America Latina y el Caribe*, 2000.
- CEPAL, *The Economic Relations of Latin America with Europe*, E/CEPAL/G.1116, Santiago, 1980.
- Cervo, Amado & Jose Calvet de Magalhaes, *Depois das Caravelas. As Relacoes entre Portugal e Brasil 1808-2000*, Editora UnB, 2000.
- Cervo, Amado Luiz & Mario Rapoport, *História do Cone Sul*, Editora UnB, Brasília, 1998.

- Chaire Mercosur (edited by Paolo Giodano), *An integrated approach to the EU-Mercosur Association* Sciences Po, Paris, 2002.
- Chaire Mercosur, *Annual Report 1999*, Sciences Po, Paris, 1999.
- Chaire Mercosur, *Annual Report 2000*, Sciences Po, Paris, 2000.
- Chaire Mercosur, *Annual Report 2001-2002*, Sciences Po, Paris, 2002.
- Chaire Mercosur, *Towards an agreement between Europe and Mercosur*, Sciences Po, Paris, 2001.
- Checkel, Jeffrey T., *International Norms and Domestic Politics: Bridging the Rationalist-Constructivist Divide*, in: European Journal of International Relations, Vol.3(4), 1997.
- Checkel, Jeffrey, *The Constructivist Turn in International Relations Theory*, in: World Politics, No.50, 1998.
- Christian, Shirly, *Latin American Trade Relations*, in Journal of Interamerican Studies and World Affairs, Vol.39, No.1, Special Issue: US-Latin American Relations, 1997.
- CIDSE, *Food Security and the WTO*, by Sophia Murphy, Position Paper, September 2001.
- CIDSE, *International trade as an engine for development*, Statement submited with Caritas Internationalis in consultative status with the UN Economic and Social Council to the Preparatory Committee for te International Conference Financing for Development of the General Assembly, 14-25 Januay, 2002.
- Clark, Mary, *Transnational Alliances and Development Policy in Latin America: Non-traditional export promotion in Costa Rica*, in Latin American Research Review, Vol.32, No.2, 1997.
- Clarke, Michael & B.White (eds), *Understanding Foreign Policy: The foreign policy systems approach*, Aldershot, 1989.
- Clarke, Michael, *Foreign Policy Analysis: A Theoretical Guide*, in Stavridis, Stelios & Christopher Hill (eds.), *Domestic Sources of Foreign Policy*, Oxford, Washington DC, 1996.
- Coffey, Peter & Luis Correa do Lago, *The EEC and Brazil. Trade, capital investment and the debt problem*, Pinter Publishers, London & New York, 1988.
- Coffrey, P., De Vree, J.K., Lauwaars, R.H. (eds.), *Towards a European Foreign Policy. Legal, Economic and Political Dimensions*, Martinus Nijhoff Publishers, 1987.
- Coleman, William & Stefan Tangerman, *Linked games, international organisations and agricultural trade*, Max Planck Institut fuer Gesellschaftsforshung, Discussion Paper 98/8, December 1998.
- Colombi, Pedro & Podrez, Javier, *Mercosur Protocols for Foreign Investment Promotion and Protection*, in: Investment Policies in Latin America and Multilateral rules on Investment, OECD,1997.

- Commission of European Communities, *European Union-Mercosur Relations*, in: Investment Policies in Latin America and Multilateral rules on Investment, OECD,1997.
- COPA/COGECA, *COPA's new President: The EU must not be pusehd by eternal pressures into a hurried compromise on CAP reform*, Press Release, CdP(03) 23-1e, 11 April 2003.
- Correia, Miguel Anacoreta, *Mercosur y la Unión Europea. Un Acuerdo para un Futuro Conjunto*, in: Pozo, Carlos Francisco Molina del, *Integracion Eurolatinoamericana*, Ediciones Ciudad Argentina, Buenos Aires, 1996.
- Cosgrove-Sacks, Carol (ed), *The European Union and Developing Countries. The Challenges of Globalization*, McMillan & College of Europe, 1999.
- Cox Aidan & Chapman Jenny, *The European Community External Cooperation Programmes. Policies, Management and Distribution*, Overseas Development Studies, London, 1999.
- Cremona, Marise, *EC external commercial policy after Amsterdam: authority and interpretation within interconnected legal orders*, in Weiler, J.H.H.(ed), *The EU, the WTO , and the NAFTA, Towards a Common Law of International Trade?* , Oxford University Press, 2000.
- Cruz Junior, Ademar Seabre, Antonio R.F. Cavalcante, Luiz Pedone, *Brazil's foreign policy under Collor*, in Journal of Interamerican Studies and World Affairs, Vol35, No.1, 1993.
- Curry, Charles E., Wm.Patrick Nichols & Randall B.Purcell, *Confrontation or negotiation. United States Policy and European Agriculture*, Reports from a Public Policy Study of the Curry Foundation, 1985.
- Czempiel, Ernst-Otto, *Internationale Beziehungen: Begriff, Gegestand und Forshungsabsich*, in: Knapp, Manfred & Krell, Gert (Hrsg.), Eifnfürung in die Internationale Politik, Oldenbuch, München, 1996.
- Dabene, Olivier, *L'Integration regionale en Amerique Latine: Le Mercosur*, Les Cahiers du CERI, No8 Novembre 1995.
- Damro, Chad, *Building an international identity: the EU and extraterritorial competition policy*, in Journal of European Public Policy, Vol.8, No.2, 2001.
- Dasso, Mario, *The Argentine Automotive Sector*, in: Foreign Direct Investment Policy and Promotion in Latin America, OECD, 1999.
- Dauster, Jorio, *Mercosul – União Européia: rumo à associação inter-regional*, in: Política Externa, vol.4, No.4, 1996.
- Dauster, Jorio, *O Brasil no contexto do Acordo União Européia – Mercosul*, in: Konrad Adenauer Stiftung - Debates, No.13, 1997.
- De Mello Barreto Filho, Fernando Paulo, *O Tratamento Nacional de Investimentos Estrangeiros,* Instituto Rio Branco, 1999.
- Defraigne Pierre, *Partnership for Foreign Direct Investment: The Policies of the European Communities,* in: Foreign Direct Investment. OECD countries and Dynamic economies of Asia and Latin America, OECD, 1995.

- Defraigne, Pierre, *The EU towards a Global Economic Power*, in: Relazioni Internazionali, No.50, 1999.
- Deloitte & Touche, *Independent appraisal of the EC Investment Partners (ECIP) Financial Instrument,* European Commission, Common Service for external Relations – SCR Evaluation Unit, December 1999.
- Dessler, D., *What's at stake in the Agent-Structure Debate*, in: International Organization, No.43(3), 1989.
- Devlin, Robert, Antoni Estevadeordal, & Ekaterina Krivonos, *The trade and cooperation nexus: how does the Mercosur-EU Process Measure up*?, in Giodano, Paolo (ed), An integrated approach to the EU-Mercosur Association, Chaire Mercosur Sciences Po, 2002.
- Di Biase, Héctor N. , *Acuerdo Mercosur-Unión Europea: las oportunidades políticas, comerciales y de inversión*, in: SELA – Capítulos, No.46, 1996.
- Di Biase, Héctor N. , *Acuerdo Mersosur-Unión Europea: el paso a la segunda fase*, in: Cuadernos de Negocios Internacionales e Integración, Vol.2, No.10, 1996.
- Di Biase, Héctor N., *Mercosur-Unión-europea: un ejemplo de regionalismo abierto*, in: Cuaderno de Negocios Internacionales e Integración, Vol.1, No.3, 1995.
- Dias, Vivianne Ventura, *América Latina en la agenda de transformaciones estructurales de la Unión Europea. Una contribución de la CEPAL a la Cumbre de jefes de Estado y de Gobierno de América Latina y el Caribe y de la Unión Europea (Rio de Janeiro, 28 y 29 de junio de 1999),* Comisión Económica para América Latina y el Caribe (CEPAL), Santiago de Chile, 1999.
- Dickson, Anna K., *The demise of the Lome Protocols: Revising European Development Policy,* in European Foreign Affairs Review, Vol.5, No.2, 2000.
- Domingues, José Maurício, *Sociological Theory and Collective Subjectivity*, Macmillan (London) & St.Martin's Press (New York), 1995.
- Döpcke, Wolfgang, *Back to the future – relacoes entre a Uniao Europeia e a Africa sob o signo do neoliberalismo*, in Correio Internacional, RelNet, 12-06-2002.
- Dordi, Claudio, *Rules of origin*, Chaire Mercosur, *Annual Report 2000*, Sciences Po, Paris, 2000.
- Doty, Roxanne Lynn, *Foreign Policy as Social Construction: A Post-Positivist Analysis of US. Counterinsurgency Policy in the Philippines*, in: International Studies Quarterly, No.37, 1993.
- Doty, Roxanne Lynn, *Sovereignty and the nation: constructing the boundaries of national identity*, , in: Biersteker, Thomas & Cynthia Weber(eds), State Sovereignty as Social Construct, Cambridge University Press, 1996.
- Duchéne, F., *Europe's Role in World Peace*, in R.Mayne (ed), Europe Tomorrow: Sixteen European Look Ahead, Fontana, London, 1972.

- Durán, Esperanza, *European Interests in Latin America*, Chatham House Papers, No.28, The Royal Institute of International Affairs, Routledge & Kegan Paul, London, Boston & Henley, 1985.
- Duran, Juan Jose, *General Trends of FDI in Latin America. Special Reference to Spain,* in: Investment Policies in Latin America and Multilateral rules on Investment, OECD,1997.
- East, Maurice, Stephen Salmore & Charles Herman, *Why nations act: theoretical perspectives for comparative foreign policy studies*, London, 1978.
- Eckstein, Harry, *Case study and Theory in Political Science*, in: Greenstein, Fred & Nelson Polsby (eds), Handbook of Political Science. VII, Reading, Addision-Wesly, 1975.
- Edwards, Geoffrey, *Europe and the Falkland Islands Conflict*, , in: Stavridis, Stelios & Christopher Hill (eds.), Domestic Sources of Foreign Policy, Oxford, Washington DC, 1996.
- El-Agraa, Ali M., *Economic Integration Worldwide*, Macmillan Press Ltd, London, 1997.
- Elman, Colin, Horses *for Courses. Why not Neo-Realist Theories of Foreign Policy?* In: Security Studies 6:1, 1996.
- Erdmann-Keefer, Vera, *Agrarhandelskonflikte EG-USA. Analyze eines Dauerproblems*, Kehl, NP Engel Verlag, 1991.
- ERT, *European Industry and the Developing World. For a Global Framework of Mutual Interest and Trust*, Working papers, European Round Table of Industrialists (ERT), 1997.
- ERT, *Improved Investment Conditions. Third Survey on improvements in conditions for investment in the Developing World*, Working papers, European Round Table of Industrialists (ERT), 2000.
- ERT, *Investment in the Development World – New Openings and Challenges for European Industry*, Working papers, European Round Table of Industrialists (ERT), 1996.
- ESC, *Opinion of the Economic and Social Committee on the European Union negotiations with Mercosur and Chile: economic and social aspects,* 2001/C 260/13, June 2001.
- Estay, Jaime & Héctor Sotomayor (eds), *América Latina y México ante la Unión Europea de 1992*, Fundacion Friedrich Ebert, BUAP, IIEC-UNAM, UAM, 1992.
- Estevadeordal, Antoni, *Market Access*, Chaire Mercosur, *Annual Report 2000*, Sciences Po, Paris, 2000.
- Ethier, Wilfred, *Regionalism in a multilateral world*, in: The Journal of Political Economy, Vol.106, No.6, 1998.
- European Commission (2003a), DG Trade, *User's Guide to the European Union's Scheme of Generalised Tariff Preferences*, February 2003.
- European Commission (2003b), DG Trade, MEMO/03 from 13/02/2003.

- European Commission, DG Enterprise, *Guide to the implementation of directives based on the New Approach and the Global Approach*, 2000.
- European Commission, DG Trade, *Joint Photography of Trade Relations between the European Community and Mercosur*, 27-April, 1998.
- European Commission, DG Trade, *Trade Policy Instruments: on guard for unfair practices*, October 2001.
- European Commission, DG Trade, *What is the Community's trade barriers regulation? Opening new trade opportunities for European business*, 2000.
- European Parliament, DG Research, *Glossary of the Commom Agricultural Policy and the Agenda 2000 Reform*, Working Paper AGRI 118 EN, June 1999.
- European Parliament, *EU-Latin American Energy Cooperation*, Working Paper ENER 113 EN, 2001.
- Eurostat/ European Commission, *Euro-Mercosur statistics*, edition 2000.
- Evans, P.B., H.K.Jacobson & R.D.Putman (eds*), Double Edged Diplomacy,* University of California Press, 1993.
- FAO, *Agriculture: Toward 2000,* Conference 20th session, Rome, 10-29 November, 1979.
- FAO, *The State of food and agriculture 1984 World Review: the ten years since the World Food Conference urbanisation, agriculture and food systems*, Rome, 1985.
- Fearon, James, *Counterfactuals and Hypotheses Testing in Political Science*, in World Politics, 43:2, 1991.
- Fernandez, Carlos Garcia, *A Framework for FDI in Latin America*, in: Investment Policies in Latin America and Multilateral rules on Investment, OECD,1997.
- Ffrech-Davis, Ricardo & Reisen, Helmut, *Capital Flows and Investment Performance: An Overview,* in: Capital Flows and Investment performance. Lessons from Latin America, OECD, 1998, in: Capital Flows and Investment performance. Lessons from Latin America, OECD, 1998.
- Fishlow, Albert, *Social Sustainability of Growth in Latin America* in: Mobilising International Investment for Latin America, OECD, 1993.
- Frankel, Benjamin (ed), *Realism: Restatements and Renewal*, Frank Cass, London, Portland, 1996.
- Frediani, Ramón, *Flujo de capitales y deuda externa: el caso Argentino*, in: Dividas externas na América Latina e a crise financeira internacional, Konrad Adenauer Stiftung, Pesquisas nr.15, 1999.
- Frenkel, Roberto, Fanelli, Jose Maria & Bonvecchi, Carlos, *Capital Flows and Investment Performance in Argentina,* in: Capital Flows and Investment performance. Lessons from Latin America, OECD, 1998.

- Freres, Christian L., Van Klaveren, Alberto, Ruiz-Gimenez, Guadalupe, *Europa y América Latina: la búsqueda de nuevas formas de cooperación*, in: Sintesis, No.18, 1992.
- Freres, Christian, *The European Union as a global civilian power: develoment cooperation in EU-Latin American Relations*, in Journal of Interamerican Studies and World Affairs, Vol.42, No.2, 2000.
- Freres, Christian, *The role of civil societa in the European Union's Development policy cooperation with Mercosur*, in Giodano, Paolo (ed), An integrated approach to the EU-Mercosur Association, Chaire Mercosur Sciences Po, 2002.
- Freund, Corina, *German foreign trade policy within the EU and GATT*, in Rittberger (ed), *German foreign policy since unification*, Manchester University Press, 2001.
- Friscia A.Blake & Francoise Simon, *The Economic Relationship Between Europe and Latin America*, in: Purcell, Susan Kaufman & Francoise Simon, *Europe and Latin America in the World Economy*, Lynne Rienner Publishers, Boulder, London, 1995.
- Fritsch, Winston & Franco, Gustavo, *Foreign Direct Investment in Brazil: its impact on industrial restructuring*, OECD, 1991.
- Fritsch, Winston, *Investment and Capital Flows in Brazil* in: Mobilising International Investment for Latin America, OECD, 1993.
- Fuchs, Gerhard, *The European Commission as a Corporate Actor*, in Rhodes, Carolyn & Sonia Mazey (eds), The State of the European Union: Building a European Polity?, Lynne Rienner Publishers, 1995.
- Fuentes, Juan Alberto, *El regionalismo abierto y la integración económica*, in: Revista de la CEPAL, No.53, 1994.
- FUNAG, Noronha Advogados & OECD, *Investing in Brazil: a legal and practical guide*, OECD, 1999.
- Furtado, Celso, *Desenvolvimento e subdesenvolvimento*, Editora Fundo de Cultura, 1961.
- Furtado, Celso, *Pequena Introducao ao Desenvolvimento*, Companhia Editora Nacional, 1980.
- Gaddis, John Lewis, *International Relations Theory and the End of the Cold War*, in: International Security, Vol.17, No.3, 1993.
- Galli, Diego A. Laporte, *La Unión Europea y el Cono Sur emprenden la reconciliación*, in: Afers Internacionals, No.31, 1995.
- Galloway, David, *The Treaty of Nice and Beyond, Realities and Illusions of Power in the EU,* Sheffield Academic Press, 2001.
- Galtung, J., *The European Community: a Superpower in the making?* Allen & Unwin, Lonon, 1973.

- García, Eduardo Cuenca, *Las relaciones económicas entre Europa y América Latina*, in: Pozo, Carlos Francisco Molina del, *Integracion Eurolatinoamericana*, Ediciones Ciudad Argentina, Buenos Aires, 1996.
- Gardner, Brian, *European agriculture. Policies, production and trade,* Routledge, 1996.
- George, Stephen, *Politics and Policy in the European Union*, Oxford University Press, 1996.
- Gilpin, Robert, *US Power and the Multinational Corporation. The Political Economy of Foreign Direct Investment*, Basic Books, New York, 1975.
- Ginsberg, Roy & Featherstone, Kevin, *The United States and the European Community in the 1990s*, Macmillan Press Ltd, 1993.
- Ginsberg, Roy, *Conceptualizing the European Union as an International Actor*, in: Journal of Common Market Studies, No.37 (3), 1999.
- Ginsberg, Roy, *Foreign Policy Actions of the European Community. The Politics of Scale*. Lynne Rienner Publishers Inc., 1989.
- Ginsberg, Roy, The *European Union in International Politics. Baptism by Fire*, Rowman & Littlefield, 2001.
- Ginsberg, Roy, *Transatlantic Dimensions of CFSP: The Culture of Foreign Policy Cooperation*, in : Regelsberger, E., Philippe de Shoutheete de Tervarent & Wolfgang Wessels (eds), Foreign Policy of the European Union : from EPC to CFSP and beyond, Lynne Rienner Publishers, 1997.
- Giordano Paolo & Santiso Javier, *La course aux Ameriques: les strategies des investisseurs europeens en Argentine et au Bresi*l, Les Etudes du CERI No.52, Avril 1999.
- Giordano Paolo, *The external dimension of Mercosur : prospects for north-south integration with the European Union*, Intal, ITD-STA, Occasional paper 19, January 2003.
- Giordano, Paolo, *Economic effects of an EU-Mercosur Free Trade Agreement: a CGE Model analysis*, Chaire Mercosur, *Annual Report 2000*, Sciences Po, Paris, 2000.
- Gomes-Casseres, Benjamin & Yoffie, David B., *The International Political Economy of Direct Foreign Investment*, Edward Elgar Publishing Limited, 1993.
- Goncalves, Reinaldo, *Crise, vulnerabilidade e dívida externa: América Latina e Brasil,* in: Dividas externas na América Latina e a crise financeira internacional, Konrad Adenauer Stiftung, Pesquisas nr.15, 1999.
- Gordon, Philip, *Europe's Uncommon Foreign Policy*, in: International Security 22:3, 1997.
- Grabendorf, Wolf, *Germany and Latin America*, in: Purcell, Susan Kaufman & Francoise Simon, *Europe and Latin America in the World Economy*, Lynne Rienner Publishers, Boulder, London, 1995.

- Grabendorff, Wolf, *As relações União-Européia – Mercosul*, in: Konrad Adenauer Stiftung - Debates, No.13, 1997.
- Grabendorff, Wolf, *Mercosur and the European Union: From Cooperation to Alliance?*, in: Roett, Riordan (ed), *Mercosur: regional integration, world markets*, Lynne Rienner Publishers Inc, London & Boulder, 1999.
- Grabendorff, Wolf, *Prioritäten und Perspektiven der Beziehungen der USA zu Lateinamerika: Das Konzept der Westichen Hemisphäare der Regierung Bush*, in : Wulfdiether Zippel(Hrsg.), Die Beziehingen zwischen der EU und den Mercosur-Staaten, Nomos, Baden-Baden, 2001.
- Gradendorff, Wolf, *Germany and Latin America: a complex relationship*, in Journal of Interamerican Studies and World Affairs, Vol.35, No.4, 1993-4.
- Graham, Edwards M., *Fighting the Wrong Enemy. Antiglobal Activists and Multinational Enterprises*, Institute for International Economics, Washington, 2000.
- Granell, Francesc, *The FTAA, the United States and Europe*, Series Papers, University of Miami, October 2002.
- Granell, Francesc, *The FTAA, the United States and Europe*, Working Paper, Miami European Union Center, 2002.
- Grant, Wyn, *The Common Agricultural Policy*, European Union Series, Macmillan, 1997.
- Gratius, Susanne, *América Latina y Europa ante la Cumbre de Madrid: Intereses, Conflictos y Expectativas*, Konrad Adenauer & PEE-UFRJ, Rio de Janeiro, 2002.
- Greenwood, Justin, *Representing Interests in the European Union*, Palgrave Macmillan, 1997.
- Grieco, Joseph M., *Anarchy and the limits of cooperation: a realist critique of the newest liberal institutionalism*, in International Organization, No.42(3), 1988.
- Grieco, Joseph, *State Interests and Institutional Rule Trajectories: A Neorealist Interpretation of the Maastricht Treaty and European Economic and Monetary Union*, in Frankel, Benjamin (ed), *Realism: Restatements and Renewal*, Frank Cass, London, Portland, 1996.
- Grossman, Gene & Elhanan Helpman, *The Politics of Free-Trade Agreements*, in The American Economic Review, Vol.85, No.4, 1995.
- Guerrieri, Paolo, *As relações comerciais União Européia – Mercosul e o impacto frente a terceiros: compatibilidade com as normas GATT/OMC e a solução de controvérsias*, in *Seminário União Européia – Mercosul, Acordo Marco Inter-regional de Cooperação*, Edição: Presidência Espanhola da União Européia, Editora Palloti, Porto Alegre, 1995.
- Guillochon, Bernard, *Teorias de Comercio Internacional*, Editora Campus, Rio de Janeiro, 1979.

- Gustavsson, Jakob, *How should we study foreign policy change?*, in: Cooperation and Conflict 34(1), 1999.
- Guttry, Andrea de, *Las relaciones entre Centroamérica y la Unión Europea: Problemas y desafíos*, in: Pozo, Carlos Francisco Molina del, *Integracion Eurolatinoamericana*, Ediciones Ciudad Argentina, Buenos Aires, 1996.
- Guzman, Gabriel, *Commentaires sur límpact possible de ládhésion de l'Espagne à la CEE sur les relations avec l'Amerique Latine*, in: Institut d'Etudes Europeennes Université Libre de Bruxelles, Colloques Europeens, *La Communaute Europeenne et L'Amerique Latine*, Bruxelles, 9 et 10 mai 1980, Editions de l'Universite de Bruxelles, 1981.
- Haas, Peter M., *Introduction: Epistemic Communities and International Policy Coordination*, in: International Organization, No.46, 1992.
- Haftendorn, Helga & Christian Tuschhoff, *Causes and Consequences of Change : Contending Approaches and Competing Perspectives,* in : Haftendorn, Helga & Christian Tuschhoff (eds), America and Europe in an era of change, Westview Press, Inc., 1993.
- Hansen, Birthe, *Multiple Identities of European States,* in : Wivel, Anders (ed.), Explaining European Integration, Copenhagen Political Studies Press, 1998.
- Hansen-Kuhn, Karen, *Free Trade of the Americas*, in Foreign Policy in Focus, Vol.6, No.12, 2001.
- Hanson, Brian, *What happens to fortress Europe? External trade policy liberalisation in the European Union,* International Organisation, 1995.
- Hantke, Wolfgang, *Challenges for a Multilateral Framework on Investment*, in: Foreign Direct Investment Policy and Promotion in Latin America, OECD, 1999.
- Hart, Jeffrey A. & Aseem Prakash, *Strategic Trade and Investment Policies: Implications for the Study of International Political Economy*, in Frieden, Jeffry A. & David A.Lake (eds), International Political Economy. Perspectives on Global Power and Wealth, Routledge, 1998.
- Harteneck, Guillermo, *Privatisation as a Catalyst for FDI: The Case of Argentina*, in: Foreign Direct Investment. OECD countries and Dynamic economies of Asia and Latin America, OECD, 1995.
- Hassner, Pierre, *Beyond the Three Traditions : the Philosophy of War and Peace in Historical Perspective*, in: International Affairs, Vol. 70, No.4, 1994.
- Hayes, J.P., *Making trade policy in the European Community*, New York, St.Martins Press, 1993.
- Hayes-Renshaw, Fiona & Helen Wallace, *The Council of Ministers*, The EU Series, Macmillan, 1997.
- Heritier, Adrienne, *Policy-Making and diversity in Europe. Escaping deadlock,* Cambridge University Press, 1999.

- Heritier, Adrienne, *The accomodation of diversity in European policy-making and its outcomes: policy as a patchwork*, in Journal of European Public Policy 3(2), 1996.
- Hermann, Charles , Charles Kegley & James Rosenau (eds), *New Directions in the Study of Foreign Policy*, Boston, Allen & Unwn, 1987.
- Hermann, Charles, *Foreign Policy Behaviour: that which is to be explained*, in, East, Salmare & Charles Hermann, Why Nations Act: Theoretical Perspectives for Comparative Foreign Policy Studies, Sagem 1978.
- Hermann, Margaret & Bengt Sundelius (eds), *Comparative Foreign Policy Analysis*, Prentice-Hall, 2003.
- Herrera, Carlos, *Latin American Investment Policies: Building a Multilateral Framework for Investment*, in: Foreign Direct Investment Policy and Promotion in Latin America, OECD, 1999.
- Hette, Björn, Inotai, András & Sunkel, Osvaldo (eds.), *Globalism and the New Regionalism*, Macmillan Press LTD, London, 1999.
- Heurlin, Bertel, *Constraining and Disposing Structural Forces: the Role of the United States*, in: Wivel, Anders (ed.), Explaining European Integration, Copenhagen Political Studies Press, 1998.
- Higgott, Richard & Geoffrey Underhill & Andreas Bieler, *Non-State actors and authority in the global system*, Routledge, 2000.
- Hill, Christopher (ed.), *National Foreign Policies and European Political Cooperation*, Royal Institute of International Affairs, 1983.
- Hill, Christopher (ed.), *The Actors in Europe's Foreign Policy*, Routledge, London & New York, 1996.
- Hill, Christopher J., *Convergence, Divergence & Dialectics: National Foreign Policies & the CFSP*, in: EUI Working Papers RSC, No.97/66, 1997.
- Hill, Christopher, *Closing the capabilities-expectations gap?*, in : Peterson J & Helene Sjursen, A Common Foreign Policy for Europe ? Competing visions of the CFSP, 1998.
- Hill, Christopher, *The Actors Involved: National Perspectives*, in : Regelsberger, E., Philippe de Shoutheete de Tervarent & Wolfgang Wessels (eds), Foreign Policy of the European Union : from EPC to CFSP and beyond, Lynne Rienner Publishers, 1997.
- Hill, Christopher, *The Capability-Expectations Gap, or Conceptualizing Europe's International Role*, in: Journal of Common Market Studies, Vol.31, No.3, 1993.
- Hill, Christopher, *The Falklands War and European Foreign Policy*, in: Stavridis, Stelios & Christopher Hill (eds.), Domestic Sources of Foreign Policy, Oxford, Washington DC, 1996.
- Hindley, Brian, *Trade Policy of the European Community*, in Minford, Patrick (ed), The cost of Europe, Machester University Press, 1992.

- Hirst, Monica, *Mercosur's Complex Political Agenda*, in: Roett, Riordan (ed), *Mercosur: regional integration, world markets*, Lynne Rienner Publishers Inc, London & Boulder, 1999.
- Hix, Simon, *The Political System of the European Union*, The EU Series, Macmillan, 1999.
- Hix, Simon, *The Study of the European Community: the challenge to comparative politics*, in Western European Politics 17(1), 1994.
- Hofmeister, Wilhelm & Franklin Trein (orgs), *Anuário Brasil – Europa. Instituicoes e Integracao*, Konrad Adenauer, Sao Paulo, 2001.
- Hojman, David, *The political economy of recent conversions to market economics in Latin America*, in Journal of Latin American Studies, Vol. 26, No.1, 1994.
- Holanda Cavalcanti, Geraldo, *O Brasil e a CEE, 30 anos de relacoes*, in Albuquerque, Jose Augusto Guilon (ed), Sessenta Anos de Politica Externa Brasileira 1930-1990. Diplomacia para o desenvolvimento, Cultura Editores Associados, 1996.
- Holanda Cavalcanti, Geraldo, *O Brasil e a CEE*, in Fonseca Junior, Gelson & Sergio Henrique Nabuco de Castro (orgs), Temas de Politica Externa Brasileira II, Vol.2, Editora Paz e Terra, 1994.
- Holland, Martin, *European Union Common Foreign Policy, from EPC to CSFP Joint Action and South Africa*, St. Martin's Press, 1995.
- Hollis, M. & Smith S., *Beware of Gurus: Structure and Action in International Relations*, in: Review of International Studies, No.17, 1991.
- Hollis, M. & Smith S., *Structure and Action: further comment*, in: Review of International Studies, No.18, 1992.
- Holsti, Ole, Theories *of International Relations and Foreign Policy: Realism and its Challengers*, in Kegley, Charles (ed), Controversies in International Relations Theory. Realism and the Neoliberal Challenge, St.Martins Press, NY, 1997.
- Hooghe, Liesbet, *Supranational Activists or Intergovernmental Agents? Explaining the Orientations Toward European Integration*, in: Comparative Political Studies 32:4, 1999.
- Hoogue, Liesbet & Gary Marks, European integration from 80s, in: Journal of Common Market Studies 34, 1996.
- Hoogue, Liesbet & Gary Marks, Multi-level governance and European integration, 2001.
- Hopf, Ted, *The Promise of Constructivism in International Relations Theory*, in: International Security, Vol.23, No.1, 1998.
- Howarth, Richard, *The Common Agricultural Policy*, in Minford, Patrick (ed), The cost of Europe, Manchester University Press, 1992.
- Howell, Thomas R., Rosemary E.Gwynn & R.Michael Gadbaw, *European Community*, in Howell, Thomas, Alan Wm. Wolff, Brent L.Barlett &

R.Michael Gadbaw (eds), *Conflict among nations. Trade policies in the 1990s*, Boulder, CO Westview Press, 1992.

- Hudson, Valerie & C.Vore, *Foreign Policy Analysis yesterday, today and tomorrow*, in Mershon International Studies Review, No. 39, 1995.
- Hudson, Valerie & David Skidmore (eds.), *The Limits of State Autonomy. Societal Groups and Foreign Policy Formulation*, Westview Press, Boulder,San Francisco, Oxford, 1993.
- Huntington, Samuel, *The Clash of Civilisations?* in Foreign Affairs, Summer 1993.
- Hurrel, Andrew, *Latin America in the new world order: a regional bloc of the Americas?* in International Affairs, Vol.68, No.1, 1992.
- IIRELA (2000b), *Las negociaciones Union Europea-Mercosur: El largo camino hacia la liberalización comercial*, Madrid, 2000.
- Ikenberry, G. J, Lake & Mastaduno, The *State and American Foreign Economic Policy*. Special Issue of International Organisation, 42(1), 1988.
- Ikenberry, G. J., *The state and strategies of international adjustment*, in: World Politics, 39(1), 1986.
- IMF (2002), *World Economic Outlook. Trade and Finance*, September 2002.
- InterAmerican Development Bank (IDB*), Foreign Investment Regimes in the Americas: a Comparative Study*, 1997.
- Ipsen, Knut & Ulrich R. Haltern, *Reform des Welthandelssystems? Perspektiven zum GATT und zur Uruguay-Runde*, Frankfurt a.M., Peter Lang, 1991.
- IRELA (1993a), *El Mercado Único Europeo y su impacto en América Latina*, Madrid, 1993.
- IRELA (1993b), *Foreign Direct Investment in Latin America and the Caribbean: an overview of flows from Europe, Japan and the United States*, 1979-1990, Madrid, 1993.
- IRELA (1996a), *Foreign Direct Investment in Latin America in the 1990s*, Madrid, 1996.
- IRELA (1997a), *A challenge to the Atlantic triangle? Context and agenda of an EU-Latin America Summit*, Briefing, No.97/2, 1997.
- IRELA (1997b), *Closer European Union links with Eastern Europe: implications for Latin America*, Madrid, 1997.
- IRELA (1998a), *European Direct Investment in LA, trends and contribution to development*, Briefing, 3 November 1998.
- IRELA (1998b), *Trade between the EU and LA: Recent trends and pending problems*, Briefing 23 November, 1998.
- IRELA (1999a), *La Cumbre de Río: Hacia una asociación estratégica?*, Informe, 30 June 1999.
- IRELA (1999b), *Las relaciones entre Europa y América Latina: hacia una agenda bi-regional para el siglo XXI*, Informe Especial Cumbre de Rio, 1999.

- IRELA (1999c), *Trade and capitals flows between the EU and LA: current trends and outlook*, Special Report, 7 June 1999.
- IRELA (2000a), *La Unión Europea y el Grupo de Río: la agenda bi-regional*, Madrid, 2000.
- IRELA (2000c) ; *La Politica Europea de Desarrollo hacia America Latina : Tendencias y perspectivas,* Informe, 11 de Setembre de 2000.
- Istituto Italo-Latinoamerican (ILLA) & BID, *America Latina y la Comunidad Economica Europea,* Seminario, Roma, 24-26 de junio de 1968, Giuffré Editore, Milano, 1968.
- Istituto Italo-Latinoamericano (ILLA), *Guida per l'operatore economico italiano in America Latina, I, II, III, Appendice*, Roma, 1998.
- Istituto Italo-Latinoamericano (ILLA), *Relaciones Economicas entre la Comunidad Europea y America Latina*, Conferencia, Punta del Este, 4-6 de marzo de 1974, Aziende Tipografiche Eredi Dott. G. Bardi, Roma, 1974.
- Jaguaribe, Helio, *Potenzialità e opzioni future del Mercosud*, in: Relazioni Internazionali, Ottobre, 1995.
- Jank, Marcos, *Market access and domestic policies regulations in agriculture*, Chaire Mercosur, *Annual Report 2000*, Sciences Po, Paris, 2000.
- Jorgensen, K.(ed), Reflective *Approaches to European Governance,* Macmillan, 1997.
- Junne, Gerd, *Multinational Enterprises as Actors*, in: Carlsnaes, Walter & Steve Smith(eds), EC and Changing Perspectives in Europe, Sage Publications Ltd., London, 1994.
- Kagan, Robert, Power and Weakness. Why the United States and Europe see the World Differently, in: Policy Review Online no 113 (http://www.policyreview.org), June 2002.
- Katzenstein, Peter & Christopher Hemmer, *Collective Identity, Regionalism and Origins of Multilateralism*, in: International Organization 56, 3, Summer 2002.
- Katzenstein, Peter J & Oran, R.Young, *International Cooperation: Building Regimes for Natural Resources and the Environment*, Cornell Studies in Political Economy, 1989.
- Katzenstein, Peter J. (ed), *The Culture of National Security. Norms and Identity in World Politics*, Columbia University Press, 1996.
- Kelstrup, Morten, *Integration Theories: History, Competing Approaches and New Perspectives*, in: Wivel, Anders (ed.), Explaining European Integration, Copenhagen Political Studies Press, 1995.
- Kenneth, A.Froot, *Foreign Direct Investment*, University of Chicago Press, 1993.
- Keohane, Robert O., *After Hegemony. Cooperation and Discord in the World Political Economy*, Princeton University Press, 1984.

- Keohane, Robert O., *International Institutions: Two Approaches*, in: Keohane, R. (ed.), *International Institutions and State Power*, Westview, 1989.
- Kindleberger, Charles P., *American Business Abroad. Six Lectures on Direct Investment,* Yale University Press, 1969.
- King, Gary /Keohane, RobertO. & Verba, Sidney, *Designing Social Inquiry. Scientific Inference in Qualitative Research,* Princeton University Press, 1994.
- Kinoshita, Fernando, *Manual Bibliográfico e de Pesquisa das Relacoes entre o Mercosul e a Uniao Européia*, Papel Virtual, Rio de Janeiro, 2001.
- Kinoshita, Fernando, *Mercosur y Unión Europea: de la cooperación al libre comercio*, Papel Virtual, Rio de Janeiro, 2001.
- Kleistra, Yvonne & Igor Mayer, *Running to extremes: modelling foreign policy and organization change in Dutch policy on arms control*, paper presented at ECPR 2001.
- Kleistra, Yvonne & Igor Mayer, *What models of foreign policy change can learn from theories on public policy change (and vice versa),* Paper presents at ECPR 2001.
- Krasner, Stephen (ed.), *International Regimes*, Cornell University Press, 1983.
- Krasner, Stephen, *Defending the National Interest, Raw materials investments and US foreign policy,* Princeton University Press, 1978.
- Kratochwil, Friedrich, *Constructing a New Orthodoxy? Wendt's Social Theory of international Politics and the Constructivist Challenge*, in: Millennium, Vol.29, No.1, 2000.
- Krueger, Anne, *Are preferential trading arrangements trade-liberalising or protectionist?,* in The Journal of Economic Perspectives, Vol.13, No.4, 1999.
- Lagos, Henrique & Timothy D.Rudy, *The Third Summit of the Americas and the 32nd session of the OAS General Assembly*, in American Journal of International Law, Vol.96, No.1, 2002.
- Laird, Sam, *Mercosur: Objectives and Achievements*, in: WTO Staff Working Papers, TPRD9702.wpf, World Trade Organization, June, 1997.
- Lamigeon, Sarah, *EC Investment Partners Programme*, in Cosgrove-Sacks, Carol (ed), *The European Union and Developing Countries. The Challenges of Globalization*, McMillan & College of Europe, 1999.
- Lamothe Alejandro E., *Las relaciones jurídicas entre la Unión Europea y los diferentes esquemas de integración latinoamericanos*, in: Pozo, Carlos Francisco Molina del, *Integracion Eurolatinoamericana*, Ediciones Ciudad Argentina, Buenos Aires, 1996.
- Larsen, Henrik, *British and Danish European Policies in the 1990's: A Discourse Approach*, in: European Journal of International Relations, 5:4, 1999.
- Larsen, Henrik, *Explaining the Common Foreign and Security Policy - The New Research Agenda*, in: Wivel, Anders (ed.), Explaining European Integration, Copenhagen Political Studies Press, 1995.

- Larsen, Henrik, *Foreign Policy and Discourse Analysis*, France, Britain and Europe, Routlegde, 1997.
- Larson, Alan Amb., *The MAI – Origin and State of Play*, in: Investment Policies in Latin America and Multilateral rules on Investment, OECD,1997.
- Laurent, Catherine, *Multifunctionality in agriculture*, Chaire Mercosur, *Annual Report 2000*, Sciences Po, Paris, 2000.
- Lavagna, Roberto, *Foreign Direct Investment, in* Chaire Mercosur, *Annual Report 2000*, Sciences Po, Paris, 2000.
- Leal-Arcas, Rafael, *The European Community and Mixed Agreements*, in European Foreign Affairs Review, Vol.6, Issue 4, 2001.
- Leon Hurwitz & Christian Lequesne (eds), *The State of the European Community, Policies. Institutions, and Debates in the Transition Years*, Lynne Rienner Publishers Inc., 1991.
- Lessa, Antônio Carlos, *O Triângulo Inperfeito: as relacoes Franca-Brasil-Europa Ocidental na década de noventa*, in: Cena Internacional, Ano 4, No.1, 2002.
- Light, Margot, *Foreign Policy Analysis*, in A.J.R. Groom & Margot Light (eds.), Contemporary International Relations: A Guide to Theory, London, Frances Pinter, 1994.
- Lim, Ewe-Ghee, *Determinants of, and the relations between Foreign Direct Investment and Growth: a summary of the recent literature*, IMF Working Paper WP 01/175, 2001.
- Lim, Paul, *Political Issues of EU-ASEAN Relations*, Panorama 1/1999, Konrad Adenauer Stiftung, 1999.
- Lim, Paul, *The unfolding Asia-Europe Meeting (ASEM) process: issues for ASEM III,* in Peter Preston & Julir Gilson (eds), The European Union and East Asia, E.Elgar, Cheltenham, 2001.
- Lohbauer, Christian, *Oportunidades de uma relacao complementar entre Brasil e Europa*, Konrad Adenauer & PEE-UFRJ, Rio de Janeiro, 2002.
- Lorca, Roberto Mayorga, *Foreign Investment Regimes in the Americas – Legal Challenges,* in: Investment Policies in Latin America and Multilateral rules on Investment, OECD,1997.
- Maciel, Marco, *A Parceria Mercosul-UE*, in: Jornal do Brasil, Rio de Janeiro, 10/1998.
- Magalhaes, Jose Calvet de, *Breve Historia das Realcoes Diplomaticas entre Brasil e Portugal*, Editora Paz e Terra, 1999.
- Mainwaring, Scott, *Democracy in Brazil and the Southern Cone: achievements and problems,* in Journal of Interamerican Studies and World Affairs, Vol.37, No.1, 1995.
- Maior, Luiz Souto, *"Cimeira América Latina-Caribe-União Européia: estratégia e realidade*", ", in: Carta Internacional, No.77, 1999.

- Malamud, Andres, *Presidential Diplomacy or Presidential Democracy? The Institutional Underpinnings of Mercosur*, paper prepared for delivery at the 2003 meeting of the Latin American Studies Association, Dallas, Texas, March 27-29, 2003.
- Manners, Ian & Richard Whitman, *Introduction*, in Manners, Ian & Richard Whitman(eds), *The foreign policies of European Union States*, Manchester University Press, 2000.
- Manners, Ian, Normative Power Europe: A contradiction in terms? Working papers 38, Copenhagen Peace Research Institute, 2000.
- Mansfield, Edward D. & Milner, Helen V., *The New Wave of Regionalism*, in: International Organization, No.53, 3, 1999.
- Mansfield, Edward D., & Milner, Helen V., *The Political Economy of Regionalism*, Columbia University Press, New York, 1997.
- Manzetti, Luigi, *The evolution of agricultural groups in Argentina*, in Journal of Latin American Studies, Vol.24, No.3, 1992.
- Manzetti, Luigi, *The Political Economy of Mercosur*, in Journal of Interamerican Studies and World Affairs, Vol.35, No.4, 1993-4.
- Marchisio, Sergio & Antonietta di Blase, *The Food and Agriculture Organisation (FAO)*, International Organisation and the Evolution of World Society series, vol.1, Martinus Nijhoff Publishers, 1991.
- Marín, Manuel, *L'Unione europea e l'America Latina*, in: Relazioni Internazionali, 1999.
- Marín, Manuel, *Las relaciones entre la UE y AL: passado, presente y futuro*, in: Pozo, Carlos Francisco Molina del, *Integracion Eurolatinoamericana*, Ediciones Ciudad Argentina, Buenos Aires, 1996.
- Marín, Manuel, *Por uma nova relacao Europa-América*, Folha de Sao Paulo, 23/06/1999.
- Marin, Manuel, Vice-President of the European Commission, *Letter to Dr.Jürgen Strube, MEBF European Co-Chairman, Chairman and CEO BASF AG*, 23 June, 1999.
- Marón, José Manuel Peláez, *La comunidad europea: relaciones economicas con América Latina*, in: Agenda Internacional, Ano 1, No.1, 1992.
- Marsh, John & Christopher Ritson, *Agricultural Policy and the Common Market*, Chatham House, 1971.
- Marsh, John & Pamela J.Swanney, *Agriculture and the European Community*, University Association for Contemporary European Studies, George Allen & Unwin, 1980.
- Marsh, John, *The Common Agricultural Policy*, in Stavridis, Stelios, Elias Mossialos, Roger Morgan, Howards Machin, New Challenges to the European Union: policies and policy-making, Dartmouth Publishing Company, 1997.

- Martenczuk, Bernd, *From Lome to Cotonou: the ACP-EC partnership agreement in a legal perspective*, in European Foreign Affairs Review, Vol.5, No.4, 2000.
- Martin, Lisa, *Coercive Cooperation. Explaining Multilateral Economic Sanctions*, Princeton University Press, 1992.
- Martins Lima, Antonio, *Investimentos dos setores público e privado no Mercosul*, in : Plá (Ed.), O Mercosul e a Comuidade Européia. Uma Abordagem comparativa, UFRGS, 1994.
- Martins, Antonio, *FDI in Latin America in the Current Environment*, in: Foreign Direct Investment Policy and Promotion in Latin America, OECD, 1999.
- Matthews, Alan & Cathie Laroche-Dupraz, *Agricultural tariff rate quotas as a development instrument*, Trinity Economic Paper Series, Paper No.17, 2001.
- Matthews, Alan, *Multilateral Trade Reform in Agriculture and the Developing Countries*, Trinity Economic Series, Paper No.10, 2000.
- Matthews, Alan, *The WTO agricultural trade negotiations after Seattle*, Trinity Economic Paper Series, Paper No.5, 2000.
- Mattli, Walter, *The Logic of Regional Integration – Europe and Beyond*, Cambridge University Press, Cambridge, 1999.
- Matutes, Juan Abel, *España e Iberoamérica: una relación privilegiada*, in: Relazioni Internazionali, No.50, 1999.
- Mearsheimer, John, *Back to the future: instability in Europe after the Cold War*, in International Security 15:1, 1990.
- MEBF (1999a), *Rio Declaration*, February 23, 1999.
- MEBF (1999b), *Mainz Statement*, November 23, 1999.
- MEBF (2001a), *EU-Mercosur Business Facilitation and cooperation measures*, 07-07-2001.
- MEBF (2001b), *Buenos Aires Statement on Business Facilitation*, December, 2001.
- MEBF (2002), *Madrid Declaration*, May, 2002.
- Mello, Isabel Parente, *A inserção do Mercosul na economia mundial*, in: Brandão, Antônio & Lia Valls Pereira (ed.), Mercosul: Perspectivas da Integração, FGV, Rio de Janeiro, 1997.
- Meunier, Sophie & Kalypso Nicoladis, *Trade competence in the Nice Treaty*, in: ECSA Review, Vol.14, No.2, 2001.
- Meunier, Sophie & Kalypso Nicoladis, *Who speaks for Europe? The delegation of trade authority in the EU*, in: Journal of Common Market Studies, Vol.37, No.3, 1999.
- Meunier, Sophie, *Divided but United: European Trade Policy Integration and EU-US Agricultural Negotiations in the Uruguay Round*, in : Rhodes, Carolyn (ed.), *The European Union in the world community*, Lynne Rienner Publishers, 1998.

- Mix, Miguel Rojas, *La cultura en las relaciones entre la UE y AL y la especificidad de Iberoamérica*, in: Pozo, Carlos Francisco Molina del, *Integracion Eurolatinoamericana*, Ediciones Ciudad Argentina, Buenos Aires, 1996.
- Molz, Manfred, *Integration und Kooperation in zwei Kontinenten - Das Streben nach Einheit in Lateinamerika und in Südostasien*, Mainzer Philosophische Fakultät Gesellschaft, Franz Steiner Verlag, Stuttgart, 1996.
- Monar, Jörg, *Political Dialogue with Third Countries and Regional Political Groupings: The Fifteen as an Attractive Interlocutor,* in : Regelsberger, E., Philippe de Shoutheete de Tervarent & Wolfgang Wessels (eds), Foreign Policy of the European Union : from EPC to CFSP and beyond, Lynne Rienner Publishers, 1997.
- Moran, Theodore, *Investment Issues*, in Schott, Jeffrey (ed), *The WTO after Seattle,* Institute for International Economics, Washington, 2000.
- Moravcsik, Andrew, *Despotism im Brussels? Misreading the European Union*, in: Foreign Affairs 80:3, 2001.
- Moravcsik, Andrew, *Liberal International Relations Theory. A Social Scientific Assessment*, Harvard University, 2001.
- Moravcsik, Andrew, *Liberalism and International Relation Theory*, Working Paper series No29, Cambridge, Center for International Affairs, 1992.
- Moravcsik, Andrew, *Taking Preferences Seriously, A Liberal Theory of International Politics*, in; International Organisation 51:4, 1997.
- Moravcsik, Andrew, *The Choice for Europe - Social Purpose & State Power from Messina to Maastricht*, Cornell University Press, Ithaca, New York, 1998.
- Motta Veiga, Pedro da Motta, *The political economy of Mercosur and trade negotiations wit the EU*, Chaire Mercosur, *Annual Report 2000*, Sciences Po, Paris, 2000.
- Mower Jr., A.Glenn, *The European Community and Latin America. Case study in global role expansion*, Greenwood Press, Westport & London, 1982.
- Moyer, H.Wayne & Timothy E.Josling, *Agricultural Policy Reform. Politics and process in the EC and the US,* Iowa State University Press, 1990.
- Murphy, Declan, *Investment Promotion Techniques and the Role of the Investment Promotion Agencies*, in: Foreign Direct Investment Policy and Promotion in Latin America, OECD, 1999.
- Nagarajan, Nigel, *Regionalism and the WTO: New rules for the game*?, in World Bank Economic Papers No.128, June 1998.
- Neack, Laura, Jeanne Hey & Patrick Haney (eds), *Foreign Policy analysis: Continuity and Change in its Second Generation*, Prentice-Hall, 1995.
- Neville-Rolfe, Edmund, *The politics of agriculture in the European Community,* European Centre for Political Studies, 1984.

- Nordic Consulting Group a/s, Evaluation of Economic Cooperation between the European Community and partner states in Asia and Latin America, August 2001.
- Norgaard, Ole, Thomas Pedersen & Nikolaj Petersen, *The European Community in World Politics*, Pinter Publishers, 1993.
- Nugent, Neil, *The European Commission*, Palgrave, 2001.
- Nugent, Neil, *The Government and Politics of the European Union*, The European Union Series, Macmillan, 4th edition, 1999.
- Nunnenkamp, Peter, *Die EU-Osteweiterung als Bedrohung, die Entwicklungsparterschaft als Chance? – Lateinamerika im regionalen Beziehungsgeflecht der EU,* in : Wulfdiether Zippel(Hrsg.), Die Beziehungen zwischen der EU und den Mercosur-Staaten, Nomos, Baden-Baden, 2001.
- Nunnenkamp, Peter, *European FDI Strategies in Mercosur Countries,* Kiel Working Paper No.1047, May 2001.
- Nunnenkamp, Peter, *Foreign Direct Investment in Mercosur: The strategies of European Investors*, in Giodano, Paolo (ed), An integrated approach to the EU-Mercosur Association, Chaire Mercosur Sciences Po, 2002.
- Nutall, S., *The Commission and foreign policy making*, in G.Edwards & D.Spence(eds), The European Commission, Cartermill, London, 1997.
- Odell, J.S., *Understanding international trade policies: an emerging synthesis*, in World Politics, 43(1), 1990.
- OECD, *Declaration and Decisions on International Investments and Multilateral Enterprises 1991 Review, 1991.*
- OECD, *The development dimensions of trade*, Policy Brief, October 2001.
- OECD, *Capital Flows and Investment Performance. Lesson from Latin America*, 1997.
- OECD, *Development and Democracy: Aid Policies in Latin America*, 1992.
- OECD, *Development Cooperation Review Series. European Community*, no12, 1996.
- OECD, *Foreign Direct Investment Policy and Promotion in Latin America*, 1998.
- OECD, *Foreign Direct Investment. OECD countries and dynamic economies of Asia and Latin America*, 1993.
- OECD, *Investment Policies in Latin America and Multilateral Rules on Investment*, 1996.
- OECD, *Promoting private enterprise in developing countries*, 1990.
- Oman, Charles, *Emerging Policy Issues for the Dynamic Non-Member Economies; Trends in Global FDI and Latin America*, in: Foreign Direct Investment. OECD countries and Dynamic economies of Asia and Latin America, OECD, 1995.
- Oman, Charles, *New Forms of International Investment in developing Countries*, OECD, 1984.

- Orden, David, Rashid Kaukab & Eugenio Diaz-Bonilla, *Liberalising Agricultural Trade and Developing Countries*, Carnegie Endowment for International Peace, Trade, Equity and Development series, No.6, 2003.
- Ossio, Bernardino, *La dimensión cultural de las relaciones entre la Unión Europea y América Latina: especial referencia a Mercosur*, in: Pozo, Carlos Francisco Molina del, *Integracion Eurolatinoamericana*, Ediciones Ciudad Argentina, Buenos Aires, 1996.
- Otten, Adrian, *Investment Provisions I the Agreement Establishing the WTO*, in: Investment Policies in Latin America and Multilateral rules on Investment, OECD,1997.
- Paarlberg, Robert, *Agricultural policy reform and the Uruguay round; synergistic linkage in a two-level game?*, in: International Organisation, 51,1997.
- Page, Sheila, *The existing EU trade agreements: what to learn for Mercosur*, Chaire Mercosur, *Annual Report 2000*, Sciences Po, Paris, 2000.
- Page, Shila, *Trade and Foreign Policy in the EU*, in Giodano, Paolo (ed), An integrated approach to the EU-Mercosur Association, Chaire Mercosur Sciences Po, 2002.
- Paiva Abreu, Marcelo de, *O Brasil e o GATT: 1947-1990*, in Albuquerque, Jose Augusto Guilon (ed), Sessenta Anos de Politica Externa Brasileira 1930-1990. Diplomacia para o desenvolvimento, Cultura Editores Associados, 1996.
- Paiva Abreu, Marcelo de, *O Brasil na Rodada Uruguay do Gatt,* in Fonseca Junior, Gelson & Sergio Henrique Nabuco de Castro (orgs), Temas de Politica Externa Brasileira II, Vol.2, Editora Paz e Terra, 1994.
- Pappas, Spyros & Vanhoonacker, Sophie (eds.), *La Politique Étrangère et de Sécurité Commune de l'Union Européenne: les Défis du Futur*, Actes du colloque de l'IAP Maastricht, les 19 et 20 octobre 1995, Institut Européen d'Administration Publique, Maastricht, 1996.
- Parlamento Europeo, *El Parlamento Europeo impulsa la cooperación interregional con Mercosur*, in: Tribuna del Parlamento Europeo, Ano VIII, No.5, 1995.
- Pastor, Robert, *The Clinton Administration and the Americas: the post-war rhythm and blues*, in Journal of Interamerican Studies and World Affairs, Vol.38, No.4, 1996.
- Patterson, Lee Ann, *Agricultural policy reforms in the European Community; a three-level game analysis*, in: International Organisation, 51, 1997.
- Pena, Felix, *For and against an EU-Mercosur FTA: the interest of Mercosur*, Chaire Mercosur, *Annual Report 2000*, Sciences Po, Paris, 2000.
- Petersen, Hans J.(Hrsg), *Die Beziehungen zwischen der Europaeischen Gemeinschaft und Lateinamerika. Bestandsaufnahme und Perspektiven*, Nomos, Baden-Baden, 1983.

- Peterson J & Helene Sjursen, *A Common Foreign Policy for Europe ? Competing visions of the CFSP*, 1998.
- Peterson, J, *The European Union as a Global Actor*, in : Peterson J & Helene Sjursen, A Common Foreign Policy for Europe ? Competing visions of the CFSP, 1998.
- Peterson, John & Elizabeth Bomberg, *Decision-Making in the European Union,* European Union Series, Macmillan, 1999.
- Peterson, John, *Get away from me closer, you're near me too far: Europe and America after the Uruguay Round*, in Pollack, Mark & Gregory Shaffer (eds), *Transatlantic governance in the global economy,* Rowman & Littlefield, 2001.
- Petrochilos, George, *Foreign Direct Investment and the Development Process*, Avebury, 1989.
- Pfetsch, Frank, *Tensions in Sovereignty : Foreign Policies of EC Members Compared*, in: Carlsnaes, Walter & Steve Smith(eds), EC and Changing Perspectives in Europe, Sage Publications Ltd., London, 1994.
- Phinnemore, David, *Association: Stepping-Stone or Alternative to EU membership?* Sheffield Academic Press, 1999.
- Picerno, Alfredo & Gutiérrz, Pablo, *Notas sobre la convergencia entre el Mercosur y la Unión europea*, in: Cuadernos del Centro Latinoamericano de Economia Humana (CLAEH), Montevideo, No.77, 1996.
- Piening, Christopher, *Global Europe: The European Union in World Affairs,* Boulder, Lynne Rienner, 1997.
- Plá, Juan Agorta (coord), *O Mercosul e a Comunidade Européia: uma abordagem comparativa*, Editora da Universidade Federal do Rio Grande do Sul, Goethe Institut, Rio Grande do Sul, 1994.
- Pletcher, David M., *The diplomacy of trade and investment: American economic expansion in the Hemisphere*, 1865-1900, University Missouri Press, 1998.
- Poelmans, J. & J.Lecomte, *L'agriculture europeene et les pays tiers*, Presses Universitaires de Bruxelles, 1972.
- Pollack, Mark, Delegation, *Agency and Agenda Setting in the European Community*, in: International Organisation 51:1, 1997.
- Pollack, Mark, *Delegation, Agency and Agenda Setting in the Treaty of Amsterdam*, in: European Integration Online Papers 3:6, http//eiop.or.at/eiop/texte/1999-006a.htm, 1999.
- Pollack, Mark, *The Political Economy of the Transatlantic Partnership*, RSCAS- BP Chair in Transatlantic Relations, 2002.
- Posada, Edgar Vieira, *Un exercicio de prospectiva: los esquemas regionales latinoamericanos, el ALCA y la Unión Europea en el año 2020*, exposição preparada para o Seminário "*Escenarios estratégicos de la integración en el umbral del siglo XXI:persppectivas americanas y europeas*", organizado pelo

Centro de Formación para la Integración Regional (CEFIR), Montevideo; em colaboração com o Centro de Estudos Estratégicos, Secretaria de Assuntos Estratégicos da Presidência da República Federativa do Brasil; e a Escola de Administração da Fazenda, Ministério da Fazenda da República federativa do Brasil, Brasília, 6-8 de outubro de 1998.

- Prat, Juan, *New Dynamics in Latin America and New Intensity in European-Latin American Economic Relations*, in: Mobilising International Investment for Latin America, OECD, 1993.
- Prebish, Raul, *O desenvolvimento economico da America Latina e alguns de seus problemas principais*, 1949, reprinted in Bielschowsky, *Cinquenta anos de pensamento na CEPAL*, Editora Record, 2000.
- Priyadarshi, Shishir, *Reforming Global Trade in Agriculture: A developing-country perspective,* Carnegie Endowment for International Peace, Trade, Equity and Development series, No.6, 2003.
- Purcell, Randall & Elizabeth Morrison, *US Agriculture and Third World Development, The critical linkage,* Lynne Rienner, 1987.
- Purcell, Susan Kaufman & Francoise Simon, *The Impact of Regional Integration on European-Latin American Relations*, in: Purcell, Susan Kaufman & Francoise Simon, *Europe and Latin America in the World Economy*, Lynne Rienner Publishers, Boulder, London, 1995.
- Putnam, Robert D., *Two-Level Games : The Impact of Domestic Politics on Transatlantic Bargaining*, in : Haftendorn, Helga & Christian Tuschhoff (eds), America and Europe in an era of Change, Westview Press, Inc., 1993.
- Putnam, Robert, *Diplomacy and Domestic Politics: The logic of two level games*, in: International Organisation, 42.3, 1988.
- Quadros, Salomao, *Dívidas externas na América Latina: os anos 30 e 80 revisitados*, in: Dividas externas na América Latina e a crise financeira internacional, Konrad Adenauer Stiftung, Pesquisas nr.15, 1999.
- Ramjas, Gabriel Arthur, *Las relaciones Unión Europea-América Latina: hacia una nueva era de entendimiento*, in: Análises Político, No.28, 1996.
- Regelsberger, E., Philippe de Shoutheete de Tervarent & Wolfgang Wessels, *From EPC to CFSP : Does Maastricht Push the EU Toward a Role as a Global Power ?*, in : Regelsberger, E., Philippe de Shoutheete de Tervarent & Wolfgang Wessels (eds), Foreign Policy of the European Union : from EPC to CFSP and beyond, Lynne Rienner Publishers, 1997.
- Retout, Olivier, Directorate-General for External Relations of the Commission of the European Communities, *The Europe-Asia and Latin America Dialogue*, 1991.
- Rhi-Sausi, Jose Luis, *The internationalisation strategies of European Agribusiness*, Chaire Mercosur, *Annual Report 2000*, Sciences Po, Paris, 2000.

- Rhodes, Carolyn (ed.), *The European Union in the World Community*, Lynne Rienner., 1998.
- Rhodes, Carolyn, *The Identity of the European Union in International Affairs*, in : Rhodes, Carolyn (ed.), *The European Union in the World Community*, Lynne Rienner, 1998.
- Ribeiro Hoffmann, Andrea, *Os imigrantes alemaes no Brasil e as relacoes comerciais Brasil-Alemanha entre 1815 e 1871: uma analise das subjetividades coletivas*, in Contexto Internacional,Vol.23, 2001.
- Ribeiro, Fernando, *Indicadores estatísticos e outras consideracoes sobre o endividamento externo do Brasil e da América Latina*, in: Dividas externas na América Latina e a crise financeira internacional, Konrad Adenauer Stiftung, Pesquisas nr.15, 1999.
- Richards, Donald, *Dependent Development and Regional Integration: a critical examination of the Southern Cone Common Market*, in Latin American Perspectives, Vol.24, No.6, 1997.
- Richardson, Jeremy, *European Union. Power and policy-making*, Routledge, 1996.
- Richarson, Keith, *Big Business and the European Agenda,* SEI Working Paper No.35, Sussex European Institute, University of Sussex, September 2000.
- Ricupero, Rubens, *I processi d'integrazione in America Latina*, in: Relazioni Internazionali, Ottobre, 1995.
- Rieger, Elmar, *The common agricultural policy: external and internal dimensions*, in Wallace & Wallace(eds), Policy-making in the European Union, Oxford University Pres, 1996.
- Risse, Thomas, *Exploring the Nature of the Beast: International Relations Theory and Comparative Policy Analysis Meet the European Union*, in: Journal of Common Market Studies, Vol.34, No.1, 1996.
- Risse, Thomas, *The Long-Term Future of European Security*, in: Carlsnaes, Walter & Steve Smith(eds), EC and Changing Perspectives in Europe, Sage Publications Ltd., London, 1994.
- Risse-Kappen, Thomas (ed.), *Bringing transnational relations back in: non-state actors, domestic structures and international institutions*, Cambridge Studies in International Relations, 1995.
- Risse-Kappen, Thomas, *Democratic Peace - Warlike Democracies? A Social Constructivist Interpretation of the Liberal Argument,* in: European Journal of International Relations, Vol.1, No.4, 1995.
- Rittberger, Volker & Mayer, Peter (eds.), *Regime Theory and International Relations*, Clarendon Press Oxford, 1993.
- Rittberger, Volker (ed), *German foreign policy since unification. Theories and case-studies*, Manchester University Press, 2001.

- Rittberger, Volker, *Approaches to the Study of Foreign Policy derived from International Relations Theory*, in: Hermann, Margaret & Bengt Sundelius (eds), *Comparative Foreign Policy Analysis*, Prentice-Hall, 2003.
- Rittberger, Volker; Hasenclever, Andreas & Mayer, Peter, *Theories of International Regimes*, Cambridge Studies in International Relations, 1997.
- Robert, Maryse & Wetter, Theresa, *Bilateral Investment Treaties in the Western Hemisphere,* in: Investment Policies in Latin America and Multilateral rules on Investment, OECD,1997
- Robert, Maryse, *Investment Agreements in the Americas: Convergence of Rules*, in: Foreign Direct Investment Policy and Promotion in Latin America, OECD, 1999.
- Robert, Maryse, Pierre Sauve & Karsten Steinfatt, *Negotiating Investment Rules: Possible Scenarios for an EU-Mercosur Agreement*, in Giodano, Paolo (ed), An integrated approach to the EU-Mercosur Association, Chaire Mercosur Sciences Po, 2002.
- Robinson, Richard, (ed), *Direct Foreign Investment: costs and benefits*, Greenwood Press INC, NY, 1987.
- Robson, Peter, *The Economics of International Integration*, Routledge, London & New York, 1998.
- Rodrigues, Stéphane, *Les Nouveaux Enjeux de l'OMC*, in: Relazioni Internazionali, No.50, 1999.
- Roett, Riordan, *La relacion trilateral América Latina, Europa y Estados Unidos*, in: America Latina / Internacional, Vol.1, No.2, 1994.
- Roloff, Ralf, *Die Aussenbeziehungen der Europäische Union zwishen Globalisierung und Regionalisierung,* in: Zeitschrift für Politikwissenschaft 11:3, 2001.
- Rose, Gideon, *Neoclassical Realism and Theories of Foreign Policy*, in: World Politics 51:1, 1998.
- Rosecrance, R., *The European Union: A New Type of International Actor*, in: EUI Working Papers RSC, No.97/64, 1997.
- Ruggiero, Renato, *Beyond the Multilateral Trading System*, in: Relazioni Internazionali, No.50, 1999.
- Ruggiero, Renato, *La política de comercio internacional en la era de la OMC*, in: SELA – Capítulos, No.47, 1996.
- Rummel, R. & Wiedemann, J., *Identifying Institutional Paradoxes of CFSP*, in: EUI Working Papers RSC, No.97/67, 1997.
- Rummel, Reinhart (ed.), *Toward Political Union. Planning a Common Foreign and Security Policy in the European Community*, Nomos Verlagsgesellschaft, Baden-Baden, 1992.
- Rummel, Reinhart, *Zusammengesetzte Aussenpolitik Westeuropa als Internationaler Akteur*, N.P. Engel Verlag, Kehl am Rhein, Strassburg, 1982.

- Sabóia, Eduardo Paes, *Cooperação Mercosul-CEE*, in: Boletim de Diplomacia Econômica, No.14, 1993.
- Sandholz, Wayne & Alec Sweet Stone (eds), European *Integration and Supranational Governance*, Oxford, 1998.
- Sangmeister, Hartmut, *Wirtschaftliche Rahmenbedingungen und ökonomische Bewertung des Mercosur*, in : Wulfdiether Zippel(Hrsg.), Die Beziehungen zwischen der EU und den Mercosur-Staaten, Nomos, Baden-Baden, 2001.
- Santagostino, A & G.Culla, *I rapporti tra la Comunità e l'America Latina e gli effetti del secondo allargamento della CEE*, in: Pio, Alessandro, *Europa-America Latina: Nuove Forme di Cooperazione*, Edizioni Unicopli, Milano, 1997.
- Santander, Sebastian, *Strategia di integrazione regionale e intercontinentale: Argentina, Mercosur e Unione Europea*, in: Relazioni Internazionali, 1999.
- Santiso, Javier, *In Search of a New El Dorado: The return of European Investors in Latin America*, SAIS John Hopkins Bologna Center, April 2001.
- Saraiva, Jose Flavio Sombra (ed), *CPLP – Comunidade dos Paises de Lingua Portuguesa*, Instituto Brasilerio de Relacoes Internacionais (IBRI), 2001.
- Saraiva, Miriam Gomes, *Política Externa Europea: el caso del los Diálogos Grupo a Grupo con América Latina de 1984 a 1992*, Nuevohacer, Buenos Aires, 1996.
- Schirm, Stefan A., *Europe's Common Foreign and Security Policy: The Polices of Necessity, Viability, and Adequacy*, in : Rhodes, Carolyn (ed.), The European Union in the world community, Lynne Rienner Publishers, Inc., 1998.
- Schirm, Stefan, *Kooperation in der Amerikas: NAFTA, Mercosur und die neue dynamik regionaler Zusammenarbeit*, Nomos, Baden-Baden, 1997.
- Schmitter, Philippe C., *Examining the Present Euro-Polity with the Help of Past Theories*, in Scharpf, Fritz, Philippe Schmitter & Wolfgang Streeck (eds), Sage Publications, London, 1996.
- Schmitter, Philippe C., *Imagining the Future of the Euro-Polity with the Help of New Concepts*, in Scharpf, Fritz, Philippe Schmitter & Wolfgang Streeck, Sage Publications, London, 1996.
- Schott, Jeffrey, *The WTO after Seattle*, Institute for International Economics, Washington, 2000.
- Schumacher, Edward, *Spain and Latin America: The Resurgence of a Special Relationship,* in: Purcell, Susan Kaufman & Francoise Simon, *Europe and Latin America in the World Economy*, Lynne Rienner Publishers, Boulder, London, 1995.
- Seabra, Maria Joao, *For and against an EU-Mercour FTA: the interests in the EU*, Chaire Mercosur, *Annual Report 2000*, Sciences Po, Paris, 2000.
- Secchi, Carlo, *Factos Influencing Private Investment in Argentina* in: Mobilising International Investment for Latin America, OECD, 1993.

- Seitz, Klaus & Michael Windfuhr, *Landwirtschaft unde Welthandelsordnung: handbuch zu den Agrarverhandlungen der Uruguay-Runde im GATT*, Texte 45, Hamburg, Verlag Diente in Übersee, 1989.
- Seixas Correia, Luiz Felipe, *As conferencias de Cupula Ibero-Americanas: um formato em busca de substancia*, in Fonseca Junior, Gelson & Sergio Henrique Nabuco de Castro (orgs), Temas de Politica Externa Brasileira II, Vol.2, Editora Paz e Terra, 1994.
- Senti, Richard, *The role of the EU as an economic actor within the WTO, in:* European Foreign Affairs Review No.7, 2002.
- Sirc, L., *Comercio Internacional, Fluxos de Bens e Divisao da Producao entre Nacoes*, Zahar Editores, Rio de Janeiro, 1975.
- Sjöstedt, Gunnar, *The External role of the European Community*, Saxon House, 1977.
- Sjursen, Helene, *Missed opportunity or eternal fantasy?: the idea of a European security and defence policy*, in : Peterson J & Helene Sjursen, A Common Foreign Policy for Europe ? Competing visions of the CFSP, 1998.
- Smith, Hazel, *Actually existing foreign policy - or not ? the EU in Latin America and Central America*, in : Peterson J & Helene Sjursen, A Common Foreign Policy for Europe ? Competing visions of the CFSP, 1998.
- Smith, Hazel, *European Union Foreign Policy and Central America*, St.Martin's Press Inc, New York & Macmillan Press Ltd, London, 1995.
- Smith, K.E., *The Instruments of European Union Foreign Policy*, in: EUI Working Papers RSC, No.97/68, 1997.
- Smith, K.E., The *Making of EU Foreign Policy*, Basingstone, Macmillan, 1999.
- Smith, K.E., *The Use of Political Conditionality in the EU's Relations with Third Countries: How Effective?,* in: EUI Working Papers SPS, No.97/7, 1997.
- Smith, Michael, *Beyond the Stable State? Foreign Policy Challenges and Opportunities in the New Europe*, in: Carlsnaes, Walter & Steve Smith (eds), EC and Changing Perspectives in Europe, Sage Publications Ltd., London, 1994.
- Smith, Michael, *Does the flag follow trade?: ,politisation and the emergence of a European foreign policy*, in : Peterson J & Helene Sjursen, A Common Foreign Policy for Europe ? Competing visions of the CFSP, 1998.
- Smith, Michael, *The EU, Foreign Economic Policy and the changing world economy,* in: Journal of European Public Policy 1(2),1994.
- Smith, S., *Theories of foreign policy: a historical overview*, in: Review of International Studies, 12, 1986.
- Smith, Steve, *Foreign Policy Theory and the New Europe*, in: Carlsnaes, Walter & Steve Smith (eds), EC and Changing Perspectives in Europe, Sage Publications Ltd., London, 1994.

- Snyder, R., H.Bruck & B.Sapin (eds), *Foreign Policy Decision Making: an approach to the study of international politics*, Free Press of Glencoe, NY, 1962.
- Soares, Maria Regina & Monica Hirst, *O Brasil e os Estados Unidos: dilemas e desafios de uma relacao complexa,* in Fonseca Junior, Gelson & Sergio Henrique Nabuco de Castro (orgs), Temas de Politica Externa Brasileira II, Vol.2, Editora Paz e Terra, 1994.
- Sobrino, Sergio A.A.L. Florencio, Antonio Jose Ferreira Simoes & Glivanea Maria de Oliveira, *Liberalizacao do Comercio Internacional de Productos Agricolas Temperados*, in: Cadernos do IPRI, n.4, 1990.
- Soetendorp, Ben, *Foreign Policy in the European Union*, Longman, London & New York, 1999.
- Soetendorp, Ben, *The Evolution of the EC/EU as a Single Foreign Policy Actor*, in: Carlsnaes, Walter & Steve Smith(eds), EC and Changing Perspectives in Europe, Sage Publications Ltd., London, 1994.
- Sorensen, Georg, *An analysis of contemporary statehood: consequences for conflict and cooperation*, in: Review of International Studies, No.23, 1997.
- Stern, Eric, *Towards Futures Past: Foreign Policy Analysis 2025*, Paper presented at ECPR 2001.
- Stuart, Ana Maria, *Valores e interesses na Cimeira América Latina-Caribe e União Européia: do texto ao contexto*, in: Carta Internacional, No.77, 1999.
- Tavares, Maria da Conceicao, *Auge e declinio do processo de substituicao de importacoes no Brasil*, 1964, reprinted in Bielschowsky, *Cinquenta anos de pensamento na CEPAL*, Editora Record, 2000.
- Telo, Mario, *European Union and New Regionalism (ed),* Ashgate, 2001.
- Thompson-Flores Netto, Francisco, *Relacoes Brasil-Alemanha*, in Fonseca Junior, Gelson & Sergio Henrique Nabuco de Castro (orgs), Temas de Politica Externa Brasileira II, Vol.2, Editora Paz e Terra, 1994.
- Toia, Patrizia, *Italia e America Latina: un dinamico dialogo*, in: Relazioni Internazionali, 199
- Tooze, Roger, *Foreign Economic Policy in the New Europe*, in: Carlsnaes, Walter & Steve Smith(eds), EC and Changing Perspectives in Europe, Sage Publications Ltd., London, 1994.
- Torrent, Ramon, *Derecho y Práctica de las Relaciones Exeriores en la Unión Europea*, Cedecs Editorial, Barcelona, 1998.
- Torrent, Ramon, *Regional Integration in Europe and the Americas and Bilateral Transatlantic Relations*, in Giodano, Paolo (ed), An integrated approach to the EU-Mercosur Association, Chaire Mercosur Sciences Po, 2002.
- Trebilcock, Michael & Robert Howse, *The regulation of international trade*, Routledge, 1999.

- Tsebelis, George & Xenopon Yataganas, Veto *Players and Decision-Making in the EU after Nice*, in: Journal of Common Market Studies, 40:2, 2002.
- UNCTAD, *Bilateral Investment Treaties*, 1959-1999, 1999.
- UNCTAD, *Impact of International Investment flows on development: the impact of FDI policies on industrialisation, local entrepreneurship and the development of supply capacity of developing countries, in particular the LDCs*, 2002.
- UNCTAD, *Should countries promote FDI?, Gordon H.Hanson, G-24 Discussion Paper Series*, 2001.
- UNCTAD, *The world of Investment Promotion at a glance*, 2001.
- UNCTAD, *World Investment Report*, 2001.
- Uthoff, Andras & Titelman, Daniel, *The Relationship between Foreign and National Saving under Financial Liberalisation*, in: Capital Flows and Investment performance. Lessons from Latin America, OECD, 1998.
- Vacchine, Juan Mario, *La Cumbre entre la Unión Europea y América Latina y el Caribe y sus Perspectivas*, exposição preparada para o Seminário "*Escenarios estratégicos de la integración en el umbral del siglo XXI:perspectivas americanas y europeas*", organizado pelo Centro de Formación para la Integración Regional (CEFIR), Montevideo; em colaboração com o Centro de Estudos Estratégicos, Secretaria de Assuntos Estratégicos da Presidência da República Federativa do Brasil; e a Escola de Administração da Fazenda, Ministério da Fazenda da república federativa do Brasil, Brasília, 6-8 de outubro de 1998.
- Vaillant, Amrcel & Alejandro Nin, *International Coalitions for Agriculture Trade Liberalisation*, in Giodano, Paolo (ed), An integrated approach to the EU-Mercosur Association, Chaire Mercosur Sciences Po, 2002.
- Vaillant, Marcel, *Trade specialisation and trade policy in agriculture in bilateral trade between the EU and Mercosur*, Chaire Mercosur, *Annual Report 2000*, Sciences Po, Paris, 2000.
- Valdes, Alberto, *The role of agricultural exports in development,* in Timmer, C.Peter (ed), Agriculture and the State. Growth, employment, and poverty in developing countries, Cornell University Press, 1991.
- Van Vera, Stephen, *Guide to Methods for Students of Political Sciences*, Cornell University Press, 1997.
- Vasconcelos, Álvaro de, *Parceiros Naturais. Europa – América Latina*, in *Europa-América Latina: A Convergência Natural*, Instituto de Estudos Estratégicos e Internacionais (IEEI), Lisboa, 1993.
- Vaz, Alcides Costa, *Cooperacao, Integracao e Processo Negociador. A Construcao do Mercosul,* IBRI, 2002.
- Vengoa, Hugo Fazio, *La Política Exterior de la Integración Europea*, in: Análises Político, No.27, 1996.

- Vigevani, Tullo, *Mercosul: impactos para trabalhadores s sindicatos*, Editora LTr, São Paulo, 1998.
- Viola, Donatella M., *European Foreign Policy and the European Parliament in the 1990s: an investigation into the role and voting behaviour of the European Parliament's political groups*, 2000.
- Vizentini, Paulo Fagundes, *As negociações Mercosul-União Européia*, in: Carta Internacional, No.77, 1999.
- Waever, Ole, *Resisting the Temptation of Post Foreign Policy Analysis*, in: Carlsnaes, Walter & Steve Smith, EC and Changing Perspectives in Europe, Sage Publications Ltd., London, 1994.
- Walker, S., *Role Theory and Foreign Policy Analysis*, Duke University Press, 1987.
- Wallace, Cynthia (ed), *Foreign Direct Investment in the 1990s. A new Climate in the Third World,* Martinus Hijhoff Publishers, 1990.
- Wallace, H., W.Wallace, C.Webb (eds), *Policy Making in the European Communities*, Chichester, John Wiley, 1977.
- Wallace, Helen & Willian Wallace (eds), *Policy Making in the European Union*, Oxford, 2000.
- Wallace, William & W. Paterson (eds), *Foreign Policy Making in Western Europe*, Farnborough, Saxon House, 1978.
- Walt, Stephen, *International Relations: One World, Many Theories*, in: Foreign Policy, 110, 1998.
- Walter, Andrew, *Globalisation and policy convergence: the case of direct investment rules*, in: Higgott, Richard & Geoffrey Underhill & Andreas Bieler, *Non-State actors and authority in the global system*, Routledge, 2000.
- Waltz, Kenneth, *Structural Realism after the Cold War*, in: International Security 25:1, 2000.
- Waltz, Kenneth, *Theory of International Politics*, Random House, NY, 1979.
- Weaver, Ole, *Explaining Europe by Decoding Discourses*, in: Wivel, Anders (ed.), Explaining European Integration, Copenhagen Political Studies Press, 1998.
- Weaver, Ole, *Figures of International Thought: introducing persons instead of paradigms*, in: Weaver, Ole & Neumann & Iver, B. (eds*), The Future of International Relations – Masters in the Making*, Routledge, 1997.
- Wehner, Ulrich, *Spezifische Rechtsfragen des Mercosul und der EU-Mercosul Beziehungen*, in : Wulfdiether Zippel(Hrsg.), Die Beziehungen zwischen der EU und den Mercosur-Staaten, Nomos, Baden-Baden, 2001.
- Weiler, J.H.H.(ed), *The EU, the WTO , and the NAFTA, Towards a Common Law of International Trade?* , Oxford University Press, 2000.
- Weiler, J.H.H., *Cain and Abel, Convergence and divergence in international trade law*, in Weiler, J.H.H.(ed), *The EU, the WTO , and the NAFTA, Towards a Common Law of International Trade?* , Oxford University Press, 2000.

- Weiler, J.H.H., *Epilogue: Towards a common law of international trade*, in Weiler, J.H.H.(ed), *The EU, the WTO , and the NAFTA, Towards a Common Law of International Trade?* , Oxford University Press, 2000.
- Weiler, Joseph, *The European Parliament and Foreign Affairs: External Relations of the European Economic Community*, 1980.
- Weldes, Juta, *Constructing National Interests*, in: European Journal of International Relations, 1996.
- Weldes, Jutta, *Constructing National Interests*, in: European Journal of International Relations, Vol.2(3), 1996.
- Wendt, Alexander & James Fearon, *Rationalism vs. Constructivism: A Sceptical View*, in Carlsnaes (ed), Handbook of International Relations, Sage, 2002.
- Wendt, Alexander, *Bridging the Theory/Meta-Theory gap in International Relations*, in: Review of International Studies, No.17, 1991.
- Wendt, Alexander, *Collective Identity Formation and the International State*, in: American Political Science Review, Vol.88, No.2, 1994.
- Wendt, Alexander, *Constructing International Politics*, in: International Security, Vo.20, No.1, 1995.
- Wendt, Alexander, *Level of Analysis vs. Agents and Structures: part III*, in: Review of International Studies, No.18, 1992.
- Wendt, Alexander, *Social Theory of International Politics*, Cambridge Studies in International Relations, 1999.
- Wendt, Alexander, *The Agent-Structure problem in IR Theory*, in: International Organization, Vol.41, No.3, 1987.
- White, Brian, *Analysing Foreign Policy: Problems and Approaches*, in Clarke, Michael & B.White (eds), *Understanding Foreign Policy: The foreign policy systems approach*, Aldershot, 1989.
- White, Brian, *The European Challenge to Foreign Policy Analysis*, in: European Journal of International Relations, 5:1, 1999.
- White, Brian, *Understanding European Foreign Policy*, Palgrave, NY, 2001.
- Whitman, Richard, *From Civilian Power to Superpower? The International Identity of the European Union*, Macmillan, NY, 1998.
- Wionczek, Miguel S., *The relations between the European Economic Community and Latin America in the Context of a Global Economic Crisis*, in: Institut d'Etudes Europeennes Université Libre de Bruxelles, Colloques Europeens, *La Communaute Europeenne et L'Amerique Latine*, Bruxelles, 9 et 10 mai 1980, Editions de l'Universite de Bruxelles, 1981.
- Wivel, Anders, *New Threats and Ols Dilemmas: European Integration in the International System*, in: Wivel, Anders (ed.), Explaining European Integration, Copenhagen Political Studies Press, 1995.

- Woolcock, Stephen, *European trade policy – global pressures and domestic constraints*, in Wallace & Wallace (eds), Policy-making in the European Union, Oxford University Press, 2001.
- WTO, *Developing countries and the Uruguay Round: An overview, Note by the Secretariat*, 10 November 1994.
- WTO, *Preparations for the 1999 Ministerial Conference, EC approach to duty-free market access for the least developed countries, Communication from the European Communities,* WT/GC/W/195, 2nd June 1999.
- WTO, *Preparations for the 1999 Ministerial Conference, Trade and Sustainable development, Communication from the United States*, WT/GC/W/304, 6 August 1999.
- WTO, *Trade and Foreign Direct Investment*, Press/57, 9th October 1996.
- WTO, Trade Policy Reviews, *Argentina 1999,* First & Second Press Release, 1999.
- WTO, Trade Policy Reviews, *Brazil 1996,* First & Second Press Release, 1996.
- WTO, Trade Policy Reviews, *Brazil 2000,* First & Second Press Release, 2000.
- WTO, Trade Policy Reviews, *European Union 1997,* First & Second Press Release, 1997.
- WTO, Trade Policy Reviews, *European Union 2000,* First & Second Press Release, 2000.
- WTO, Trade Policy Reviews, *European Union 2002,* First & Second Press Release, 2002.
- WTO, Trade Policy Reviews, *Paraguay 1997,* First & Second Press Release, 1997.
- WTO, Trade Policy Reviews, *Uruguay 1998,* First & Second Press Release, 1998.
- WTO, *Trading into the future: The World Trade Organisation*, 2nd ed., March 2001.
- Young, Alasdair, *The Adaptation of European Foreign Economic Policy: from Rome to Seattle*, in: Journal of Common Market Studies, Vol.38, nr.1, 2000.
- Young, Alasdair, *The adaptation of European foreign economic policy: from Rome to Seatlle*, in: Journal of Common Market Studies, Vol.38, No.1, 2000.
- Yrigoyen, Martín, *El Dialogo America Latina - CEE*, Lluvia Editores, Lima, 1985.
- Zielonka, Jan (ed.), *Paradoxes of European Foreign Policy*, Kluwer Law International, 1998.
- Zielonka, Jan, *Explaining Euro-Paralysis. Why Europe is Unable to Act in International Politics*, Macmillan Press Ltd (London) & St.Martin's Press (New York),1998.